Macau in Transition

Also by Herbert S. Yee

A STUDY OF MACAU'S POLITICS AND PUBLIC POLICY

A TALE OF TWO CITIES: A Comparative Study of Political, Economic and Social Developments in Hong Kong and Macau

CHINA IN TRANSITION: Issues and Policies (*co-editor*)

MACAU AT THE HANDOVER: Problems and Policies

MACAU BEYOND 1999

THE MODERNIZATION OF TIBETAN REGIONS: Theory, Practice and Policies (*co-editor*)

THE POLITICAL CULTURE OF CHINA'S UNIVERSITY STUDENTS

THE POLITICAL CULTURE OF THE MACAU CHINESE (*co-author*)

Macau in Transition

From Colony to Autonomous Region

Herbert S. Yee
Professor
Government and International Studies
Hong Kong Baptist University
Hong Kong

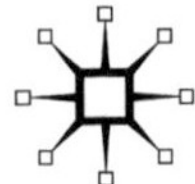

First published 2001 by
PALGRAVE
Houndmills, Basingstoke, Hampshire RG21 6XS and
175 Fifth Avenue, New York, N.Y. 10010
Companies and representatives throughout the world

PALGRAVE is the new global academic imprint of
St. Martin's Press LLC Scholarly and Reference Division and
Palgrave Publishers Ltd (formerly Macmillan Press Ltd).

ISBN 0–333–75009–8

This book is printed on paper suitable for recycling and made from fully managed and sustained forest sources.

A catalogue record for this book is available from the British Library.

Library of Congress Cataloging-in-Publication Data
Yee, Herbert S.
    Macau in transition : from colony to autonomous region /
    Herbert S. Yee.
        p. cm.
    Includes bibliographical references and index.
    ISBN 0–333–75009–8
    1. Macau (China : Special Administrative Region)—History—
    —Transfer of Sovereignty from Portugal, 1999. I. Title.
    DS796.M257 Y44 2001
    951.26′06—dc21
                                                        2001021729

10 9 8 7 6 5 4 3 2 1
10 09 08 07 06 05 04 03 02 01

Printed and bound in Great Britain by
Antony Rowe Ltd, Chippenham, Wiltshire

To my loving children

Tien-wei (Tianhui)
Tien-mien (Tianmin)
Tien-zong (Tiancong)
Tin-heng (Tianxing)
Tin-weng (Tianying)

Contents

List of Tables

Acknowledgements

The author would like to thank all the people and institutions who have helped to make this book possible, in particular former Macau governors, Vasco Almeida e Costa and Carlos Montez Melancia, and former members of the Portuguese negotiation team on Macau's reversion, Joao de Deus Ramos and Carlos Gaspar, as well as the enclave's legislators, municipal councillors, community leaders, academics and civil servants who have granted me interviews.

Many people, including my former students at the University of Macau, helped the research of this book with telephone surveys, interviews and information collection. Among these helpers are Chen Mingmin, Shen Dongqing, Feng Jinming, Tan xian, Ou Kaiyi and Yu Zongjie. Thanks to Miss Ada To, Secretary of the China Studies Programme of Hong Kong Baptist University (HKBU), who assisted me throughout, and Tam Chunyuk who prepared the entire typescript.

Special thanks are also due to Jo Campling who provided generous professional advice in preparing the typescript for publication and Sally Crawford whose excellent editing makes the book much more readable.

Chapters 5, 6 and 7 and part of the Introduction and Chapter 8 are derived from my previous articles on Macau: Chapter 5 is a revised and expanded version of my article published in *Issues and Studies* in 1999; Chapter 6 is a revised and updated version of my article in the *Asian Survey* in 1997; Chapter 7 is a revised and updated version of another article published by *Issues and Studies* in 1997; part of the Introduction and Chapter 8 is derived from my article in *China Perspectives* in 1999. I would like to acknowledge the following copyright sources:

Copyright 1997 by The Regents of the University of California. Reprinted from *Asian Survey*, Vol. 37, No. 10, pp. 944–60, by permission of the Regents.

Reprinted from *China Perspectives*, No. 26 (November–December 1999), pp. 28–38, by permission of French Centre for Research on Contemporary China, Hong Kong.

Reprinted from *Issues & Studies*, Vol. 33, No. 6, pp. 113–32; and Vol. 35, No. 2, pp. 174–97, by permission of the editor.

I also wish to offer my grateful thanks to HKBU which funded the research of this book.
Lastly, I wish to dedicate this book to my five loving children.

Introduction

In the aftermath of the Portuguese revolution of 1974, when Portugal divested herself of her colonies, it might have seemed that Macao, most anomalous of all Portuguese possessions, would be the first to have its flag hauled down. An anomaly from the start, however, anomaly at this juncture piled on anomaly. Regardless of Portuguese revolutionary opinion, Lisbon was informed that China wished Macao to remain as it was.

Austin Coates[1]

The Macau question is not urgent. We can wait for another 3 or 5 years. There is still 13 years before 1997. The [Macau] question can wait for another 7 or 8 years. Tell the Macau people to feel at ease. There is no urgent need to solve the Macau question. . . . Now it is more important to maintain stability and prosperity in the Hong Kong/Macau region. The Macau question can be solved only when it does not affect Hong Kong's prosperity and stability.

Deng Xiaoping[2]

The reversion of Macau (in 1999) was not the major concern of Zhongnanhai leaders, at least not in the early 1980s. When Deng Xiaoping, China's paramount leader, met Ma Man Kei (or Ma Wanqi) in Beijing in October 1984, shortly before the signing of the Joint Sino-British Declaration on the Hong Kong question, and told the latter that there was no urgent need to solve the Macau question, he was clearly himself preoccupied with the Hong Kong question. As noted by Coates, although the Macau question was first raised by the Portuguese several years prior to the Sino-British negotiations over Hong Kong's future, the Chinese leaders chose to keep Macau's status unchanged. Beijing was apparently afraid that an early return of Macau, if not handled properly, would prompt foreign capital to leave Hong Kong or cause an exodus of people and hence harm Hong Kong's economy and stability.

Needless to say, Macau in comparison to Hong Kong is far less important to Beijing, or to Lisbon, than Hong Kong is to London. The limelight of international attention also focused on Hong Kong's reversion and the practice of 'one-country, two systems' in the former British colony. Macau was treated by Beijing as an afterthought and of secondary – and a distant second – importance in the policy considerations of Zhongnanhai leaders. Indeed, when Deng told Ma that there was no rush for the Macau question to be solved he probably thought that Macau's reversion process was, in comparison to Hong Kong's, simple and apparently forgot that Macau, like Hong Kong, would need a long transitional period before the handover. In any event, Zhongnanhai changed its plan, something Beijing and Lisbon agreed in May 1985, six months after London and Beijing had inked in an agreement on Hong Kong's reversion, to start negotiating over Macau's reversion in 1986.

After eight months and four rounds of relatively smooth talks, in contrast to the 13 months and 22 rounds of rough sailing in Sino-British negotiations, the People's Republic of China (PRC) and the Republic of Portugal signed on 13 April 1987 a Joint Declaration on the question of Macau, agreeing that the PRC would resume the exercise of sovereignty over the territory from 20 December 1999. In the Joint Declaration, the PRC promised that the Macau Special Administrative Region (SAR) would enjoy a high degree of autonomy, except in foreign and defence affairs which are the responsibilities of Beijing, as was to be the case for the Hong Kong Special Administrative Region. The Joint Declaration further stipulated that the government and legislature of the Macau SAR be composed of local inhabitants and be vested with legislative and independent judicial power.[3] This marked the beginning of the transition period for Macau to move from Portuguese to Chinese administration.

The objective of this book is to analyse the process of Macau's transition, the actors involved in the process and the dynamics of interactions between the actors, as well as the concurring political and social changes in the enclave that have direct or indirect impact on the transition.

The Portuguese legacy[4]

When the Portuguese first landed in Macau in 1553 they found only a few hundred local inhabitants.[5] The first Portuguese settled in 1557 and rented the enclave from the Ming officials. At times, particularly during the sixteenth and the first half of the seventeenth century, when Macau was an important entrepôt for East–West trade, the size of the Portuguese settlement far exceeded the local population. The settlement's link with the parent country was weak. Indeed, for 70 years after the first settlement was established, Macau was without a governor. The first governor, D. Francisco Mascarenhas, who was appointed by the governor of Portuguese Goa, arrived in the enclave in 1623. The local Portuguese settlement, however, was resentful of influence from Portugal and continued to maintain a highly autonomous citizen assembly (*Leal Senado*). Influence from the Chinese authorities was weak, indeed nominal, and the local Chinese inhabitants were separately ruled by Chinese officials.[6] It was not until 1849, when the Qing Dynasty was considerably weakened by the Opium Wars, that Governor João Ferreira do Amaral succeeded in colonizing Macau after expelling the local Chinese customs officials. Lisbon then increased its influence at the expense of the local Portuguese inhabitants and the *Leal Senado* was downgraded to an urban council. Strictly speaking, however, Portugal had never possessed the sovereignty of Macau and, unlike Hong Kong, Macau was never ceded to the Portuguese. Nonetheless, Macau had become a *de facto* Portuguese colony, at least since 1849.

Unlike the situation in its colonies in Africa, in Macau, Portugal was confronted with a powerful, if not superior, Chinese civilization. The Chinese had little incentive to learn Portuguese and the Portuguese made little effort to popularize their language among the Chinese, perhaps due to a lack of resources. As a result, few Chinese were able to speak fluent Portuguese and communicate directly with the Portuguese government. The government had to rely on the Cantonese-speaking Macanese (people of mixed Portuguese and East Asian descent) who often occupied the middle-ranking positions in the government bureaucracy as its intermediaries. There was thus little direct communication between the Chinese community and government officials and the local Chinese inhabitants were by and large alienated from politics. Owing to this language barrier, few Chinese had a chance to become high- or middle-ranking officials in the government bureaucracy. As a non-elected, Portuguese-dominated government, the legitimacy of the Portuguese government had always been challenged by the local Chinese residents and the lack of direct communication between the local Chinese and the government authorities had over time created tension and misunderstanding between the two groups. The riots of 3 December 1966 were the eruption of longstanding grievances against Portuguese rule. For two years after the riots, the Portuguese government was crippled and lost its will and capability to govern Macau. What is more significant, perhaps, in the light of Macau's long-term political development, was the expulsion of pro-Taiwan social groups and organizations from the enclave following the riots. Since that time the enclave's Chinese community has been dominated by pro-Peking groups and organizations. The April 1974 revolution in Portugal was another turning point in Macau's political development. As a far east Portuguese outpost, politics in Macau had always been influenced by the political developments in Lisbon.

Macau's political scene at the beginning of the transition

Two years after the April 1974 revolution when the political situation in Lisbon had become more stable the Portuguese parliament passed the Organic Statute of Macau (*Estatuto Organico de Macau*) and established the Legislative Assembly in Macau. According to the statute, the legislature was to be composed of 17 members of which six were to be directly elected by the people, six indirectly elected by the functional constituencies[7] and five appointed by the governor. Elections for the Legislative Assembly were to be held every four years. The statute was revised in 1990 to expand the Legislative Assembly to 23 members with eight directly elected, eight indirectly elected and seven appointed seats.

When the Legislative Assembly's elections were first held in 1976, the electoral law was biased in favour of Portuguese nationals; there was no residency requirements for Portuguese nationals while a minimum of five years' residency in Macau was required for local Chinese nationals to be entitled to register as voters. At the same time, after centuries of political apathy, few local Chinese aspired to participate in the elections or to run for legislature seats. As a result, the Macanese took all but one of the directly elected seats in the 1976 election and all the directly elected seats in the 1980 elections. The only ethnic Chinese who made it into the legislature through the 1976 direct elections was Susana Chou, who had obtained Portuguese nationality and spoke fluent Portuguese. Only four local Chinese community leaders had succeeded in entering the legislature in 1976 and 1980 through indirect functional constituencies. Indeed, the governor had to appoint two Chinese community leaders to the 1976 and 1980 legislatures to counterbalance the Macanese influence.

It was in 1984 when Governor Vasco Almeida e Costa, who was engaged in a political power struggle with the Macanese and dissolved the Macanese-dominated legislature,[8] lifted the residency requirements for Chinese nationals and mobilized the Chinese to actively participate in elections and run for seats in the legislature that the enclave's political scene changed. In the 1984 elections, two Chinese, Alexandre Ho and Lau Cheok Va (or Liu Zhuohua), won seats through direct election while all six indirectly elected seats were won unopposed by local Chinese community leaders. In the 1988 elections, the Chinese won four directly elected seats and took all the indirectly elected seats.

In fact, since 1988, the Macanese influence in Macau politics has significantly declined. In the 1988 election, only two Macanese, Carlos D'Assumpcao, the chairman of the Legislative Assembly, and Leonel Alberto Alves, a young lawyer, won their seats through direct ballot. The Macanese won only one directly elected seat in the 1992 elections and none in 1996. The end of the Macanese era signalled the beginning of Chinese domination.

Another significant trend in the enclave's political scene in the last two decades is the increase in number of registered voters and the increasing voter turnout. Under the active mobilization of Governor Costa, with the apparent approval of the mainland Chinese authorities, more than 45 000 local Chinese residents registered as voters in 1984 and slightly more than half of them actually cast their ballots in the election. Voter turnout, however, dropped significantly in the 1988 elections and 1991 by-election. The drop in voter turnout was partly a result of insufficient mobilization or propaganda from the government authorities when both Governors Melancia's and Vieira's administrations were largely indifferent to the elections. However, the turnout rate increased significantly in the 1992 and 1996 elections. Rapid economic development and social change in Macau in the 1980s and early 1990s had contributed to the rise in citizen participation in the last two elections.

Rapid economic growth gave birth to a new middle class of professionals in the 1980s and a *nouveau riche* business elite in the 1990s. Alexandre Ho, a senior civil servant, Leong Kam Chuen (or Liang

Jinquan), an accountant, and Wong Cheong Nam (Wang Changnan), a laboratory technician, won three seats in the 1988 legislature direct elections under the banner of 'improving people's livelihood'. The trio succeeded in mobilizing the grassroots population, in particular the new immigrants, to vote in the elections. Antonio Ng Kuok Cheong (Wu Gongchang), a bank branch-manager, who ran for the direct election and campaigned under the banner of 'Democratic Macau', won the support of the middle class and professionals and a seat in the 1992 legislature. The *nouveaux riches*, a product of the boom years in the 1980s and early 1990s, were big winners in the 1996 legislature elections, winning four directly elected seats. Indeed, an increasingly diversified society has been emerging in Macau since the 1980s.

In short, when the transition period for Macau began in the late 1980s, the enclave was no longer a backwater town of the 1960s and 1970s. Partly due to the large inflow of new immigrants since 1979 and the double-digit economic growth of the 1980s and coinciding with the process of transition, Macau was under significant social and political transformation.

The process of transition

One special feature of the process of Macau's transition is the absence of open dispute – at least until the final years – between Lisbon and Beijing, in sharp contrast to the relatively rough Hong Kong transition. Throughout the transitional period until 1997, the progress of Macau's transition was to different degrees affected by the Hong Kong transition. Indeed, the process of Macau's transition can be divided into three stages: pre-1989, 1989–97 and post-1997. It was smooth sailing in the respective Anglo-Chinese and Luso-Chinese negotiations over the transition of Hong Kong and Macau prior to the 4 June 1989, Tiananmen Square Incident. Beijing's crackdown on the student demonstrators, however, had serious negative repercussions on Sino-British relations. The United Kingdom joined the West in imposing economic sanctions against the PRC and was highly critical of the latter's human rights record. The open confrontation between Beijing and London was escalated after Chris Patten had succeeded David Wilson in 1991 as the last governor of Hong Kong. Patten was determined to quicken Hong Kong's democratization process and to strengthen the enclave's political autonomy before the handover despite strong opposition from Beijing. Portugal, on the other hand, refrained from openly criticizing the PRC's human rights record and the Portuguese Macau administration under Melancia or his successor Vieira was indifferent to Macau's democratic development. Beijing rewarded Lisbon's 'friendly' attitude by giving concessions on nationality and localization issues while maintaining a confrontation strategy against the British over Hong Kong's transition. In a sense, the smooth Macau transition was a product of the rough Hong Kong transition. After the reversion of Hong Kong, however, Beijing's attention was shifted to Macau. Conflicts of interests between Beijing and Lisbon, which were previously hidden under the banner of Sino-Portuguese friendship, emerged and caused open disputes between the two capitals in the final years of Macau's transition.

Like other colonial regimes in their final years of rule, the Portuguese Macau administration had faced a crisis of eroding governance legitimacy. As a non-elective, colonial government, the Portuguese administration was weak in procedure legitimacy. It could count only on its policy performance to enhance its legitimacy of governance. Rapid economic growth in the late 1970s and 1980s had assisted the Portuguese administration to recover from the aftermath of the 1966 anti-government riot. But the collapse of the local real estate market in 1994 and the subsequent economic recession had plunged the Portuguese administration into another crisis of performance legitimacy. The Portuguese governance was further challenged by the erosion of law and order in the enclave, partly as a result of in-fighting between triads or other gangs for gambling customers because of decreasing revenue in Macau's casinos due to economic recession.

Understandably, the Portuguese Macau administration wanted to strengthen its governance and maintain an image of a viable, not a 'lame-duck', government in the final years of its rule. It therefore was reluctant to quicken the pace of localizing the enclave's civil service by promoting local Chinese to senior government positions, despite increasing pressure from the Chinese government. Indeed, by the end of 1998, one year prior to the handover, the majority of positions of office director or equivalent rank were still held by Portuguese expatriates. Furthermore, the seven under-secretaries retained their posts until the handover. At the same time, the Portuguese administration was lukewarm in its attitude to implementing Chinese as a working language in government offices or departments when their own heads could not read or write Chinese.

Equally understandably, Beijing wanted to quicken the pace of localization, especially the promotion of local Chinese to key positions and the use of Chinese as a working language in the government civil service. Beijing was apparently concerned about a smooth transition as well as political and social stability in post-1999 Macau. A sudden withdrawal of senior expatriate civil servants at the handover would no doubt cause discontinuity or instability in the SAR administration. Yet, paradoxically, Beijing's pressuring for a quicker pace of localization was likely to further weaken the Portuguese legitimacy and hence capability to curb the deterioration in law and order or to boost the enclave's depressed economy. In the end, Beijing failed to persuade the Portuguese administration to quicken the pace of localization and fell short of assisting the latter to maintain public order or improve the economy.

The dynamics of this process produced an outcome that probably no one wanted.[9] The slow start to localization and the Portuguese strategy of maintaining a post-1999 cultural presence in Macau, resulted in the promotion of a large number of young and inexperienced administrators. The small group of local Chinese promoted to director or deputy director rank were still in their 30s. Most lacked experience at lower levels and were generalists without professional expertise. Many were promoted because of their proficiency in Portuguese or their pro-government stand. The result could well be a mediocre bureaucracy, with the power vacuum left at the end of 1999 by the departing Portuguese making it possible for the pro-Beijing elite effectively to secure power without a fight. The new chief executive of the SAR, Edmund Ho Hau Wah, hand-picked by the Chinese government, will find it hard to resist pressure from the local pro-Beijing groups for their favoured political appointments. The more radical of these are likely to try to erase the remnants of Portuguese influence and cultural heritage.[10] Thus the Portuguese could become victims of a situation of their own making.

Another special feature of the enclave's reversion is Macau citizens' jubilant attitude toward the handover, in sharp contrast to Hongkongers' largely indifferent attitude at Hong Kong's handover.

The difference could be partly explained by the local residents' attitudes towards the respective colonial governments: while more than two-thirds of the Hongkongers were satisfied with the British administration's performance before the reversion of Hong Kong,[11] less than one-quarter of the Macau citizens were happy with the performance of the sunset Portuguese administration.[12] Another factor that partly explains the different mood towards the handover in Hong Kong and Macau is the latter's prevailing pro-Beijing attitude, while Hongkongers were split into pro-China and pro-British groups at the handover. Indeed, thousands of Macau residents went out to the street and welcomed the People's Liberation Army at noon 20 December 1999 as if Macau were 'liberated' from the Portuguese.

The organization of the book

This book consists of eight chapters. Chapter 1 discusses the PRC's attitude and strategy towards the process of Macau's transition, as reflected in the evolving Sino-Portuguese negotiations over the enclave's transition. It also compares Macau's reversion to that of Hong Kong, especially the impact of change in Anglo-Chinese relations on Macau's handover. Chapter 2 describes the special features of Macau's political system as inherited from the Portuguese and the implications for the post-1999 SAR government. Chapter 3 gives a detailed account of the process of localization, the focal point of contention between the Chinese and the Portuguese during the transition process. Chapter 4, primarily based on data from a telephone survey conducted by the author in December 1998, examines Macau citizens' attitudes towards the transition. Chapter 5 compares two sets of data from surveys conducted in 1991 and 1999, respectively, and highlights the continuity and change of Macau's mass political culture in the last decade. Chapter 6 presents a case study of political participation and mobilization in the enclave's 1996 Legislative Assembly election. This book takes a close look at the Eurasian (Macanese) issue, something which has been neglected by both Beijing and Lisbon (Chapter 7). Finally, Chapter 8 concludes the book by highlighting the major actors involved in the transition process as well as the limitations and prospects of Macau's democratic development.

1

Beijing's Attitude and Strategy toward the Transition

Macau's transition from Portuguese autonomous territory to Chinese Special Administrative Region (SAR) had started when the Chinese and Portuguese delegations first met in Beijing in June 1986 while negotiating the reversion of Macau. For better or worse, the territory's future was in the hands of Beijing and Lisbon. The course of Macau's transition was to be shaped by the outcome of negotiations between the People's Republic of China (PRC) and Portugal, which in turn was affected by the change in Sino-Portuguese relations. Largely due to the asymmetrical power relations between the PRC and Portugal, Beijing rather than Lisbon had always taken the initiative in monitoring Macau's transition. Beijing's strategies towards the transition aimed at (1) quickening the pace of localization, especially in promoting local Chinese to senior positions in the civil service; (2) ensuring a smooth and stable handover in 1999; and (3) tightening the PRC's control of Macau society through the co-opting of the local elites.

Beijing's strategies towards the transition process in Macau can be divided into three stages: pre-1989, from 1989–97, and post-1997. Before the 1989 Tiananmen massacre, Beijing's policy towards Macau was similar to its policy towards Hong Kong. Perhaps to some degree this was a result of the central authorities' lack of knowledge of the local conditions in the two territories which it assumed were European colonies, and, therefore, more or less the same. In any event, Beijing was eager to use both Hong Kong and Macau as examples of its 'one country, two systems' model to lure Taiwan and tried to accommodate the wishes of the local Hong Kong and Macau populace as well as those of the European governments.

After the Tiananmen massacre, Beijing changed strategy in an attempt to seek the support of the Portuguese and isolate the 'hostile' British. Friendship and good relations between China and Portugal were stressed as indications of Beijing's good will and cooperation. Portugal was depicted as 'reasonable' in comparison with the United Kingdom. In the name of friendship, Beijing also restrained from interfering in and criticizing the Portuguese Macau administration.

The Chinese government changed its tone towards the Portuguese after the reversion of Hong Kong to China in July 1997. Macau was no longer a bargaining card in Sino-British relations, if it ever was. Beijing increased its pressure on the Macau government to follow Beijing's own plans for the transfer of administration. Perhaps the greatest pressure from Beijing came in September 1998 when the Chinese government unilaterally declared that, in order to help the future SAR government maintain order, China would station troops from the People's Liberation Army (PLA) in the Macau SAR.[1] The Chinese decision was a complete turnabout from the agreement reached between Portugal and the PRC in the Joint Declaration of 1987.[2] The Portuguese had not stationed any troops in Macau since 1975 and they felt Macau to be too small to accommodate a PLA garrison – a fact now partially acknowledged by Beijing which decided to station a larger force on the border in Zhuhai which can be called into Macau to reinforce the PLA garrison planned for the SAR. Beijing's decision was applauded by the pro-Beijing groups but provoked minor protest from the Portuguese government.[3] In any event, Beijing's unilateral decision to station troops in Macau clearly suggests that the Chinese rather than the Portuguese were in control of Macau's transition process.

A comparison of Sino-British and Sino-Portuguese relations during the transitions of Hong Kong and Macau

Macau was returned to China two and a half years after the reversion of Hong Kong. The two territories' transitional periods were almost overlapping. It will certainly enlighten our understanding of Macau's transition process if we compare it to that of Hong Kong. Indeed, the two territories' different courses towards the handover tended to affect each other. Nonetheless, it is equally important to note the similarities of the two transitions.

First and foremost, on the one hand, the Chinese leadership had regarded both Hong Kong and Macau as 'lost' territories, despite the fact that the former was ceded to the British by a treaty while the Portuguese ruled Macau by sufferance. Beijing was determined to close this chapter of humiliating history before the end of the twentieth century.[4] This mainly explains Beijing's inflexibility towards the timing of the two enclaves' reversion. Secondly, Beijing intended to implement the so-called 'one country two systems' concept in the two territories, presumably as a prelude to the eventual re-unification of Taiwan. Ensuring a smooth transition to Chinese rule as well as establishing a mechanism to monitor the proper functioning of the two SARs were thus the prime concerns of the Chinese leadership. Thirdly, Beijing reiterated the significance of sovereignty transfer and heralded the reversion as China's recovery of its lost sovereignty over the two territories. The United Kingdom and Portugal were to hand over the sovereignty to China, *not* to the local residents of Hong Kong/Macau. Both Hong Kong and Macau citizens were thus excluded from the process of negotiations which directly affected their future well-being.

On the other hand, there are striking contrasts between Hong Kong's and Macau's respective processes of transition. First, the power relations between China and the United Kingdom – as compared to that between China and Portugal – are clearly different. Although the UK, as compared to China, is much smaller in terms of area and population, it is a developed country with a GNP even greater than the PRC. Moreover, the UK enjoys an equal, if not higher, international status as that of China because of its influence in the British Commonwealth and its close relations with the United States. Portugal, by comparison, is merely a small underdeveloped European state with relatively little international influence. Nonetheless, Portugal is not an insignificant state. It has substantial influence in Portuguese-speaking countries or regions in Africa, Latin America and Asia, with an area larger and a population equal to Europe. Its cultural connection with the Latinate world has enabled Portugal to play a role very different from the UK in the European Union (EU). The above facts have somewhat moderated the power imbalance between Beijing and Lisbon. In any event, power symmetry between London and Beijing had provided the former with a leverage which Lisbon did not possess in negotiating with the PRC. Indeed, London rather than Beijing had often taken the initiatives and controlled the rhythm of Hong Kong's transitional process, while the rhythm of the Macau transition was largely controlled by Beijing.[5]

Secondly, partly due to historical reasons, London and Lisbon had adopted different strategies towards the transition. Partly feeling the need to enhance the legitimacy of British rule over Hong Kong prior to the handover,[6] the Hong Kong British administration had opened its decision-making process, promoted democracy and increased the autonomy of the legislature.[7] By contrast, the Portuguese administration in Macau had taken little initiative in promoting democracy or subjecting its governance to the scrutiny of the Macau citizens. The Macau legislature was dominated by the pro-China political force. Following its tradition of ruling Macau with Chinese consent, the Portuguese administration chose to rely on the cooperation of pro-China social groups to enhance its legitimacy. In the end, the Portuguese had unintendedly helped the pro-China groups to consolidate their domination over the local community at the expense of the pro-democracy groups. Arguably, Lisbon appeared to be more interested in maintaining a harmonious relationship with Beijing and/or preserving Portugal's interests in post-1999 Macau than in negotiating with Beijing for the betterment of the citizens of Macau.

Thirdly, Hong Kong is far more important to the UK than Macau is to Portugal. British capital had for a long time dominated Hong Kong's commercial sector and local capital only gradually caught up with this dominance in the 1970s and 1980s and mainland Chinese capital in the 1990s. Hong Kong had also served as an important base in the Far East for the British navy until the latter's withdrawal from the region in the 1970s. By comparison, the Macau economy is dominated by mainland companies with less than 5 per cent of its capital coming from Portugal.[8] Portuguese business-people would rather invest in Brazil or Portugal's ex-colonies in Africa than in Macau. According to a noted Portuguese historian, Portugal had and has no economic, cultural or military interest in Macau.[9] When President Mário Soares proclaimed, during the process of Sino-Portuguese negotiation, that the Macau question was a 'national interest' of Portugal, he meant 'national prestige', not anything of substantive or practical importance.[10] In fact, Portugal had reportedly offered to return Macau to China after the 1966 anti-government riot and in the aftermath of the 1974 Portuguese revolution.[11] Ironically, Portugal's relative disinterest in the enclave had enabled Lisbon to threaten to terminate the process of negotiation over Macau's reversion when it did not proceed smoothly.[12] Nonetheless, the few, if not insignificant, Portuguese interests both in Macau and in the region had contributed to the serenity that marked Macau's transition prior to the mid-1990s, in contrast to Hong Kong's rough transition mentioned above.[13]

Fourthly, few people will question the relative importance to the Beijing regime of Hong Kong in comparison to Macau, although the latter greatly assisted the PRC to survive the hardships of the 1950s and 1960s when China was isolated in international terms.[14] Because of China's vested interests in Hong Kong, the Chinese leadership was apparently more concerned about the progression of transition in Hong Kong than in Macau. Sino-British negotiations over the Hong Kong transition were directly supervised by President Jiang Zemin while Macau's transition was monitored only by Vice-Premier Qian Qichen. Beijing was particularly alarmed when the British, with the apparent approval and support of the Americans, had the intention of turning Hong Kong into a full democracy with high political autonomy, which, if it succeeded, would make it extremely difficult for Beijing to control Hong Kong after the handover. Beijing thus pressed hard on negotiations with and at times directly confronted London. By comparison, Beijing did not have much to lose in going easy with Lisbon over the Macau transition. After all, the PRC had already been in control of Macau. Lisbon apparently took advantage of Beijing's disinterest in Macau and thus scored points in the negotiations.

Fifthly, Hong Kong is a large metropolis of international status and a financial centre of Asia while Macau is merely a small gambling city little known to the world outside of Asia. Hong Kong's transition to the Chinese rule, especially the open Sino-British dispute over the territory's political reform, was widely reported by the international mass media and drew worldwide attention. Hong Kong's transition was thus highly politicized and partly subject to the change in global and regional political environment. For instance, after Beijing's crackdown on student demonstrators at Tiananmen Square in June 1989, London followed the Western world's economic sanctions against the PRC and, partly in response to the world's concerns about Hong Kong's political future, quickened the pace of democratization in Hong Kong. By comparison, the Tiananmen Square incident had little impact on Macau's transition. There was little international pressure on Portugal to strengthen Macau's political autonomy *vis-à-vis* mainland China.

Lastly, the Hong Kong and Macau handovers were only two-and-a-half years apart. The progress of Sino-British negotiations over Hong Kong's transition apparently had some impact on the progress of Sino-Portuguese negotiations over Macau's transition, and vice versa (albeit to a much lesser extent). As has been said, Beijing had contrasted the 'friendly' Sino-Portuguese relations with the conflictual Sino-British relations and rewarded the cooperative Portuguese with an immediate green light in terms of constructing Macau's airport while deliberately delaying the construction of the new airport at Hong Kong. Furthermore, the Portuguese had apparently learned from the British experience and avoided mentioning politically sensitive issues such as human rights with the Chinese concentrating instead on Portugal's interests in Macau.

Cooperation and conflict between Beijing and Lisbon over Macau's transition

The inevitability of Macau's reversion had ensured at the outset of Sino-Portuguese negotiations that the outcome would not be a 'winner takes all' situation. If both sides were willing to compromise and to cooperate, in the end a 'win-win' situation could be reached. Moreover, maintaining an amicable relationship between the two countries is in the interests of both Beijing and Lisbon. Sino-Portuguese relations during Macau's transition were thus largely characterized by co-operation rather then confrontation. Yet, mainly due to different policy objectives as well as cultural biases, conflicts between the two countries did arise, especially in the final years of the transition.

On the one hand, the Portuguese were apparently more concerned about maintaining a viable and effective administration before the handover than in preparing for the handover itself. They wanted to avoid a 'lame-duck' sunset government image. As mentioned above, this partly explains the Portuguese Macau administration's lukewarm effort to promote local Chinese to senior positions in the civil service or to make Chinese a working language in government offices and departments. In hindsight, apparently realizing that Portuguese influence and culture would soon disappear in Macau after their departure,[15] the Portuguese were probably not genuinely concerned about preserving Portuguese language and culture in post-1999 Macau but used the above as a bargaining tool against Beijing for short-term economic and/or political gains. On the other hand, Beijing was more concerned about establishing an effective post-1999 administration, comprising mainly local Chinese, to replace the departing Portuguese, although Beijing also wanted to ensure a smooth handover. In sum, in comparison to Lisbon, Beijing tended to see the handover from a longer term perspective and, arguably, from the long-term interests of Macau.[16] In order to ensure the effective implementation of the Joint Declaration and create appropriate conditions for the smooth transfer of sovereignty, the PRC and Portugal agreed to set up a Sino-Portuguese Joint Liaison Group and a Sino-Portuguese Land Group. The Joint Liaison Group was to conduct consultation and exchanges on the implementation of the Joint Declaration and its Annexes and on matters relating to the transfer of administration.[17] Each side of the Joint Liaison Group included an official of ambassadorial rank and four other members. The Land Group dealt with land leases in Macau and related matters. Land proved lucrative for the government as the territory is small and shallow waters have made reclamation easy.

However, the Portuguese and Chinese sometimes resolved their differences at a higher, diplomatic level or even at summit meetings between the two countries' top leaders. The Macau governor and his under-secretaries also played a vital role in the process of transition, especially in administrating the day-to-day affairs in Macau in the run-up to 1999 and in providing the necessary personnel and auxiliary supports for a smooth handover.

On the diplomatic front

In the early 1950s, the outbreak of the Korea War had ended any hope of diplomatic recognition between Beijing and Lisbon. The anti-Communist Salazar regime had followed the American policy of containment against the PRC and imposed an embargo on strategic goods to China.[18] It was only after the April 1974 Portuguese revolution that Lisbon began to approach Beijing for the normalization of relations between the two countries. After three years of informal exchange of views and 13 months of official negotiations, Portugal and the PRC established diplomatic relations on 8 February 1979. In the following year, Governor Melo Egidio was invited by the Chinese government to visit China. Egidio was received in Beijing by Deng Xiaoping, the paramount Chinese leader, and the two had discussed issues concerning Macau and Sino-Portuguese relations.[19] The question of Macau's reversion, however, was first mentioned by Chinese foreign minister Huang Hua when he visited Lisbon and met President Ramalho Eanes in June 1982. Two years later President Li Xiannian of the PRC visited Portugal.

President Ramalho Eane's visit to Beijing in May 1985, the first head of Portugal ever to visit China, was instrumental in setting the date for Sino-Portuguese negotiation over the question of Macau's future. The Chinese delegation headed by vice-foreign minister Zhou Nan, who also represented China in negotiating with the United Kingdom over Hong Kong's reversion, was apparently well-prepared while, in comparison, the Portuguese were poorly prepared.[20] The Portuguese delegation was also handicapped by the absence of China experts who could give advice on Chinese negotiation styles and tactics. Indeed, China studies is so undeveloped in Portugal that its foreign ministry simply does not have a China expert.[21] By contrast, some members of the Chinese negotiation team were very knowledgeable about Portugal and fluent in the Portuguese language. In any event, as admitted by Portugal's former Prime Minister Cavaco Silva who co-signed the 1987 Joint Declaration with the then Chinese Prime Minister Zhao Ziyang, it was not easy for a small country like Portugal to negotiate with a big and powerful country like China.[22] Furthermore, the Portuguese had to deal with Zhou Nan whom Silva regarded as a very tough negotiator. Silva pointed out that the Chinese had respected the Portuguese view of not having Macau's handover at the same time of Hong Kong's, although the chosen date fell short of Portuguese wish to extend Portuguese rule in Macau to the twenty-first century.[23] After the first round of Sino-Portuguese negotiation which was held in June and July 1986 and the deadlock over the handover date, Beijing had sent Zhou Nan to Lisbon to explain to President Mária Soares and Prime Minister Cavaco Silva the Chinese decision to take back both Hong Kong and Macau before the end of the twentieth century.[24] Since then high level diplomatic visits had become a pattern in resolving major differences or conflicts between Beijing and Lisbon over Macau.

Prime Minister Li Peng's February 1992 visit to Portugal, the first made by a top Chinese leader, was significant in ensuring Portugal's cooperation in Macau's transition process and seeking Lisbon's support in improving relations with European Union in the aftermath of the Tiananmen crackdown. While other European leaders were cool to Li Peng and embarrassed him with reference to China's human rights record, Cavaco Silva warmly received Li and only mentioned in passing his concerns about human rights in Macau.[25] In fact, Silva had tried to persuade other European leaders to end boycotting the PRC.[26] Silva returned an official visit to Beijing in April 1994, marking the seventh anniversary of the Joint Declaration. One year later, President Mária Soares visited Beijing. Thus, for the first half of the 1990s, Beijing and Lisbon had a friendly and close relationship.

However, the two countries' relations were clouded by the turn of events in Macau since the mid-1990s, namely the declining economy,[27] the erosion of law and order,[28] and the Portuguese administration's incompetence to deal with the above. Beijing was also unhappy with the slow pace of localization.[29] President Jorge Sampaio's visit to the PRC in February 1997 was poorly timed and clouded by the death of China's paramount leader Deng Xiaoping. Sino-Portuguese relations were under further stress when Beijing unilaterally declared that the PLA would be stationed in Macau after the handover. Lisbon was also unhappy with Beijing's refusal to invite a representative from the Vatican to the handover ceremony and Beijing's ambivalent attitude towards the East Timor question.[30] Indeed, it was unclear two months before the handover whether President Sampaio would actually attend the handover ceremony. It was only after President Jiang Zemin's visit to Portugal in October 1999 and Jiang's promise not to send an advance group of PLA to Macau before December 20 that the last hurdle of the transition process was cleared. In the end, both Jiang and Sampaio attended the handover ceremony and the PLA entered Macau at noon on 20 December after the departure of Sampaio and, unlike the Hong Kong handover which had created mutual distrust between Beijing and London, Sino-Portuguese relations were not tarnished by the reversion of Macau.

Sino-Portuguese Joint Liaison Group

While the overall direction and policy of Macau's transition was monitored at the diplomatic level, differences over actual policy implementations and the technicality of related problems were settled at meetings of the Sino-Portuguese Joint Liaison Group (JLG) as well as at its sub-committee meetings. Since the JLG's inauguration in January 1988, it had held 37 meetings. In addition, in the run-up to 1999, its sub-committees dealing with specific issues such as localization, international organizations, civil servants' retirement funds as well as the working group for the handover ceremony had held numerous meetings. The JLG's schedule was extremely tight, especially towards the final years of the handover.

Despite all the diplomatic fanfares and the banner of Sino-Portuguese friendship, there were serious disagreements between Lisbon and Beijing over Macau's transition process as indicated by the hot debates in the JLG meetings.[31] The most contentious issue during the 12 years of the JLG's existence was the so-called 'three big problems' (*sanda wenti*), namely the localization of the civil service, law, and the legalization of Chinese as an official language. The Chinese side insisted that localization of the civil service must aim at promoting the local ethnic Chinese, who constitute more than 96 per cent of Macau's population, to middle-rank and senior positions and that 'Macanization'[32] could not replace localization.[33] The Portuguese argued that localization should not have any racial bias and that only those local civil servants including Macanese who were qualified and competent would be promoted.[34] Other issues related to localization of the civil service such as the integration of Macau's civil servants into Portugal's civil service[35] and the arrangement of civil servants' retirement funds, which affected both Chinese and Portuguese interests, were also hotly debated at JLG meetings. The localization of Macau's laws – largely extended from laws enacted in Portugal – were less contentious, except on the question of capital punishment. The Portuguese Constitution and 'Criminal Code' forbid capital punishment as well as any punishment that indefinitely deprives an individual of their freedom.[36] The Chinese delegation refused to discuss the above issue at the JLG meeting and suggested that the SAR government be left to enact the related law.[37]

Another 'big problem', the localization of Chinese as an official language, was, at least in the beginning, not a contentious issue. The JLG reached a consensus in 1991 regarding the language issue and the Portuguese parliament passed a law in that year establishing Chinese as another official language in Macau with the same legal status as Portuguese. The Portuguese delegation, however, again brought up the language issue at the JLG meeting in 1997 by introducing a 'Bilingual Regulations' (*zhuangyu tongze*) for government operation, in an apparent attempt to strengthen the official status of Portuguese language in post-1999 Macau.[38] The Chinese delegation refused to discuss the Portuguese proposal at the JLG meeting, arguing that both the Joint Declaration and Macau's Basic Law clearly stipulated the official status of the Portuguese language after the handover and that any specific regulations related to that matter should be enacted by the SAR government.[39] The Portuguese did not give up and threatened to unilaterally enact and promulgate the 'Bilingual Regulations'.[40] Lisbon had apparently used this issue as a form of leverage, pressing Beijing to make concession on the issue of stationing a garrison of PLA troops in post-1999 Macau. In the end, the Chinese agreed to include the bilingual issue in the agenda of JLG meetings and the two sides appeared to have reached some kind of understanding on the issue.[41]

The nagging nationality issue was another contentious issue at JLG meetings. The issue concerned two groups of local residents: the first group involved an estimated 100000 locally born ethnic Chinese who possessed Portuguese passports and the second group an estimated 10000 Eurasian Macanese. Unlike the United Kingdom, which does not give the right of abode to Hong Kong's British National Overseas (BNO) passport holders, Portugal does not distinguish its passport holders according to place of residence. The local Chinese Portuguese passport holders, like any Portuguese passport holder, have the right of abode in Portugal. Lisbon does not have any problem with the nationality issue because the Portuguese Constitution recognizes multinationality. The problem lies with the PRC which does not recognize dual nationality. The Portuguese delegation of the JLG argued that all Portuguese passport holders, including the local ethnic Chinese, should be given the right to choose their nationality. The Chinese side argued that, according to the PRC's Nationality Law, all local Macau inhabitants with Chinese blood are Chinese nationals and their Portuguese passports are merely regarded as travelling documents with no consular protection in any Chinese territory. For the 10000 Eurasian Macanese, the majority of which have both Chinese and Portuguese blood, Beijing adopts a flexible policy allowing them to choose either the Chinese or Portuguese nationality with no deadline being imposed for the decision.[42] The Portuguese delegation, however, was not satisfied with the Chinese concession and stood firm on its position; it insisted that the nationality issue be included in the agenda until the final JLG meetings.[43] Not to discount Portugal's genuine concerns about consular protection in Chinese territory of Macau's Portuguese passport holders,[44] Lisbon, well aware of Beijing's bottom-line, appeared to use the nationality issue as a bargaining tool, pressing the Chinese side for concessions on other issues.

One particular issue which the Portuguese refused to include in the agenda was the question of the Orient Foundation. The Orient Foundation was registered in Lisbon in 1988 and its aim was to develop Portuguese culture and its continuity in the Orient. The financial source of the Foundation came mainly from the annual contributions of the local casinos (5 per cent of the net profit), that is, the Sociedade de Tourismo e Diversoes de Macau (STDM).[45] The Chinese side raised the issue at the JLG meetings and argued that the Orient Foundation should be based in Macau and managed by a team of local citizens since its financial source mainly came from Macau.[46] The Portuguese argued that since the Foundation was a private non-governmental organization its problems should not be discussed at JLG meetings.[47] The Chinese, however, insisted that the issue be included in the JLG agenda and refused to meet Carlos Monjardino, the President of the Foundation.[48] In the end, the Portuguese side agreed to discuss the issue at JLG meetings. It was reported that a mutual understanding on the issue was reached between President Mário Soares and President Jiang Zemin when the former visited Beijing in April 1995.[49] The two sides agreed to terminate the annual contributions from STDM to the Orient Foundation effective from January 1996 and to set up a new local foundation which receives the annual contributions from STDM.[50]

In the final two years of the transition process, disputes between the two sides became open in press conferences held after the JLG meetings. This was in sharp contrast to the early years of the transition process when differences between the two sides were disguised under the banner of Sino-Portuguese friendship. The Chinese side was apparently impatient with the slow process of localization, particularly the promotion of local Chinese to senior positions in the civil service,[51] the Portuguese administration's reportedly less than cooperative efforts in handing over the government documents and properties,[52] and the slow progress in preparing for the handover ceremony.[53] On the other side, the Portuguese were, as mentioned above, worried about the official status of the Portuguese language in post-1999 Macau and upset by Beijing's unilateral decision to station a garrison of PLA troops in Macau. In the end, the above disputes were eventually settled, albeit at the last minute and often not to the satisfaction of both sides, at the JLG meetings or at the diplomatic level by the exchange of visits between leaders in Beijing and Lisbon.

Overall, the two sides were more cooperative on issues not directly affecting their respective interests: these included issues such as Macau's membership in international or regional organizations, the extension of international treaties or agreements to Macau, as well as Macau's aviation agreements with other countries or regions.[54] Despite the power asymmetry between Portugal and the PRC, the former was often not necessarily being cornered or put at a disadvantageous bargaining position. Indeed, fearing nothing to lose after the handover, the Portuguese were able to bargain from a position of relative strength by threatening to become uncooperative during the transition, a strategy similar to the one used in the 1986 negotiations over Macau's reversion when the Portuguese threatened to leave Macau. In the end, the Portuguese were able to score points in gaining political concessions[55] and/or economic interests,[56] arguably at the expense of Macau's long-term interests.

The Sino-Portuguese Land Group

Macau comprises a small peninsula and two small islands. Land area has increased over the years through land reclamation. The pace of reclamation was quickened in the 1970s when Macau's economy began to take off. In the period 1972–94, Macau had expanded by one-third from 15 to 21.3 square kilometers.[57] The scarcity of land implies that reclamation and land leases in Macau provide potential revenue. The Joint Declaration set up a Sino-

Portuguese Land Group to deal with land leases in Macau together with related matters.

The land issue mainly affected the economic and not the political interests of the Portuguese Macau administration and the future SAR government. The Joint Declaration stipulates: 'From the entry into force of the Joint Declaration until 19 December 1999, all incomes obtained by the Portuguese Macau government from granting new leases and renewing leases shall, after deduction of the average cost of land production, be shared equally between the Portuguese Macau government and the future government of the Macau Special Administrative Region. All the income so obtained from land by the Portuguese Macau Government, including the amount of the above-mentioned deduction, shall be used for financing land development and public works in Macau'.[58]

The Chinese strategy to protect Macau's interests was threefold: (1) to limit the total amount of new land, including fields reclaimed from the sea and undeveloped land, to be granted to 20 hectares a year;[59] (2) to ensure that all land be sold at a good price in open biddings; and (3) to monitor the efforts of the Portuguese administration in spending the money from land leases on land development and public works in Macau. By and large, the Chinese side usually took the initiative in raising issues concerning land leases and other related matters at the Land Group meetings. Unlike their colleagues in the Joint Liaison Group, the Portuguese rarely voiced their opposition in public. In fact, during the 12-year existence of the Land Group, there were only a few contentious issues, namely the Chinese disapproval of the leasing of seven pieces of newly reclaimed land which was sold through secret biddings in February 1991,[60] the controversial development project in Praia Grande (*Nan Wan* or South Bay),[61] and the row over the reclamation of land between Taipa and Coloane islands.[62] The Chinese clearly wanted to stop corrupt officials from selling the land at lower than market prices through secret biddings or giving land development contracts to their friends. In the end, the Vieira administration had complied with most of the Chinese requests. Nonetheless, it was not all smooth sailing for the Land Group during the transition process because of the Portuguese administration's incompetence in collecting the premiums of land leases.[63] The Land Group had handed the Macau SAR administration with nearly 10 billion patacas (or 1.25 billion US dollars) of reserve fund from land leases at the handover, yet nearly 1 billion of premiums remained to be collected.[64]

The role of the Macau governor

The Macau governor was Portugal's representative in the territory. His relation with mainland China was thus affected by the change in Sino-Portuguese relations. When Beijing and Lisbon were still negotiating diplomatic relations in Paris, Governor José Leandro was invited to visit China in April 1978 by Ke Zhengping, head of the Nam Kwong (or Nan Guang) Company, PRC's semi-official agency in Macau. Leandro was the first Macau governor to visit China in 30 years. After Lisbon and Beijing established diplomatic relations in February 1979 a new era of Macau–mainland relations had begun. Leandro's successors had all been officially invited by the Chinese government to visit China. They had also exchanged visits with provincial leaders of Guangtong and the mayor of Zhuhai. The above visits had provided opportunities for the Macau governor, who was directly responsible for overseeing the process of Macau's transition, to exchange views with Chinese leaders. The mutual visits were particularly useful in facilitating cooperation between the Macau Portuguese administration and Chinese authorities in major construction projects such as Macau airport, the new Macau–Taipa bridge and the bridge linking Taipa to Zhuhai as well as in combating cross-border and organized crimes in the run-up to 1999.

Almeida e Costa, who served as Macau's governor from 1981 to 1986 prior to the Sino-Portuguese negotiations on the question of Macau's reversion, had been credited with modernizing the territory's infrastructure such as telecommunication and urban development and its administration.[65] Partly realizing that Macau would sooner or later be returned to China and partly as a measure to counterbalance the Macanese (Eurasian) domination of the local legislature and administrative bureaucracy, Costa bad tried to improve relations with the PRC and local Chinese elites.[66] He had consulted the Chinese government on important policies, including the decision to dissolve the Legislative Assembly in 1984[67] and the move to encourage the local Chinese to participate in politics, by removing the residential requirements for Chinese nationals in legislative elections.[68]

Governor Carlos Melancia who succeeded the ineffective Joaquim Pinto Machado[69] in July 1987 right after the signing of the Joint

Declaration, had adopted a cooperative attitude towards the PRC government. However, Melancia's handling of China–Macau relations was severely criticized by opposition party members in the Portuguese parliament and suggestions were made to set up a special committee composed of politicians from different parties to supervise Sino-Portuguese relations in Macau.[70] Melancia was forced to publicly rebuke China's interference in Macau's internal affairs, notably China's objection to the name of the Taipei Trade and Tourism Office in Macau[71] and the Portuguese administration's policy to privatize some public corporations and transfer their ownership to Portuguese companies in Macau.[72] Yet Melancia appeared to be quite cooperative in implementing the localization policy. After his visit to China in May 1988, Melancia had designed a tentative timetable under which the civil service 'leadership staffs' would consist of 50 per cent of local people in 1993, 70 per cent by 1995, 80 per cent by 1997, and 100 per cent by 1999.[73] He also created a new position of Under-Secretary for Transitional Affairs to work on matters concerning localization, and an inter-departmental committee had been set up to coordinate measures to train and upgrade the qualifications of local Chinese and Macanese civil servants.[74] Melancia, however, was forced to resign in September 1990 due to his alleged involvement in a bribery scandal; many believed he was a victim of Portuguese party politics.[75]

Vasco Rocha Vieira, the enclave's last governor, succeeded Melancia in April 1991. He was hailed by some of his colleagues[76] as well as local Chinese commentators[77] as the right man for the position.[78] Vieira had apparently pleased the Chinese government by complying with the Chinese wishes to adopt open biddings for land and construction projects, his promises to quicken the process of localization, the appointment of a High Commissioner for Anti-Corruption and his invitation of the mayor of Zhuhai, who had a row with Melancia over the construction of Macau airport, to visit Macau. Unlike his predecessor, Vieira had avoided confronting the Chinese authorities with controversial issues or publicly rebuking the Chinese. He was regarded by a noted pro-China legislator, Tong Chi Kin (or Tang Zhijian),[79] as a skilful politician who had given priority to maintaining Sino-Portuguese friendship and ensuring a smooth handover,[80] despite the fact that Vieira had failed to fulfil his promises to quicken the pace of localizing the civil service[81] and refused to replace his expatriate under-secretaries by local residents.[82] Ironically, the Vieira administration turned out to be an incompetent and inefficient administration which could do little to curb the deteriorating law and order or to pull Macau out of the economic recession in the final years of the transition. In any event, the sunset Vieira administration's overall performance was judged to have failed in the eyes of Macau citizens.[83]

The role of Xinhua during Macau's transition

Macau is a small, conservative and relatively closed society. Macau's small economy and population makes it highly vulnerable to outside influence, especially from the mainland. Its conservative population, comprised mainly of immigrants from neighbouring mainland regions, is largely apathetic towards politics; people were merely mobilized to vote by political groups, especially pro-China forces, in the elections. Macau is a free entrepôt and a capitalist society yet its economy is relatively closed and monopolized by mainland and Hong Kong capital. Furthermore, pro-China forces have dominated the political scene of Macau since the December 1966 anti-government riot.[84] Compared to Hong Kong, Macau's pro-democracy or independent forces are relatively weak due to the absence of a strong middle and professional class in the enclave. Due to its small economy, there is not much open space for the survival of Macau's democrats, who will have difficulty even to secure a stable job in an economy monopolized by pro-China companies.[85] On the other hand, the above social and political environments have made Beijing's effort to co-opt Macau's local elites a much easier job than similar efforts in Hong Kong.

The Nam Kwong Trading Company, established in June 1950, had been the official or semi-official representation of the PRC in Macau; it was led by the Hong Kong branch of the New China News Agency (NCNA or *Xinhua*) until the Macau branch of NCNA was inaugurated in September 1987.[86] The organization of Macau's NCNA is similar to Hong Kong's, comprising a director, four deputy directors, a general secretary, 11 departments and three offices.[87] However, the official rank of the head of Macau's NCNA is only equivalent to a vice-minister in the PRC's State Council while Hong Kong's NCNA director is equivalent to a minister. Furthermore, Beijing was and still is clearly more concerned about Hong Kong than Macau. President Jiang Zemin and Prime Minister Zhu Rongji are responsible for policies related to Hong Kong while Vice-Premier Qian Qichen is mainly responsible for Macau affairs.

The NCNA acted as the PRC's official organization in Macau implementing the central government's policy towards the enclave during the transition. Macau's Xinhua was given six major tasks or assignments during the process of transition. First, Xinhua is responsible for overseeing the operation of and providing political leadership for mainland companies which have dominated the Macau economy since the early 1990s.[88] Secondly, Xinhua acts as a coordinator for local pro-China groups. There are three major pro-China forces in Macau society, namely the Chinese Chamber of Commerce and its affiliated associations representing business and employer's interests, the labour unions representing the worker's and employee's interests, and the *kaifong* (*jiefang* or neighbourhood) associations representing grassroots citizens. Inevitably, there are conflicts of interests among and between pro-China groups. Xinhua has played a vital role in settling the conflicts and reaching a consensus among pro-China groups in regard to policies and strategies during the transitional period. Thirdly, Xinhua has monitored the implementation of Beijing's united front strategy by co-opting local social, economic and political elites into China's national or provincial people's congresses or political consultative committees, or into various committees set up for the preparations of Macau's handover. For reasons mentioned above, Macau's NCNA has been far more successful in co-opting local elites than its counterpart in Hong Kong. Fourthly, Xinhua has provided leadership for Macau's underground Chinese Communist Party (CCP) members.[89] Fifthly, it oversees the territory's Chinese official newspaper, the *Macau Daily News*, and is responsible for monitoring the latter's role as an instrument of propaganda for the CCP and PRC. Lastly, the local Xinhua branch cooperated with the Chinese members of the Joint Liaison Group in ensuring a smooth process of transition in the run-up to 1999 by: (1) controlling the local legislature and municipal council elections through pro-China forces;[90] (2) publicly involving itself in the drafting of Macau Basic Law and other preparatory works for the handover; and (3) monitoring the Portuguese Macau administration to comply with agreements reached at the JLG meetings – especially the progress of localization.

In sum, NCNA's Macau branch had been instrumental in securing a smooth transition to post-1999 Macau SAR. Xinhua's task had been greatly assisted by the generally pro-China political and social environments in Macau. Unlike Hong Kong's Xinhua, which had attempted to co-opt Hong Kong's democrats by including them in the process of Hong Kong Basic Law drafting, the local Xinhua branch in Macau simply excluded the then insignificant democratic voice in Macau's Basic Law drafting process.[91] The Macau democrats had also been excluded from the Preparation Committee for the handover and the Election Committee for the SAR's first chief executive. On the other hand, Xinhua had maintained a low political profile and refrained from publicly criticizing the outgoing Portuguese administration. It merely reiterated Chinese JLG members' concerns about the slow pace of localization,[92] Macau's depressed economy and deteriorating law and order,[93] and the Portuguese administration's reluctance to cooperate on the arrangements for stationing PLA troops in the territory.[94]

Conclusion

This chapter argues that partly due to the asymmetry of power between the PRC and Portugal Beijing had adopted a strategy in negotiating with Lisbon over the reversion of Macau that was very different from the one used in Sino-British negotiations over Hong Kong's reversion. Beijing took the initiatives and sometimes made unilateral decisions during the negotiations with Lisbon. The latter, however, was not without influence. Lisbon at times was able to capitalize on Beijing's stress on friendly Sino-Portuguese relations and the latter's concerns about a smooth transition by pressuring Beijing to make concessions on construction or land development projects which the Portuguese Macau administration normally gave to Portuguese companies.

The process of transition was often affected by the change in China–Portugal relations, especially at the summit or at high diplomatic levels. Deadlocks over issues of nationality and the stationing of PLA troops in the territory were resolved at summit meetings between Beijing and Lisbon leaders. However, the actual monitoring of the process of transition was the responsibility of the Sino-Portuguese Joint Liaison Group. Since the Group's inception in early

1988 it had held 37 general meetings and numerous sub-committee meetings. The Joint Liaison Group had discussed such nagging issues as the pace of localization, nationality, the Orient Foundation, retirement fund, bilingual policy and preparations for the handover. The Sino-Portuguese Land Group had monitored land leases and development during the transitional period.

Moreover, the Macau branch of Xinhua News Agency, the PRC's official representation in Macau, had closely monitored the process of transition by, *inter alia*, overseeing and coordinating the pro-China forces, co-opting Macau's social, economic and political elites, and pressing the Portuguese Macau administration to quicken the pace of localization and preparations for the handover. After Macau's reversion, the PRC has changed the names of the Xinhua News Agency in Hong Kong and Macau to Central Government's Liaison Office in Hong Kong SAR and Central Government's Liaison Office in Macau SAR, respectively.[95] It remains to be seen whether the new Liaison Office will play an important role in Macau's politics.

There is little doubt that the central government of PRC had taken positive attitudes and strategies to ensure a smooth process of transition in the run-up to 1999. Beijing also appears to be genuinely concerned about long-term economic development and social stability and public order in the post-1999 Macau SAR. By comparison, the Portuguese Macau administration appeared to be more interested in making short-term economic gains and/or preserving Portuguese culture and language in post-1999 Macau. In retrospect, the Chinese had apparently underestimated the Portuguese and failed to pressure the latter to quicken the pace of localization, curb the deterioration of law and order, improve the investment environment and pull Macau out of economic depression. Arguably, the sunset Portuguese Macau administration was simply incompetent or lost its will to accomplish the above. In any event, Beijing's overt concerns about a smooth handover had to some extent sacrificed Macau's long-term interests, an example of this being Beijing's approval to renew the contract with the Telecommunication Company of Macau when Hong Kong and the region have already opened the telecommunication services up to free market competition.

2
The Colonial Heritage and the Crisis of Government Legitimacy

The 1987 Joint Declaration of the PRC and Portugal stipulates that Macau's current social and economic systems, lifestyle and laws currently in force will remain basically unchanged for 50 years. Article 5 of the Basic Law of the Macau SAR further stipulates that 'the socialist system and policies shall not be practised in the Macau Special Administrative Region, and the previous capitalist system and way of life shall remain unchanged for 50 years'. It is interesting to note that neither the Joint Declaration nor the Basic Law has specifically mentioned the status of the enclave's current political system in post-1999 Macau. Arguably, the political system is part of the social or capitalist system and thus Beijing's promise not to practise 'socialist system and policies' in Macau implies that the current political system will also remain largely unchanged. However, it is probable that the Chinese government has some reservations about the colonial political system and has deliberately omitted to mention its future status in either of the two documents. Nonetheless, the fact that the Macau SAR government cannot possibly create a political system from scratch and Beijing's concerns about political stability in the enclave almost ensure that the political system inherited from the Portuguese will remain – at least in the short-term – largely intact after the handover.

This chapter examines various aspects of the political system, together with it special features, under the Portuguese rule and the perpetual crises of legitimacy of the former Portuguese administration as well as their implications for the post-1999 Macau SAR government.

The political heritage of Macau

According to Wu Zhiliang[1], the evolution of Macau's political system has three distinctive stages: (1) an era of self-rule by the local Portuguese after the Loyal Senate (*Leal Senado*) was established in 1583; (2) an era of colonial rule by Portugal when it declared in 1844 that Macau, Timor and Solor were to be administratively united as one Portuguese province; and (3) an era of regional self-rule after the promulgation of the Organic Statute of Macau (*Estatuto Organico de Macau*) in 1976. According to Wu, during the first era, the Portuguese enjoyed a certain degree of political autonomy such as having their own laws and ways of living; nevertheless, they had to obey the Chinese authorities and Chinese laws especially when involved in disputes with the local Chinese. During the colonial era, especially after the expulsion of local Chinese officials and the closing of the Chinese customs office in 1849, the Portuguese ended all direct political interventions from across the border. The Chinese authorities, however, never stopped interferring in the Portuguese administration of Macau. It was only in the wake of Portugal's 1974 revolution, after the Portuguese had officially recognized Chinese sovereignty and the Portuguese had only administration rights over Macau, that self-rule and political autonomy was granted to the enclave by both Beijing and Lisbon. The Macau political system as stipulated in the 1976 Organic Statute had remained intact until the handover.

Macau's political system[2]

Governor[3]

According to the Organic Statute of Macau, the governor was the centre of political power in Macau. He was the head of the Portuguese administration. He represented the president, parliament and government of Portugal. Only Portugal's judicial system and its extension in Macau was independent from the governor. The governor was politically accountable to the president who had appointed him. The official rank of governor was equivalent to a minister or secretary in the Portuguese government. The governor did not have a fixed tenure; his term of office usually terminated at the same time as the president who had appointed him had finished his own term of service.[4] The Macau governorship was a political appointment. A new president normally awarded that post to the person (friend or political ally) who had assisted him in the presidential election – although he normally consulted the local legislature and community on the appointment. Local opinion provided general qualification requirements without naming specific candidates but in any event the consultation results had little bearing on the president's final decision. Moreover, the governor could be dismissed only by the president of Portugal. In short, the source of the governor's political power came solely from Lisbon.

The Organic Statute had also given the governor a share of the law-making power which normally belongs to the legislature in a modern, democratic government. He and his administration often took the initiative in drafting laws, with the exception of those within the exclusive authority of the legislature such as electoral laws, for discussion and approval in the legislature. The governor could also issue decrees and these enjoyed the same hierarchical status as laws in Macau's own legal system. Moreover, both the governor and the Legislative Assembly had the power to amend or repeal legislation issued by the other provided that it did not fall within the reserved area of competency.[5] Inevitably this created conflict and tense relations between the governor and the legislature, which a subject will be dealt with below.

Under-secretaries

The Organic Statute provided no specific authority to the seven under-secretaries (*secretarios-adjuntos*); they held no executive power except to the extent of that freely delegated to them by the governor.[6] They were nominated by the governor but appointed by the president of Portugal; their official rank was equivalent to a deputy minister/secretary in Portugal. When the governor or his under-secretaries were involved in legal disputes, their cases could be only put on trial in a court in Portugal.[7] Unlike their counterparts in Hong Kong, Macau's under-secretaries held political positions; they were not civil servants in the enclave's civil service yet each headed six to 11 government offices.[8] In terms of the actual functioning of the Portuguese administration, the seven under-secretaries were real policy-makers in their respective areas of responsibility. As has been said, their term of office was normally terminated when the tenure of the governor who had nominated them expired.[9] This could cause serious problems in terms of policy continuity and result in great waste of public resources when a new governor and his team of under-secretaries terminated or changed the policy commitments of the former administration.

Legislature

The Legislative Assembly shares the law-making power with the governor.[10] Prior to 1976, Macau's legislature was merely a consultative body of the governor with limited legislative power.[11] It was only after the promulgation of the 1976 Organic Statute that the local legislature had begun to share the law-making power with the governor and became an autonomous organ. However, every statute enacted by the legislature had to be submitted to the governor for promulgation before it could be considered as having legal effect.

The 1976 legislature comprised of 17 members including six directly elected by Macau citizens, six indirectly elected through functional constituencies[12] and five appointed by the governor. The Organic Statute was revised in 1990 to expand the legislature to 23 seats of which eight were directly elected, eight were indirectly elected[13] and seven appointed. The 16 elected seats, especially the eight directly elected seats, had made the legislative body partially representative and accountable to the Macau citizens. In fact, the Legislative Assembly has, since 1993, arranged 'legislator office hours' to receive complaints from and provide consultation to local residents. Some directly elected members have also rendered their respective offices accessible to Macau citizens. Arguably, the inauguration of the 1976 legislature had started the process of democratization in the enclave; legislature elections have since inspired increasing citizen participation in politics. However, Macau's democratization process has been severely limited by various factors, particularly the enclave's conservative political and social environments.[14]

The legislature can also be considered to have performed unsatisfactorily in terms of legislation, partly due to the sharing of the law-making power with the governor. The Portuguese administration, assisted by appointed legislators, had often effectively defeated laws proposed by individual legislators that contradicted the administration's interests. More importantly, the Portuguese administration did not provide sufficient legal personnel to the legislature and few directly elected legislators (who were often outspoken against the administration) had the legal competence to draft laws.

Consultative Council

Article 4 of the Organic Statute stipulates that the 'Consultative Council functions together with the Governor'. The governor or his designate chairs the Council's meetings. The Consultative Council comprises ten members including five indirectly elected and five appointed by the governor.[15] Two of the former are elected from the existing municipal councillors, while the other three represent, respectively, employers' interests, labour interests, as well as professional, charity, culture, education and sport interests. The appointed members are normally notable members of the social and economic elites. It is worth noting that after the 1990 revision of the Organic Statute, no government official sat in the Consultative Committee,[16] a body which had since become the governor's personal consultation body.

Article 48 of the Organic Statute stipulates that the governor must consult the Consultative Council on law drafts to be submitted to the legislature, decrees and regulations before their promulgation, the general direction of economic, social, fiscal and executive policies, the decision to refuse the entrance of or to expel unwelcome personnel to the territory as well as other legal matters. Unlike the Legislative Assembly, Consultative Council meetings are not open to the public. All proceedings and minutes of Council meetings are thus confidential and the Council is responsible only to the governor. However, opinions or resolutions of the Council are not binding on the governor who is not even required to give explanation if he does not follow the Council's advice. Nevertheless, the organization and functioning of the Consultative Council suggest that the organ apparently exists to enhance the legitimacy of governance of the Portuguese administration. It is nevertheless wise for a politically astute governor to reach a consensus in the Consultative Council before issuing important decrees and/or policies. Indeed, the Portuguese administration had set up a dozen specialized consultative committees on economic, social, educational, cultural, youth, language and sport affairs as well as matters pertaining to the transition of sovereignty in 1999. The governor or his designate normally chaired these consultative committees which are attached to concerned government offices. Through the above committees, then, the governor co-opted the economic and social elites into the political system and significantly enhanced the legitimacy of the Portuguese administration.

Judicial system

Macau's current legal system is based on and derives from Portugal's own legal system. Portugal's 'Civil Code', 'Criminal Code', 'Commercial Code', 'Civil Procedure Code' and 'Criminal Procedure Code' have thus extended to Macau. Although, increasingly after 1976, laws and decrees were enacted in Macau by the governor and the local legislature, Macau's judicial organs as stipulated in the Organic Statute of Macau were still under the Portuguese judicial system, a component of Portugal's judicial organization.[17] Portugal's Court of Final Appeal had retained its jurisdiction over Macau until several months before the handover,[18] yet the governor and his under-secretaries, if involved in legal disputes, were still subject to trial in a court in Portugal.

As commonly practised in Western democracies, Macau's judicial system is independent from the executive administration. As stipulated in Article 53 of the Organic Statute, all courts in Macau are independent and subject to law only. The judges were directly appointed in Portugal and could not be removed by the local Portuguese administration. They are not required to obey orders or instructions from the administration. Moreover, they are not responsible for the trial decisions except those stipulated by law. The Western legal tradition of an independent judiciary is probably the most valuable heritage left to the Macau SAR government by the Portuguese. Yet it is far from clear whether this Western tradition can survive in a Chinese-dominated political and judicial system.

Municipal councils

Despite its comparatively small area and population, Macau has a central government and two local municipal councils, the Leal Senado and Municipio das Ilhas which are responsible for urban planning and development, public sanitary works, cultural and sport activities, as well as maintenance and protection of the environment and quality of living in the Macau Peninsular and the two islands (Taipa and Coloane), respectively. As mentioned above, Leal Senado was first established in 1583 by the local Portuguese residents as an autonomous assembly and had functioned both as a central and local administrative organ until 1848 when Portugal enforced colonial rule in the enclave.[19] Leal Senado had since become merely a local municipal organ. Surprisingly, the 1976 Organic Statute and its subsequent revisions do not stipulate the organization and functions of the two municipal councils. The existing municipal management system is still, to some extent, based on Portugal's 1933 'Overseas Administration Reform Law'.[20] However, some tasks previously assigned to the two municipal councils – such as construction of public roads and urban planning – have been moved to other offices or departments of the central administration.[21]

On 3 October 1988, a new law (Law no. 24/88/M) was promulgated to replace the 1933 law and to provide a new structure to the two local municipal administrations, that of an assembly (*Assembleia Municipal*) and an executive committee (*Camara Municipal*). The Municipal Assembly of Leal Senado comprises of 13 members of which five are directly elected, five are indirectly elected[22] and three appointed; the Assembly of Municipio Das Ilhas comprises of nine members, distributed evenly between direct, indirect and appointed seats.[23] The first elections for the two Municipal Assemblies were held in April 1989. Like the Legislative Assembly, elected members of the Municipal Assemblies serve a term of 4 years. The *Camara Municipal* of the two municipal administrations comprises of a president, a vice-president, a full-time member and two part-time members. The former three are normally appointed members while the latter two are elected members of the Municipal Assemblies. The official rank of the president of the two municipal organs was equivalent to an office director in the Portuguese administration. Both organs are administered under the supervision of the Under-Secretary for Administration, Education and Youth.

Article 95 of the Macau Basic Law stipulates that 'municipal organization which are not organs of political power may be established in the Macau Special Administrative Region'. Arguably, in the view of some local pro-China commentators, the two municipal organizations are in fact 'organs of political power' because both have elected members and a high degree of administrative and fiscal autonomy and hence contravene the Basic Law.[24] If the real objective behind this argument is to strengthen the 'executive-led' SAR government by killing off the two partially elected Municipal Assemblies, it will be a major set-back to the enclave's democratization process.

Civil service

Article 68 of the Organic Statute stipulates that Macau has its own civil service system which is subject only to the supervision of the territory's administration. Articles 69 stipulates that personnel from Portugal's civil service can apply to work in Macau's civil service for a fixed period of time while keeping their original posts in Portugal; they can also apply to join Macau's civil service in a permanent basis. The above arrangement is reciprocal in that Macau's civil servants who wish to work in Portugal's civil service for a fixed period of time or join the latter permanently can do so (Article 70). This provisions in the Organic Statute facilitated the recruitment of Portuguese expatriates to the enclave's civil service. Indeed, in the 1980s and the early 1990s about 10 per cent of Macau's civil servants were recruited from Portugal or its former colonies in Africa and Asia. The Portuguese expatriates had occupied most of the upper echelons in the bureaucratic hierarchy until the eve of handover. However, the stipulations of Articles 69 and 70 had also served as a basis for the later government scheme to integrate those local civil servants who had little confidence in post-1999 Macau to Portugal's civil service system.

Macau has a large team of civil servants in comparison to its relatively small population. According to statistics provided by the government, as of March 1999, Macau had 17 128 civil servants,[25] or a ratio of 1 civil servant to 24 local residents, far higher than the ratio of 1:36 in Hong Kong. Indeed, the number of Macau's civil servants has increased fourfold over the last two decades while the population has increased by merely a two-thirds over the same period of time. Moreover, the salary of civil servants has greatly increased over the last two decades, by a two-digit figure growth rate in the 1980s and early 1990s. As a result, the average salary of civil servants is more than double that in the private sectors. However, the civil servants' high income is not matched by their performance. Macau's civil service is notorious for its low efficiency and incompetence.

Macau has a large and complicated public administration. During the pre-handover era under the Portuguese administration, the governor and his seven under-secretaries had headed, respectively, a total of 56 government offices. There was insufficient, or a complete lack of, co-ordination between under-secretaries as well as between government offices and this often resulted in overlapping as well as unclear duties and responsibilities in policy implementation among and between offices and departments. Moreover, some important government functions and policy implementations were shared by different offices or departments which were under the supervision of different under-secretaries. For example, the police force is comprised of the security force, the marine and the municipal police, all under the supervision of the Under-Secretary for Security as well as the judicial police which was supervised by the Under-Secretary for Justice. The responsibility for implementing the immigration policy is shared between the Office of Service for Identification of Macau which was under the supervision of the Under-Secretary for Justice as well as the Department of Immigration which was supervised by the Under-Secretary for Security. Administration redundancy and incompetence can be seen to have had a clearly, adverse effect on Macau's economic development. A business person from Taiwan who intends to invest in Macau, for example, may have to go to several government offices or departments and take two years or longer to complete the complicated process of application.

Relations between the executive and legislative branches

In spite of the share of legislative functions granted to the governor, the Legislative Assembly remains constitutionally the foremost holder of law-making power.[26] Arguably, at least since the beginning of the transition in the late 1980s, the local legislature could have had a much more significant role in the creation of law. Yet statistics of the last two decades show that the number of statutes enacted yearly by the governor was more than eight times the number of statutes enacted by the Legislative Assembly.[27] Moreover, even in the area of the legislature's competence, where the governor could only make law where duly authorized, the governor had presented many more legislative proposals than had legislators.

Indeed, it appears that the legislature had been reluctant to legislate during the transitional period. Several explanations have been forwarded.[28] First and foremost, as mentioned above, few directly elected legislators have the legal competence to draft laws and were further handicapped by the inadequate legal support provided by the Portuguese administration. The legislature has been notorious for its slow pace of enacting laws. In the 1997–98 legislature, for example, only one law and three legislative proposals were endorsed.[29] Secondly, many pro-Beijing legislators would be ill at ease drafting law in areas where no position had as yet been made clear by the PRC.[30] In any event, the conservative-dominated body would hardly be sensitive to the changing social and political environments that required the enactment of new laws. Lastly, there seemed to be a tacit agreement among and between pro-Beijing and pro-Portuguese legislators that prominence should be given to the governor.[31] The governorship was largely an appointed position while the legislators themselves, apparently having in mind the future 'executive-led' post-1999 SAR administration as stipulated in the Basic Law, have preferred a low profile.

Nevertheless, both the checks and balances, or unbalances, between the executive and legislative power branches as stipulated in the Organic Statute of Macau, especially the governor's option to request the President of Portugal to dissolve the legislature and the latter's power to censor the governor and to ratify legislation enacted by the governor, do not necessarily lead to harmonious relations between the two. Indeed, conflict between the governor and the Legislative Assembly did erupt in 1980 and 1984, when a Macanese-dominated legislature tried to expand its power at the expense of the governor.[32] The then legislature had also exercised its prerogative to ratify legislation enacted by the governor as many as ten times, yet this right has not been exercised since 1983.[33] During the same period of time, the governor had four times refused to sign legislation enacted by the Legislative Assembly; this has since happened only twice, both in the third legislature (1984–88).[34] However, the above conflicts between the two bodies have proved to be exceptions. Indeed, in the enclave's tradition of informal politics,[35] the relationship between the legislative and executive power branches has been for the most part smooth and based on a search for consensus even where the law does not demand this.[36]

No doubt the relationship between the legislative and executive power branches will continue to evolve in the post-1999 SAR government. The Macau Basic Law, which largely copies the Hong Kong Basic Law and ignores Macau's political tradition, gives the sole law-making power to the legislature. It is doubtful, however, in light of the organ's past record, whether the existing legislature has the capability to carry out its new assignments. As has acutely pointed out by Ng Kuok Cheong (or Wu Guochang), a pro-democracy legislator, the SAR legislature needs to increase its capacity by eight times to handle the anticipated increase in work-load.[37] It is uncertain if the SAR administration is willing to provide the necessary back-up for the legislature's new role.

Special features of Macau's inherited political system

First and foremost, Macau's political system as inherited from the former Portuguese rule is executive-dominated. As commonly practised in any colonial regime, the Macau governor was entrusted by Portugal to represent the latter's interests in the enclave. The governor was the head of the administration and his under-secretaries had no formal constitutional power except executive power delegated by the governor. The governor was also responsible for enacting laws for the enclave until 1976 when he has since had to share the law-making power with the Legislative Assembly. Even after 1976, however, as mentioned above, the governor had enacted more laws and decrees than the statutes enacted by the legislature. Although Macau's political system has adopted the Western model of checks and balances between the executive, legislative and judicial power branches, the balance or unbalance of power between the administration and legislature clearly favours the former. Nonetheless, the actual political power and influence of the governor depends to a large extent on the personality and political prowess of a particular governor. Governor Joaquim Pinto Machado was often at loggerheads with his under-secretaries, especially Carlos Monjardino, the Under-Secretary for Economics and a trusted friend of President Mário Soares. Machado found it impossible to implement his policies and was forced to resign after one year (1986–87) in office. However, the above is an exception. Most post-1976 governors had a firm grip of power in the administration.

Secondly, the Portuguese administration was characterized by the personal, patron-client networks established by the governor, his under-secretaries and office directors. The governor often nominated his friends to be his under-secretaries; these in turn appointed their close friends or trusted civil servants to the posts of office director/deputy director or department chief and established their respective personal, patron-client networks. Following their superior's example, office directors had also established their own respective patron-client networks by appointing their friends or relatives to the government bureaucracy. Indeed, the revised 1992 'Regulations for the Recruitment of Expatriates' (No. 60/92/M decree) had provided green light for the above practice by inserting a clause which gave priority to hiring expatriates' spouses in the civil service. This practice was further helped by the loopholes and the lack of a unified recruitment policy in the civil service and Macau citizens' tolerance of personal or back-door politics. This has created unjust competition and low morale among civil servants, especially those who are talented and qualified but barred from promotion to a higher rank because of the lack of personal connections.

Thirdly, partly because of the above, bureaucratic corruption and incompetence were pervasive in the Portuguese administration. Although rampant corruption was often linked to the enclave's casino business,[38] the Portuguese administration's intransparent decision-making process and personal patron-client networks had facilitated as well as provided the opportunities for corruption. Bureaucratic corruption is a major obstacle to the development of a modern, efficient and competent civil service. The incompetence of the Portuguese administration had been demonstrated by its failure to maintain law and order to attract foreign investment and to pull the enclave out of economic depression.

Fourthly, the Portuguese administration had done little to establish good relations with the citizens of Macau. Partly due to the language barrier where very few of the local Chinese can speak Portuguese, there was little direct communication between the Portuguese administration and the public as a whole. The Portuguese had first relied on the Cantonese-speaking Macanese and later, after the agreement in 1987 with Beijing on the reversion of Macau, on the pro-China organizations as the intermediary between the administration and the masses. As a result, Macau's mass public were alienated from politics. Even after the pro-China forces have, since the mid-1980s, come to gradually dominate the enclave's political scene, a significant portion of the Macau populace are apathetic towards political participation.[39] The high voter turnout rate in the last two legislature elections was merely the result of political mobilization by the pro-China and pro-business forces.[40] The absence of effective public supervision over the administration has in turn indirectly encouraged bureaucratic corruption and incompetence.

Lastly, consensus politics has a strong tradition in Macau. Under the Portuguese administration, the governor and his under-secretaries had always tried to reach a consensus with the legislators before proposing laws to the Legislative Assembly. If the administration sensed strong opposition in the legislature it would withdraw the law proposal. However, the Portuguese administration's legislation effort was normally supported by both the appointed legislators and the pro-China legislators who were more concerned about political stability than law-making. In fact, different political forces within the legislature had normally first reached a compromise and then reached a consensus before formally voting on a piece of legislation. The pro-China forces which constitute conflicting business and labour interests have the practice of trying to compromise and reach a consensus among themselves, sometimes assisted by the PRC's local New China News Agency,[41] before taking an official stand. Yet this consensus, or 'conspiracy' politics, as the local democrat Ng Kuok Cheong has coined it,[42] is very different from 'corporatist' politics commonly practised in some Western democracies, where a strong civil society has provided effective supervision over the government and the organized interests. The unintended, or intended, consequence of consensus politics in Macau thus represents the exclusion of the mass public from participating in government policy-making.[43]

The crisis of government legitimacy

Like other colonial administrations including Hong Kong,[44] the Portuguese Macau administration had suffered perpetual crises of governance legitimacy. In the official Chinese view, the sovereignty of the territory of Macau, unlike Hong Kong, was never ceded to Portugal by a treaty; the Sino-Portuguese Treaty of 1887 only transferred administrative rights over the territory to the Portuguese.[45] Macau's border with the mainland and its coastal waters had never been officially demarcated. However, according to international law, the 1887 Treaty is ambiguous on the question of sovereignty.[46] Portugal's legitimacy to rule Macau was further handicapped by its vulnerability to influence from the Chinese authorities. A small enclave of 23.5 square kilometers, with virtually no resources, Macau is totally dependent on outside sources for such basics as food and water. In the 400 years of the Portuguese presence in Macau, Chinese authorities had several times (in 1748, 1778, 1787, 1922, 1952 and 1966) imposed, or threatened to impose, economic sanctions against the enclave, and on each occasion the Macau government had no alternative but to yield to Chinese pressure.[47] The Chinese had never failed to remind the Portuguese that sovereignty over the territory belongs to China. Portuguese authorities did not even have control over the inflow of people from the mainland until it was agreed in 1990 at meetings of the Sino-Portuguese Liaison Group that, in order to stop illegal immigrants from entering Macau, the Portuguese administration would set up a customs office at the Zhuhai-Macau border.[48]

In an enclave where over 96 per cent of the population is ethnic Chinese, the legitimacy of a non-elected, Portuguese-dominated government was continually challenged by the Chinese community.[49] Unlike their colonies in Africa, the Portuguese had no plans to popularize the Portuguese language among the native population. The Portuguese regarded Macau as a Far East entrepôt rather than as a colony for Portuguese settlers. Portuguese was only taught in government schools set up for Portuguese and Macanese (Portuguese-Chinese and Portuguese-Malay mixed blood) children.[50] Chinese children who attended Chinese or English private schools never got the chance to learn Portuguese. As a result, few local Chinese could become middle- or high-ranking civil servants. Those positions were normally occupied by either Portuguese expatriates or by Macanese. As mentioned above, the Portuguese from Portugal had to rely on the Macanese who could speak Portuguese and the local dialect (Cantonese) to communicate with the Chinese. The lack of direct communication between the government and the general public resulted in mutual misunderstanding and suspicion. The Chinese were also resentful of the Macanese, especially those who had demonstrated a condescending attitude towards the local Chinese. A crisis of legitimacy regarding the government occurred in the December 1966 anti-government riots in which eight local Chinese were killed and hundreds injured.[51] For two years after the incident, Macau was without an effective government: police officers rarely ventured into the streets for fear of being attacked and the government virtually stopped functioning. Public order was maintained by neighbourhood societies and by other influential social, religious and economic organizations such as the Chinese Chamber of Commerce.

The Portuguese revolution in 1974 brought political reform to Macau. In 1976, the Portuguese parliament ratified the Organic Statute of Macau, under which the Legislative Assembly was given the constitutional power to make laws, scrutinize public expenditure and amend the Organic Statue. About one-third of the seats in the Assembly were directly elected by the citizens of Macau. The procedure legitimacy of the Macau government had thus been improved somewhat by the introduction of direct elections in the legislature in 1976 and in the municipal councils in 1989. By the mid-1990s, more than half the eligible voters had registered and a record high of 64.5 per cent of voters turned out to cast their ballots in the 1996 legislature election.

However, the crisis of legitimacy of the colonial government had worsened in the run-up to 1999.[52] Unlike the response from London, Lisbon did not condemn or criticize Beijing's massacre of student demonstrators at the 1989 June Fourth Tiananmen Square incident. China's human rights records were rarely mentioned at meetings between Chinese and Portuguese leaders. Lisbon was apparently more willing than London to co-operate with Beijing's wish for a smooth transfer of sovereignty of Macau.[53] It was quietly accepted in Lisbon that the Macau government could not rule the enclave without the consent of China, despite the assurance in the Joint Declaration that the Portuguese could continue to govern the territory until 20 December 1999.[54] To avoid irritating the Chinese government, the Macau government – unlike the Hong Kong government under Chris Patten, who wanted to enhance the legitimacy of the British rule by quickening the process of democratization in Hong Kong[55] – had not taken any steps to promote democracy in the territory. It opted instead to let pro-Beijing social groups, such as the *kaifong* or neighbourhood associations or labour unions to mobilize the Macau citizens to register as voters and to vote in the elections.[56] The government had thus unintendedly assisted the pro-Beijing groups to consolidate their power in the Legislative Assembly and the municipal councils (*Leal Senado* and *Camara Municipal das Ilhas*) at the expense of the democratic groups. It appeared to the Macau public that there existed a shadow government run by the PRC's local Xinhua branch and pro-Beijing force.

However, the Portuguese administration had made some efforts to improve its image among the Macau populace. The Public Service and Information Centre was inaugurated in 1987 and attempted to bridge the communication gap between the government and the public. Yet the service rendered by the Centre was far from satisfactory. It has since been criticized by some observers as being too bureaucratic.[57] The centre does not help citizens to solve problems but only refers citizen complaints or requests to the government offices or departments concerned. Indeed, being merely a department under the Office of Public Service and Administration, the centre has difficulty even in getting the co-operation from government offices to respond to citizen grievances. In any event more local residents have visited the offices of individual legislators than those of the centre for assistance. In the first eight months of 1999, the centre had filed 150 cases, while in 1998 democrat Ng Kuok Cheong's office and pro-China legislator Tong Chi Kin's office had received 326 and 423 cases, respectively.[58] The Portuguese administration since the mid-1980s had also attempted to enhance its legitimacy of governance by making its decision-making process more open through the establishment of policy consultative bodies. Yet the Portuguese appeared to be more interested in appeasing the Chinese government by co-opting pro-China elites into the consultative bodies than in soliciting public responses to government policies. In the final analysis, the consultative bodies had done little to improve the public image of the sunset government.

Policy performance, especially in the economic area, was the Portuguese Macau administration's only source of political legitimacy. The Costa and Melancia administrations had contributed to the rapid economic growth of the 1980s and early 1990s by providing the necessary infrastructure such as electricity, telecommunications, and reclamation of land for development. In the early 1990s, many Macau people were proud of the enclave's rapid economic growth.[59] Yet the collapse of the real estate market in 1994 had plunged Macau into economic recession. Furthermore, in the final years of colonial rule, the Portuguese appeared only to be interested in maintaining the status quo and in getting the best out of their economic and political interests.[60] In the 1990s, all major construction projects, such as the airport and the second Macau-Taipa Bridge, were awarded to Portuguese companies. The government had done little to alleviate the depressed economy or curb the deteriorating public order and corruption among government officials, especially among the police force. In the eyes of the Macau citizens, the sunset colonial government had simply lost its will and hence its legitimacy to govern Macau.

Implications for the post-1999 Macau SAR government

After more than 400 years of presence in Macau, the Portuguese have left a political system which has both strengths and shortcomings. On the positive side, Macau has inherited a Western, partial democracy with a framework of separation of power between the executive, legislative and judicial branches of power. It is a partial democracy because, on the one hand, freedom of expression and publication, freedom of association as well as fundamental rights and freedoms were guaranteed by the Portuguese Constitution and are now protected by the Macau Basic Law.[61] Furthermore, Macau has inherited an independent judicial system. On the other hand, power distribution in the political system clearly favours the executive branch while the legislature plays a subordinate role. Although the Basic Law has granted the new legislature the sole law-making power, initiatives relating to the proposing of laws are in the hands of the administration. In addition, law proposals concerning government policies from individual legislators need the written approval of the SAR's chief executive.[62] By and large, the authoritarian nature of an executive-dominated Portuguese regime has been inherited by the new SAR administration.

On the negative side, the Portuguese have bequeathed an inefficient, incompetent and many would say corrupted bureaucracy to the SAR government. The lack of co-ordination between and among government offices has resulted in overlapping responsibilities, or irresponsibilities, and redundancy in government bureaucracy. Recruitment and promotion irregularities have caused low morale among civil servants. There are signs that the practice of establishing personal patron-client networks has continued in some offices or departments headed by newly promoted local Chinese.[63] Moreover, the new administration has the urgent task to bridge the gap of communication between the government and the mass public, which had been previously ignored by the Portuguese administration. The general political apathy among the Macau citizens is another obstacle to political development in post-1999 Macau.

The foremost task for the new administration, however, is to enhance its legitimacy of government. Like its predecessor, the non-elected SAR administration is weak in procedure legitimacy.[64] While the Portuguese never really had the *de jure* sovereignty over Macau and hence had suffered perpetual crises of legitimacy of governance in a Chinese territory, neither does the SAR government possess such a sovereignty. The 'Preamble' of the Macau Basic Law stipulates that the PRC, *not* the Macau people, 'will resume the exercise of sovereignty over Macau with effect from 20 December 1999'. The chief executive of the SAR, like his predecessors, is not popularly elected by the local residents but appointed by a central government, albeit this time it is based in Beijing instead of Lisbon. The new administration can thus only hope to increase its legitimacy through policy performance. It can enhance its legitimacy of governance by taking concrete steps to solve the so-called 'three big problems', namely law and order, economic depression and bureaucratic inefficiency. Equally important, however, the new administration must strengthen its anti-corruption effort and open its decision-making process to the public by soliciting citizens' opinions through opinion polls, public forums or other channels. The chief executive should also follow the convention of the former Portuguese governor to respect the legislature[65] and not to interfere the enclave's judicial system. Last but not least, the new administration must carry out political reforms, especially measures to streamline government bureaucracy and standardize the processes of recruitment, training, evaluation and promotion of civil servants. A good, efficient and responsive government, no doubt, will continue to enhance its legitimacy among its citizens.

The Macau Basic Law has streamlined the government bureaucracy by reducing the former six levels of senior official ranks to four, namely the general secretary (equivalent to the former under-secretary), office or service director, department and division heads. By deleting the ranks of section and sector chiefs, it certainly helps to simplify and quicken the process of administration, yet the size and the original number of offices remains largely unchanged.[66] The structure and organization of the government bureaucracy remain a redundant one with overlapping functions. However, the re-structuring of the secretariat from seven under-secretaries in the Portuguese administration to the current five general secretaries is a clear improvement. It has made the government organization look more reasonable by putting offices and/or departments performing similar functions under one general secretary.[67] Yet this represents a comparatively small step in reforming the still inefficient and lowly esteemed bureaucracy.

3
The Politics of Localization

Localization is an important process in decolonization of any sovereignty transfer. Macau is no exception. After the signing of the Joint Sino-Portuguese Declaration in 1987 on the reversion of Macau, localization had become a contentious issue between Beijing and Lisbon. A special subcommittee was set up in the Sino-Portuguese Joint Liaison Group to monitor the process of localization. To the Chinese government, the localization of Macau's civil service, the legalization of Chinese as an official language, and the localization of law are the 'three big issues' (*sanda wenti*) during the transitional period. Indeed, the so-called three big issues are closely related. The progress, or the lack of, in one issue is bound to affect the other two. The progress in the localization of Macau's civil service in particular was regarded by the Chinese government as the core of the localization process. The Chinese believe that when the senior positions in the government are occupied by ethnic Chinese the language issue will be automatically resolved. At the same time, the major obstacle hindering the localization of law can be removed by replacing Portuguese judges, procurators and lawyers with local Chinese. This chapter analyses various aspects of the localization process especially the conflicting views of Beijing and Lisbon on the three big issues.

Macau's civil service in transition

There are three perspectives of localization of Macau's civil service. The first view tends to equate localization with 'Sinification', that is, the promotion and recruitment of local Chinese residents to higher positions in the civil service. It argues for a more 'representative bureaucracy',[1] that is, that localization should accurately reflect the ethnic composition of Macau's citizens. This 'Sinification' interpretation of localization was held by the local Chinese who constitute 96 per cent of Macau's population. The second perspective of localization, or 'Macanization', which argues that promotion priority should be given to bilingual Macanese, was held by some radical Macanese. The Macanese are of Portuguese–Chinese or Portuguese–Asian mixed-blood. The Macanese population is estimated to be around 10 000 or about 2 per cent of Macau's population. Understandably, the Macanese, who speak Portuguese and Chinese (Cantonese) and occupied most of the middle rank posts in the civil service, wanted to be promoted to higher ranks after the withdrawal of Portuguese expatriates. The third perspective is a mixture of 'Sinification' and 'Macanization'. This view argues that recruitment and promotion of civil servants should be based on qualification and merit only, regardless of race and nationality.

The Chinese government have tended to side with the 'Sinification' interpretation, although realizing the important role of the Macanese in a smooth transition to the post-1999 administration. The Portuguese government in Macau, on the other hand, was sympathetic to the Macanese view, although it shied away from the radical 'Macanization' view and adopted the more moderate view of emphasizing qualification and performance. Different interpretations of localization had led to policy conflicts and mistrust between the Chinese and Portuguese authorities. The Chinese often complained about the slow pace of localization, particularly the lukewarm efforts of the Portuguese administration to promote local Chinese to higher ranks. The Portuguese defended their policy by pointing out the generally low educational level and language proficiency among the local Chinese.

The main features of Macau's civil service

Macau had an executive-led, colonial style administration. The governor was directly appointed by the President of Portugal and was not accountable to the Macau populace. The governor was usually a close friend of the president and a member of the same political party. The territory's chief administrators, the seven under-secretaries, were also political appointees. They were appointed by the president, with the tacit agreement of the governor. Normally, as has been mentioned, the complete upper echelon of the leadership changed when a governor was replaced. Moreover, although the directors and deputy directors of government offices and departments are permanent civil servants, many were personal friends of the under-secretaries and were recruited from Portugal on a three-year contract. They usually returned to Portugal after their patrons were replaced.

The politicization of appointments at the upper ranks had profound impact on the process and pace of localization. Firstly, there were few openings at the director level for the local Chinese or Macanese. In 1987, the year when the Sino-Portuguese Joint Declaration was signed, none of the directors or deputy directors was a locally-born Chinese. Twenty-nine (85 per cent) of the directors and deputy directors were Portuguese expatriates or from former Portuguese colonies; the rest were local Macanese (Table 3.1). Of the department/division chief posts, 85 per cent were also held by non-local Portuguese while the local Macanese dominated the lower section chief rank. Secondly, the practice of political appointments had led the Portuguese administration to neglect training programmes, particularly leadership training for local civil servants. It

Table 3.1 The distribution of place of birth for the director/chief ranking civil servants (1987)

	Macau	*Portugal*	*PRC*	*Hong Kong*	*Other**	*Total*
Director	2	16	0	0	3	21
Deputy director	3	8	0	0	2	13
Department chief	8	27	0	0	7	42
Division chief	2	20	0	0	2	24
Sector chief	8	12	0	0	1	21
Sub-sector chief	14	1	0	0	1	16
Chief secretary	6	4	0	0	0	10
Section chief	57	1	0	0	1	59
Other	24	19	0	0	6	49
Total	124	108	0	0	23	255

* About one-third were born in Portugal's former colonies.
Source: Office of Administration and Civil Service, Government of Macau.

had in effect blocked the promotion of bright local civil servants to leadership positions.

A majority (59.7 per cent) of the senior technician category (lawyers, physicians, engineers, etc.) was composed of Portuguese expatriates or those from its former colonies, while technicians, low rank security forces, workers and auxiliary personnel were mostly local-born or mainland-born Chinese (Table 3.2). The explanation partly lies in the generally low educational qualifications of the local Chinese. In 1991, when detailed information regarding educational qualifications of civil servants was made available, only 2251 or 14.6 per cent of the civil servants had a BA or a professional degree, out of which about half were Portuguese expatriates who constituted 13.1 per cent of the civil servants (Table 3.3). In fact, more than half (55.3 per cent) of the Portuguese expatriates had a BA or professional degree while only 9.1 per cent of the local-born and 5.7 per cent of the mainland-born had an equivalent degree. The Portuguese administration had often referred to the low educational standard of the local Chinese as an excuse not to recruit or promote them to higher positions in the civil service and to justify the continued hiring of Portuguese expatriates.

Another peculiar feature of Macau's civil service is the common practice of recruiting temporary and/or contracted/commissioned

Table 3.2 Professional groups and place of birth (1987)

Place of birth	Macau	Portugal	PRC	Hong Kong	Other*	Total
Director/chief	124	108	0	0	23	255
Senior technician	158	212	29	6	74	479
Teacher	114	190	13	2	49	368
Technician	894	147	84	16	90	1231
Inspector	155	1	4	0	8	168
Administrator	722	113	22	5	99	961
Auxiliary personnel	1105	32	937	4	173	2251
Security force	2128	59	427	5	167	2786
Worker	367	5	191	0	26	589
Other	161	101	368	1	46	677
Total	5928	968	2075	39	755	9765

* About one-third were born in Portugal's former colonies.
Source: as for Table 3.1.

Table 3.3 Educational level and place of birth (1991)

Place of birth	Macau	Portugal	PRC	Hong Kong	Former portuguese colonies	Other	Unknown	Total
No education	152	0	289	4	2	17	0	470
Primary school	2915	175	1378	44	39	198	2	4751
Grade 9/equivalent	2801	221	732	20	70	191	2	4037
Grade 11/12	740	160	156	18	45	64	5	1188
Medical/professional	322	189	63	10	39	23	0	646
Bacharelato*	158	54	54	10	15	30	0	321
Licenciatura	304	714	93	25	104	44	0	1284
Other	307	85	80	31	10	28	0	541
Unknown	949	75	822	102	13	78	94	2133
Total	8648	1697	3667	264	337	673	103	15371

* *Bacharelato* is a three-year degree programme and *Licenciatura* a four-year degree programme in the Portuguese higher education system.
Source: as for Table 3.1.

appointments. In 1987, only 42.7 per cent of civil servants were hired on a permanent basis, while 42.2 per cent were temporary appointments and 15.1 per cent were contracted/commissioned or other appointments. This recruitment practice continued during the transitional period and indeed the proportion of permanent appointments dropped to its all-time low, 31.6 per cent, in 1991 before its gradual rise to 49.5 per cent in 1998. The recruitment of permanent staff is monitored by the Office of Administration and Civil Service. Applicants have to go through a formal process of written examinations and interviews. Although the recruiting process does not rule out improper activities such as bribery or 'back-door' connections, it does impose certain objective criteria and restraints on the ever expanding bureaucracy. Yet the written examinations for permanent staff applicants were set only in Portuguese prior to 1993, thus effectively excluding the majority of local Chinese from entering the bureaucratic system and becoming permanent staff. The contracted or commissioned appointments were normally political (including people's own relatives) and favoured Portuguese expatriates before the handover. Such applicants not go through the formal recruiting process and were not required to take examinations. There is thus little control over the qualifications and standards of the contracted or commissioned appointees. Moreover, government departments were often restructured and new positions created to accommodate political or personal friends. The recruitment of temporary appointments was also not subject to formal tests and interviews and there is little control over the qualifications and standards of temporary appointees. One reason for this recruitment policy is that the colonial government wanted to reduce the commitment of retirement funds; only permanent staff qualify for retirement benefit.

Recruitment policy has dealt a heavy blow to the morale of Macau's civil service. Macau's civil service is notorious for its low efficiency and poor working attitudes. In a survey conducted in 1991, only 13.1 per cent and 14.9 per cent of respondents respectively expressed satisfaction with government efficiency and civil servants' working attitudes.[2] Low morale among civil servants was due partly to the lack of promotion opportunities and partly to the uncertainty about post-1999 Macau. Many were frustrated by the slow pace of localization. In a survey conducted in 1991 among local senior technicians in the civil service, 69.2 per cent expressed dissatisfaction with the pace of government's localization efforts, particularly the localization of high ranking government officials.[3]

The phasing out of Portuguese expatriates

To both the Macanese and the local Chinese the major issue of localization is to phase out the Portuguese expatriates. Only after the Portuguese had left would there be vacant positions in the upper administrative ranks. Yet the pace of localization was not very encouraging. Since the signing of the Sino-Portuguese Joint Declaration in 1987, the pace of phasing out the Portuguese expatriates had not picked up momentum until 1997, two years before the handover. Indeed, the proportion of expatriates from Portugal in Macau's civil service had shown no sign of decline after 1987 and reached 11 per cent in 1992, more than triple the figure in 1980 (Table 3.4). Governor Costa deliberately brought in more Portuguese expatriates in the first half of the 1980s to balance the Macanese-dominated administration. His successors continued this practice despite the call for localization from the local residents.

Portuguese expatriates, particularly those from Portugal's former colonies in Africa, had been enticed to Macau by the good salaries and expatriate benefits such as round-trip air-tickets, long annual leave, generous housing allowance and education allowance for children. In the mid-1980s, the average salary for civil servants in Macau was about double that in Portugal and considerably more than that in Angola or Mozambique. Besides, social status for civil servants in Macau is much higher than for their counterparts in Portugal. Expatriates were all on contract or commissioned basis; they normally returned to Portugal's civil service after their contracts expired. Expatriates from Portugal's former colonies, a sizeable group, however, preferred to renew the contracts and stay in Macau. About half of them became permanent staff of Macau's civil service.

Since the late 1980s, however, especially after Portugal has joined the European Economic Community (EEC), the salary gap between Portugal and Macau's civil servants has been narrowed. Macau has become less attractive to Portuguese expatriates, particularly to medical and professional personnel. Macau has to turn to mainland China for recruiting medical and professional staff. Yet salaries for administrative positions remain competitive. There was no sign of a serious 'brain-drain' among Portuguese expatriates in the 1990s.

Table 3.4 The evolution of place of birth of Macau's civil servants (1980–98)

	Macau	%	Portugal	%	PRC	%	Hong Kong	%	Other	%	Total
1980	2821	61.3	147	3.2	1091	23.7	–	–	543	11.8	4602
1984	4568	64.9	465	6.6	1696	24.1	–	–	380	5.4	7039
1987	6073	60.3	1076	10.7	2129	21.2	68	0.7	718	7.1	10064
1988	6710	58.4	1312	11.4	2538	22.1	87	0.8	852	7.4	11499
1989	7372	56.2	1461	11.1	2920	22.3	102	0.8	1270	9.7	13125
1990	8112	55.3	1811	12.4	3344	22.8	141	0.9	1256	8.6	14664
1991	8648	56.3	1679	10.9	3667	23.9	264	1.7	1113	7.2	15391
1992	8786	58.1	1657	11.0	3483	23.1	224	1.5	961	6.4	15111
1993	9132	58.2	1617	10.3	3673	23.4	204	1.3	1053	6.7	15679
1994	9493	57.8	1602	9.8	3947	24.1	242	1.5	1131	6.9	16415
1995	9500	57.3	1593	9.6	4087	24.7	267	1.6	1127	6.8	16574
1996	9743	57.3	1517	8.9	4298	25.3	294	1.7	1140	6.7	16992
1997	10093	57.4	1443	8.2	4609	26.2	316	1.8	1128	6.4	17589
1998	10040	58.9	881	5.2	4792	28.1	341	2.0	983	5.8	17037

Source: as for Table 3.1.

Indeed, unless the Macau government took the initiative not to recruit expatriates, the proportion of expatriates in Macau's civil service was not likely to decline in the run-up to 1999.

A sudden withdrawal of all Portuguese expatriates would disrupt the smooth process of transferring administrative rights to the post-1999 government. A gradual withdrawal or phasing out was more desirable. Who was going to step into the shoes of the Portuguese expatriates after their withdrawal? Both the local Chinese and the Macanese were eager to replace the Portuguese expatriates. Beijing's policy of allowing Macau people to rule Macau seems to favour the local Chinese over the Macanese. According to Macau's Basic Law, local Chinese residents have no choice and have all become citizens of China after the handover. The Macanese, on the other hand, can choose between becoming Chinese citizens or keeping their Portuguese nationality. If they choose to keep their Portuguese nationality, a step most likely to be taken by the majority of Macanese, they will be excluded from leadership positions in the Macau SAR.

Understandably, the Portuguese administration would prefer to maintain a strong, not a 'lame-duck' position, and effective government under Portuguese control in the run-up to 1999. The Portuguese wanted to maintain a cultural and possibly political presence in post-1999 Macau. They were also apparently concerned about the possible disruption to bureaucratic operation by rapid promotions. The Portuguese administration thus continued to recruit Portuguese personnel, especially professionals such as medical, legal and judicial personnel directly from Portugal or promote Macanese or 'trusted' local Chinese with a good command of both spoken and written Portuguese to the director/chief ranks. Table 3.5 shows that the Portuguese expatriates continued to occupy the majority of deputy director and director posts until 1997 and 1998, respectively. In fact, the Portuguese were reluctant to let go the positions of department and division chiefs. By the end of 1996, the deadline promised by Governor Vieira to completely localize the division chiefs,[4] 33 or 19.4 per cent of the division chief positions were still occupied by the Portuguese expatriates (see Table 3.5). The slow pace of localization, especially of director/chief positions, was severely criticized by Beijing and the local pro-China groups. Yet the Portuguese stood firm. In the end, the colonial government left behind for the Macau

Table 3.5 The distribution of place of birth for the director/chief ranking civil servants (1987–98)

	Place of birth Year	Macau	Portugal	PRC	Hong Kong	Other*	Total
Director	1987	2	16	0	0	3	21
	1991	12	39	0	0	1	52
	1995	9	43	0	0	5	57
	1996	6	48	0	0	2	56
	1997	7	49	0	1	2	59
	1998	13	38	1	0	4	56
Deputy director	1987	3	8	0	0	2	13
	1991	11	24	0	0	4	39
	1995	16	28	1	0	5	50
	1996	18	30	2	0	5	55
	1997	18	23	3	0	6	50
	1998	30	10	6	1	3	50
Department chief	1987	8	27	0	0	7	42
	1991	19	57	0	0	15	91
	1995	29	49	2	0	18	98
	1996	41	43	3	0	15	102
	1997	68	39	1	1	13	122
	1998	96	5	5	2	6	114

Division chief	1987	2	20	0	0	2	24
	1991	36	60	1	0	3	100
	1995	77	45	7	0	10	139
	1996	114	33	13	0	10	170
	1997	151	18	23	2	11	205
	1998	158	12	31	4	9	214
Sector and lower rank chief	1987	109	37	0	0	9	155
	1991	225	76	7	1	22	331
	1995	240	37	11	7	21	316
	1996	198	28	14	7	19	266
	1997	168	24	15	7	12	226
	1998	144	14	16	2	11	187

* About one-third were born in Portugal's former colonies.
Source: as for Table 3.1.

SAR a young and inexperienced team of civil servants. At the same time they said that this was not meant to deny the various measures taken by the Portuguese administration to enhance the chance of local Chinese to enter the civil service.

In 1988, the Macau government bought the privately owned University of East Asia which was founded in 1981 and in 1991 changed its name to University of Macau. The re-structured and expanded public university has since produced more than 3000 graduates and served to stop the brain-drain of local talents. In March 1989, Governor Carlos Melancia issued a decree allowing those who were educated in non-Portuguese language regions to apply for recognition of their educational qualifications. Since degrees from mainland China, Hong Kong, Taiwan, Great Britain, the United States and other countries had previously not been recognized by the Portuguese administration, much bright young local talent was barred from entering the civil service. The above policy was clearly an important step towards localization. In February 1993, Governor Vasco Vieira issued a memorandum instructing all government offices to implement the policy of localization according to government plans and regulations. In November 1993, the governor issued a decree to set up special local assistants for expatriate directors, deputy directors or department chiefs. This was followed in January 1994 by another important despatch from the governor instructing all government offices to strengthen the training of local civil servants and to promote them to director/chief ranks. In February 1994, Governor Vieira signed a decree and announced detailed plans and regulations for integrating those qualified Portuguese nationals who wished to join Portugal's civil service after 1999, an important measure which helped to speed up the promotion of those who would stay in Macau's civil service after 1999. In addition, the Portuguese administration had taken a series of measures to strengthen the training and development of civil servants such as sending them to Portugal and/or Beijing to study language as well as to take public administration courses. Since 1995, Beijing's National Institute of Administration has offered seminars on contemporary China for Macau's senior civil servants. In 1988 the Macau government installed a Chinese public administration evening degree course at the University of East Asia for existing civil servants. It also provided scholarship to train those who had promised to stay to work in Macau's civil service after 1999. Hundreds of civil servants have benefited from the above policy measures.[5]

The Macanese issue

Macau's political scene was traditionally dominated by the Macanese of Portuguese–Asian mixed blood. Prior to Portugal's 1974 revolution, Macau was an economic backwater with little to attract the outside world. Portuguese civil servants preferred either to stay at home or to work in Portugal's African colonies. Macau was thus left in the hands of the Macanese. It was an open secret that no Portuguese governor could possibly rule Macau without the co-operation of the Macanese. Indeed, in 1980, the Macanese-dominated Legislative Assembly attempted to make the governor accountable to the assembly.[6] Ironically, 1980 turns out to be a watershed, signalling the decline of Macanese influence in Macau's politics. Governor Costa brought in Portuguese expatriates to balance the Macanese influence in the government and dissolved the Macanese-dominated assembly in 1984. Costa's effort was helped by the booming Macau economy during the 1980s. An increasing number of Portuguese were attracted to Macau by its high salaries and expatriate benefits. At the expense of the Macanese themselves, they took up most of the senior positions in the administration.

The mother tongue of the Macanese is Portuguese but Cantonese, the local dialect, is also spoken. The Macanese attended local Portuguese schools and after graduating from high school, the majority joined the civil service. The better-off may elect to continue their tertiary education in Portugal. Except for the few who had been educated in Portugal, most of the Macanese did not feel comfortable within the Portuguese social circle. Indeed, there were two distinctive Portuguese-speaking social circles in pre-1999 Macau: the Macanese and the Portuguese expatriates. On the other hand, the speed of social integration through inter-marriage between Macanese and local Chinese has accelerated in recent years.[7] An increasing number of Macanese families use Cantonese as their first language at home and send their children to English instead of Portuguese schools to study Chinese as a second language. While only one-third of the adult Chinese population were locally-born, the majority of the Macanese were born in Macau. Many are emotionally attached to Macau and regard the enclave as their home. Despite their

Portuguese heritage, they have little warmth towards Portugal. If they have to leave Macau, many would prefer to settle down in Canada, the United States, Brazil or Australia rather than in Portugal. In addition, they are worried that they might be discriminated against in Portugal.

Understandably, the Macanese were concerned about the return of Macau to China in 1999. They were afraid of being discriminated against or treated as an ethnic minority in a Chinese-dominated society. At first, the Chinese authorities were insensitive to the fears of the local Macanese. In a meeting of the Basic Law Consultative Committee, a mainland official reassured the Macanese members at the meeting that the Chinese government would protect Macanese culture and treat the Macanese as one of China's numerous national minorities. His remark aroused suspicions and fears among the Macanese. They were in general quite pessimistic about their future in post-1999 Macau and Chinese promises to protect their special interests such as cultural heritage and Portuguese nationality provided little comfort to them. Few Macanese had confidence in the Chinese government. However, their wish to be integrated into Portugal's civil service while working in Macau after 1999 was shattered by the Chinese government's decision to deny dual nationality to civil servants working in the post-1999 administration.

The Portuguese administration apparently shared the concerns and worries of the Macanese. Governor Rocha Vieira, who replaced Carlos Melancia in May 1991, appointed two Macanese under-secretaries, Ana Maria Perez and Jorge Rangel, and had since promoted or recruited about a dozen Macanese to the director or deputy director level. The Vieira administration had also succeeded in mobilizing the support of pro-China legislators to elect a Macanese legislator, Anabela Fatima Ritchi, to be the chairperson of the enclave's Legislative Assembly. There is no data on the exact number of Macanese in the civil service or in the director/chief rank of the civil service. Indeed, there is no consensus even on the definition of 'Macanese'. However, since the great majority of the Macanese can speak Cantonese but are illiterate in written Chinese and none of the ethnic Chinese senior civil servants are illiterate in written Chinese, a rough estimate of the member of Macanese in the director/chief rank can be obtained by calculating the number of government workers who can only speak Cantonese.[8] Table 3.6 shows that in 1987 about one-

Table 3.6 The changing proportion of Macanese holding director/chief ranking civil servant positions (1987–95) (percentages)

1987	1988	1989	1990	1991	1992	1993	1994	1995
34.8	31.6	32.3	28.5	27.4	26.2	29.6	23.7	14.5

Source: as for Table 3.1.

third of the director/chief positions were occupied by the Macanese and this proportion remained largely unchanged until 1994 when it dropped to 23.7 per cent and fell further to 14.5 per cent in 1995.[9] Some Macanese had chosen early retirement or to leave the civil service in the government's new integration plan which became effective in 1995.

Unlike the British, who were primarily concerned about maintaining British commercial interests in Hong Kong, the Portuguese were more concerned about preserving the Portuguese cultural heritage in Macau after their withdrawal in 1999. The Macanese are their only hope of preserving Portuguese culture in post-1999 Macau. This partly explains their readiness to accommodate the Macanese demand to be integrated into the Portuguese civil service system. The Portuguese government was reassured in private by the Macanese that not more than a select few Macanese would actually join Portugal's civil service after 1999 and hence the integration plan would not become a burden to Portugal.

The integration plan was part of the localization scheme aimed at getting a more accurate figure of civil servants who would stay in post-1999 Macau and the number of vacancies available in the civil service in the run-up to 1999. The Macau government promised that the vacancies would be filled by local residents.[10] On 23 February 1994, the Macau government issued a decree detailing the plan for integrating qualified personnel from Macau's civil service into Portugal's civil service.[11] The integration plan allows those who are permanent employees of the Macau government, Portuguese nationals, and proficient in Portuguese to choose to stay in Macau's civil service, take early retirement, leave the civil service or join Portugal's civil service after 1999. Those who were thus qualified were given one year to make up their minds. Since few local Chinese are proficient in Portuguese, the integration plan was clearly aimed at offering the

Macanese a choice in the run-up to 1999. At the end of the one-year period, of the 6400 qualified civil servants, 1928 or 30.1 per cent chose to leave Macau's civil service, of which 493 chose to join Portugal's civil service; 566 chose early retirement and 869 to leave the civil service.[12] However, partly witnessing the smooth transition accomplished by Hong Kong in 1997, many changed their minds, especially those who had chosen to leave the civil service. As of January 1999, only 1485 or 23.2 per cent, a drop of 7 per centage points, of those qualified chose to leave Macau's civil service, of which 386 chose to join Portugal's civil service, 516 chose early retirement and 583 to leave the civil service.[13]

On 13 April 1998, the Macau government issued another decree giving temporarily employed Portuguese nationals – numbering around 2000 and mostly from Portugal – to choose to join Portugal's civil service.[14] Since the great majority of Macanese are permanently employed, only a small number of Macanese benefited from the new policy. In the end, 625 chose to join Portugal's civil service.[15]

Legalization of Chinese as an official language

After 400 years of rule, the Portuguese had failed to turn Macau into a Portuguese-speaking territory. All private schools used either Chinese or English as the language of instruction; only public schools which constituted less than 10 per cent of Macau's schools used Portuguese. The local Chinese normally send their children to either Chinese or English schools. Moreover, Portuguese is used only in the government and public sectors; it is not used in the commercial and business circles. An ordinary Macau resident has little use for the Portuguese language in his daily life. In fact, English is the second language in Macau after Chinese (Cantonese) while Portuguese is a distant third.

In 1987, about 50.8 per cent of Macau's civil servants had a good or fair command of written Portuguese and 53.4 per cent had a good or fair command of spoken Portuguese.[16] As could be expected, 85 per cent can speak Cantonese, yet only 65.4 per cent had a good or fair command of written Chinese. The gap between spoken and written Chinese is due mainly to the significant proportion of Macanese in the civil service who can only speak Cantonese. Only

21.6 per cent were bilingual, that is those who had a good or fair command of written Portuguese and Chinese. It is important to note that Mandarin, the *de facto* official language of post-1999 Macau, was far from popular. Only 31.4 per cent of Macau's civil servants had a good or fair command of Mandarin in 1987.

The Portuguese parliament passed a law in late 1991 making Chinese an official language in Macau, enjoying the same status as Portuguese. Yet this move had little practical influence on the status of Portuguese as the working language of the Macau administration. All official and legal documents were in Portuguese, while only important policy announcements and decrees were translated into Chinese. This is not surprising given the fact that nearly all middle- and upper-rank positions were occupied by either Portuguese expatriates or Cantonese-speaking Macanese who could not read nor write Chinese. The use of Chinese as an official language was further handicapped by the shortage of translators within the government. According to the Office of Administration and Civil Service, there were only 199 translators working in different government offices and departments in 1991. This number was far from adequate for Macau's ever expanding civil service.

The language issue is highly political. It goes deep into the contentious interpretations of localization, namely the 'Sinification' *vis-à-vis* the 'Macanization' perspectives. Understandably, local Chinese civil servants were eager to see Chinese becoming the official working language of the government. In a survey conducted in December 1991 among the senior technicians, including physicians in the civil service whose mother tongue is Chinese, about two-thirds of the respondents indicated that the government had done a poor job in making Chinese an official language.[17] About 61 per cent believed that the best way to push up the official status of the Chinese language was to promote more bilingual civil servants, those who can read and write Chinese and Portuguese, to the upper echelon of the administration. This policy suggestion, if adopted, would clearly benefit the increasingly large number of young Chinese civil servants who had learned Portuguese through various training programmes offered by the government. It would effectively exclude the Macanese, who had little incentive to learn written Chinese in mid-career,[18] and, for that matter, the Portuguese expatriates, from being promoted to upper-rank positions. This partly explains the government's lukewarm attitude towards making Chinese a working language within the civil service. Ironically, near the end of the transitional period, the Portuguese administration had begun to realize that bilingualism was probably the only way to preserve Portuguese language and culture in the enclave after the handover. It tried to persuade Beijing to agree to set up some definite rules and regulations for implementing the bilingual policy in post-1999 Macau at the Sino-Portuguese Joint Liaison Group meetings. Yet the Chinese were more concerned about raising the official status of the Chinese language and refused to discuss the bilingual issue at the meetings.[19]

By the end of 1995, about 46.2 per cent of Macau's civil servants had a good or fair command of written Portuguese,[20] a drop of 4.6 per cent from 1987. The decrease was partly due to the departure of several hundred Macanese, those who chose early retirement or to leave the civil service as part of the integration plan. It also indicates that many Chinese were not interested in learning Portuguese. However, those who have a good or fair command of written Portuguese and Chinese had increased to 27.4 per cent in 1995, as compared to 21.6 per cent in 1987. More importantly perhaps, the proportion of civil servants who have a good or fair command of Mandarin had increased from 31.4 per cent in 1987 to 46.9 per cent in 1995. The above figures suggest that a language policy can be successful only when people find it to their advantage to comply with the policy.

Localization of law

After the handover, according to Article 8 of the Macau Basic Law, 'the laws, decrees, administrative regulations and other normative acts previously in force in Macau shall be maintained, except for any that contravenes this Law, or subject to any amendment by legislature or other relevant organs of the Macau Special Administrative Region in accordance with legal procedures'. Article 145 further stipulates: 'Upon the establishment of the Macau Special Administrative Region, the laws previously in force in Macau shall be adopted as laws of the region except for those which the Standing Committee of the National People's Congress declares to be in contravention of this Law. If any laws are later discovered to be in contravention of this Law, they shall be amended or cease to have force in accordance with the provisions of this Law and legal procedure'.

There are two major sources of Macau's laws: (1) Portuguese laws including those national laws which had been extended to Macau and those laws which were specifically made for Macau; and (2) local laws passed in Macau's legislature as well as decrees and regulations issued by the Macau governors since 1976.[21] In post-1999 Macau, Portuguese laws would become alien laws, which, according to China's legal experts, clearly violate China's sovereignty in Macau and contravene the Basic Law.[22] Indeed, any existing laws including those local laws and decrees that touch on the sensitive sovereignty issue, according to the Chinese view, have to be amended before or after the handover. Moreover, most laws emanating from Portugal are outdated and include some that date from the nineteenth century and thus need revision. In short, the localization of law is a very complicated process involving the following aspects: (1) translation of existing laws, decrees and regulations into Chinese; (2) updating and revision, or modernization, of existing laws; (3) adoption, amendment or the discarding of Portuguese laws which contravene the Basic Law; and (4) localization of the enclave's legal and judicial personnel.

Unlike localization of the civil service and legalization of Chinese as an official language, the localization of law appeared to be a less controversial issue. Both Beijing and Lisbon agreed that it needed to localize and revise those laws and decrees that were dated. Apparently realizing that if the existing laws were not amended and adapted to the local situation in accordance with the Basic Law before the handover, the laws would be amended by the Macau SAR government and the Portuguese view would then be excluded, the Portuguese government thus took the initiative in modernizing these laws.[23] The Centre for Translation of Laws was inaugurated in February 1988 and an Office for Legal Modernization was set up in October 1989. However, due to the large amount of work and the shortage of specialized legal translators and legal experts, especially bilingual legal experts who are familiar with both Portuguese and Chinese law,[24] the pace of translating the laws was painfully slow. However, the Portuguese government assured Beijing that it would complete the translation and the revision of all major laws and important decrees before the handover.[25] Unlike issues concerning the localization of civil servants and Chinese as an official language, the Chinese members of the Joint Liaison Group as well as the pro-China legislators had not pressed particularly hard for a quicker pace of localization of law. There are two possible explanations: first, the Macau Basic Law already provides a safeguard against laws that might contravene the Basic Law by giving the Macau SAR legislature the power to amend those laws; secondly, none of the pro-China legislators are legal experts capable of criticizing the localization process from a legal viewpoint. As a result, revised and translated laws proposed by the Portuguese encountered little opposition at the meetings of the Joint Liaison Group and in the legislature. The legislative adopted as Macau's laws Portuguese laws and decrees that did not contravene the Basic Law. The Portuguese government also kept its promises and delivered the so-called 'Five Major Laws' (*wuda fadian*) in or before November 1999.[26]

However, the Portuguese government was lukewarm in localizing Macau's legal and judicial personnel. In the 1980s, Macau's lawyers, judges, procurators and other legal personnel were either Portuguese expatriates or Macanese.[27] In 1988, the government set up a Portuguese law degree programme at the University of East Asia. The first cohort of 16 law students graduated in 1994 and by 1999 a total of 105 new law degree holders had been trained by the university.[28] However, since the programme is taught in Portuguese the majority of graduates were either Portuguese expatriates or Macanese. Only about 40 graduates were ethnic Chinese. However, a new law degree programme taught in Chinese was inaugurated in 1996 in the University of Macau with its first cohort of graduates in 2001. At the same time, the government set up a Training Centre for Local Judges in 1995 and the first cohort of graduates, 11 students, were appointed as judges or procurators in 1997. By July 1999 a total of 34 local judges and procurators had been trained and appointed to replace the departing Portuguese expatriates.[29] In the end, the Portuguese government's localization efforts have produced a group of young and inexperienced local judges and procurators. Even the first chief judge of the SAR's Court of Final Appeal, Cen Haohui, was only 38 years old and had only three years of court experience as a local judge at the time of appointment.

Conclusion

In summary, the major obstacle to the localization of Macau's civil service is its political nature. The Portuguese administration did not want to become a 'lame-duck' government and give up its administrative control prior to 1999. It was thus reluctant to replace the Portuguese expatriates, who had occupied most of the senior positions in the government, with local civil servants in the run-up to 1999. The administration was also slow in implementing the official status of the Chinese language, which in practice would make the Portuguese expatriates helpless in running the administration. The Portuguese, however, was more co-operative in localizing and modernizing the enclave's laws. They took the initiative in revising and translating dated Portuguese laws and decrees in a hope that the spirit and content of Portuguese law would continue to exist after their departure in post-1999 Macau. In a sense, the Portuguese have not abandoned Macau. They were concerned about preserving the valuable Portuguese heritage – namely rule of law – in Macau after 1999.

It is unfair to compare Macau to Hong Kong.[30] Due to historical and political reasons, especially the anti-government riots of 1967, the Hong Kong British administration had started the de-colonization or localization of its civil service in the late 1960s, long before the signing of the Sino-British Joint Declaration on the reversion of Hong Kong in 1984. More importantly, language was never a major issue in Hong Kong's transition. The majority of Hong Kong's senior civil servants, lawyers and judges are bilingual. Besides, the British did not have to deal with the Eurasian issue in the process of localization. By comparison, Macau's Portuguese administration was severely crippled by the 1966 riot. To co-opt a large number of local Chinese into the government would, arguably, further undermine the legitimacy of the colonial government. In any event, the language barrier had effectively barred the local Chinese from entering either the civil service or the legal profession. Moreover, the loopholes and the lack of a standardized procedure for recruiting temporary or contracted appointments had enabled Portuguese office directors to continue the recruitment of expatriates from Portugal or Macau in the run-up to 1999.[31] However, given only 12 transitional years to prepare for the handover, the Portuguese administration had taken positive steps to localize Macau's civil service and the legal and judicial systems. Although partly due to bureaucratic incompetence many training programmes relating to the localization efforts were poorly designed and problem-ridden,[32] there were no major incidents of misadministration or scandal during the whole transitional period. The Portuguese administration deserves more credit for a smooth transition than is commonly granted.

The Chinese government, on the other hand, had expressed displeasure at the slow pace of localization. In contrast to the Portuguese, the Chinese were more interested in establishing a Chinese-dominated civil service and legal and judicial system prior to the handover than in their continuity after 1999. The Chinese government even changed the normal requirement of 15 years of court experience in order to appoint a mainland Chinese who had been a local judge for only three years to be the SAR's chief judge of the Court of final appeal. In short, the Chinese government's attitude towards localization was by and large politically motivated. It did not, however, want to press too hard on the Portuguese, since this might impair the 'friendly' Sino-Portuguese relations, or to offend the Macanese, which might jeopardize the Chinese wish for a smooth transition to the post-1999 era. Likewise, the Portuguese government in Lisbon wanted to maintain cordial relations with the Beijing regime. Lisbon simply would not take any actions in Macau at the expense of Sino-Portuguese relations. After all, the two sides disagreed mainly on the pace and not the contents of localization, something which had ceased to be an issue in 1999.

4
Macau Citizens' Attitudes toward the Transition

Unlike the situation in Hong Kong, Macau does not have academic institutes or mass media that conduct regular public opinion polls on government performance and/or specific policies.[1] In December 1998, a telephone survey was conducted among Macau residents above 18 years of age who had resided in Macau for no less than one year. Telephone numbers were systematically selected from the local telephone directory and one qualified person from the residence was randomly selected by the Kish Grid method. The number of successfully completed interviews was 588. The successful response rate was 65 per cent. As Macau has a very high rate of telephone installation,[2] it is very unlikely that such a telephone survey excludes any societal group.

The sample is quite representative of the population of Macau. Table 4.1 indicates that in terms of sex distribution, both male and female respondents were adequately represented. In terms of age distribution, older people aged 60 and above were underrepresented in the survey. Many older people failed to complete the 15-minute telephone interview because of difficulties in hearing using the telephone. In terms of education distribution, people from different levels of education were well represented. Moreover, indirect comparison of income and occupation distribution also suggests that people from different income groups and occupations were well represented in the sample.

Table 4.1 Sample profiles and Macau's population profiles (percentages)

	Sample profile	Population profile*
Sex		
Male	49.1	48.0
Female	50.9	52.0
Age		
20–29	33.0**	20.0
30–39	24.4	29.1
40–49	26.3	25.8
50–59	10.8	10.4
60 and above	5.3	14.6
Education		
No education	2.0	9.2***
Some primary school	6.0	12.5
Finished primary school	14.8	27.4
Form 1–Form 4	26.0	27.0
Finished high school	34.5	16.1
University	16.7	7.8

* The population profile is based on the 1998 (estimated) data, provided by the Census and Statistics Office, Government of Macau.
** This age group includes those who were 18 and 19 years old.
*** The statistics on education provided by the Census and Statistics Department include those above 3 years of age while our sample includes only those above 18 years of age. The 'no education' figure of the population is thus naturally higher than that in our sample while the figure of university-educated in the population is likely to be under-estimated.

Evaluation of the Portuguese administration's performance

The Portuguese had ruled Macau as a *de facto* colony for more than a century and a half at the handover,[3] what is the evaluation of Macau citizens on the Portuguese administration's performance? Respondents were asked: 'Portugal is about to finish its governance of Macau, are you satisfied with the overall performance of the Portuguese?' As indicated in Table 4.2, only 22.4 per cent of the respondents were satisfied or very satisfied with the Portuguese rule. By contrast, 39.2 per cent of respondents were dissatisfied or very dissatisfied with the Portuguese administration's overall performance; 31 per cent were neutral; and 7.5 per cent had no opinion one way

Table 4.2 Evaluation of the Portuguese administration's performance (percentages)

	Very satisfied	Satisfied	Neutral	Not satisfied	Very dissatisfied	Don't know/ no opinion
Overall performance	0.9	21.5	31.0	30.7	8.5	7.5
Localization of the civil service	0.3	21.4	18.4	28.9	9.2	21.8
Localization of laws	0.2	12.8	17.7	23.1	8.8	37.4
Legalization of Chinese as an official language	0.5	30.4	14.6	26.2	6.5	21.8

or the other. In comparison, 68.6 per cent of Hong Kong's citizens were satisfied while only 7.2 per cent were dissatisfied with the British administration's performance before the reversion of Hong Kong.[4] Moreover, only 35 per cent of the Macau citizens trusted the Portuguese administration while 63 per cent of Hong Kong citizens trusted the British administration at the time of the two enclaves' respective reversions.[5] Clearly, the departing Portuguese administration was not very popular among the Macau populace. About 42 per cent of the respondents blamed the Portuguese administration for the enclave's deteriorating law and order. Nevertheless, a plurality of respondents recognized and praised Portuguese contributions to economic development and the betterment of life in Macau. Furthermore, respondents were asked whether they were satisfied with the pace of the localization process. Here public opinion appeared to be divided on the issue of localization, with a slightly higher proportion of those polled expressing dissatisfaction over the pace of localizing the civil service, laws, and legalization of Chinese as an official language; about 40 per cent were either holding a neutral view or had no opinion (see Table 4.2).

Respondents were also asked to assess the Portuguese administration's specific performance by giving marks from 0 to 100 (Table 4.3). If 60 is taken as a pass, the administration's performance in economic development, maintaining law and order, opening up its decision-making process, putting in place an anti-corruption and anti-illegal administration, localization, as well as the overall performance of Governor Vasco Rocha Vieira, had all failed. Clearly, Macau citizens

Table 4.3 Grading of the Portuguese administration's specific performance (mean)

Performance indicator	*Score*
1. Economic policy	55
2. Law and order	38
3. Transparency in decision-making	48
4. Performance of the Commissioner for Anti-corruption and Anti-illegal Administration	44
5. The progress of localization of the civil service and laws and legalization of Chinese as an official language	54
6. The overall performance of Governor Vasco Rocha Vieira	55

Table 4.4 Macau's most serious social problems (percentages)

Q: What are Macau's most serious social problems?

1. Economic recession	29.3
2. Deteriorating law and order	59.4
3. Political instability	1.9
4. Juvenile delinquency	2.7
5. Corruption	3.6
6. Other	2.0
7. Don't know/no opinion	1.0

were extremely unhappy with the declining economy, deteriorating law and order, rampant corruption, the undemocratic decision-making process, as well as with the mediocre and conservative Vieira administration. Understandably, Macau citizens are more concerned about social and economic problems that directly affected their daily livelihood. Indeed, nearly 60 per cent of the respondents indicated that the deteriorating law and order was the most serious social problem in Macau while nearly 30 per cent thought economic recession was the most serious problem (Table 4.4). By comparison, respondents were less concerned about political instability, corruption and juvenile delinquency. In other words, the Macau SAR government is confronted with the urgent task of restoring citizens' confidence in law and order and in the economy.

Confidence in the post-1999 SAR government

Our survey findings indicate that Macau citizens were disappointed by the performance of the Portuguese administration. Did they look forward to the post-1999 Macau SAR government? Did they have confidence in self-rule? It is commonly assumed that, because of the mediocre performance of the Portuguese administration, Macau's citizens generally looked forward to the new SAR government. Table 4.5 indicates that 56.2 per cent of the respondents in a survey of Macau citizens were happy and optimistic at Macau's handover; in comparison, an earlier survey in Hong Kong suggests only about one-third of Hong Kong citizens were happy and optimistic at the colony's handover. Furthermore, as indicated in Table 4.6, a majority (67.8 per cent) of respondents believed that Beijing would implement its 'one country, two systems' and 'Macau people ruling Macau' policy in the enclave for at least 50 years. Only 14.5 per

Table 4.5 A comparison of Hong Kong and Macau citizens' mood at the handover (percentages)

	Happy and optimistic	*Neutral, no special feeling*	*Heavy, pessimistic and complicated feeling*	*Don't know/ no opinion*
Hong Kong	35.1	47.8	5.9	11.5
Macau	56.2	37.0	1.9	4.9

Source: the Macau survey was conducted in December 1999 by the Centre of Social Science Research, University of Hong Kong. The Hong Kong survey was conducted in June 1997 by the same research centre. *Macau Daily News*, 3 January 2000, p. B2.

Table 4.6 Confidence in 'one country, two systems' (percentages)

Q: Do you believe Beijing's promise that Macau will practice 'one country, two systems' and 'Macau people ruling Macau' for 50 years?

Strongly believe	7.3
Believe	60.5
Don't believe	13.7
Strongly don't believe	0.7
Don't know/no opinion	17.7

cent of respondents expressed distrust of the PRC government. In other words, a clear majority of Macau citizens have cast a vote of confidence in Beijing. By comparison, 75 per cent of Hong Kong's citizens also have confidence in the 'one country, two systems' concept.[6]

Nevertheless, many Macau citizens appear to be pessimistic about the prospects for political autonomy and democratic development in post-1999 Macau or have reservations about the relevant provisions in the Macau Basic Law. Table 4.7 shows that only 31.2 per cent of respondents felt that the Basic Law has provided sufficient democracy to the Macau SAR, while 32.9 per cent of respondents were neutral or felt the opposite. Moreover, only 35.2 per cent of respondents felt that the Basic Law has guaranteed the SAR sufficient political autonomy, while 28.9 per cent were neutral or held the opposite view. It is worth noting that in both questions nearly 36 per cent of respondents had expressed no opinion or indicated that they were not familiar with the Basic Law. These findings suggest that the Macau people do not believe blindly in propaganda. The central government in Beijing and the Macau SAR government have to convince the local residents of their genuine desire to implement the 'one country, two systems' policy by making it actually work.

In fact, contrary to the common assumption, not every Macau citizen is confident of economic and social development in post-1999

Table 4.7 Confidence of post-1999 democratic development and political autonomy in Macau (percentages)

	Very sufficient	Sufficient	Neutral	Insufficient	Very insufficient	Don't know/ no opinion
1. Does the Basic Law provide sufficient democracy to the Macau SAR?	0.5	30.7	16.0	15.5	1.4	35.9
2. Does the Basic Law provide sufficient political autonomy to the Macau SAR?	1.0	34.2	15.7	12.3	0.9	35.9

Macau. As indicated in Table 4.8, only 30.6 per cent of respondents believed that Macau's overall situation will be improved after the handover while 9.5 per cent believed Macau will be worse off. By comparison, 45.6 per cent of respondents expected little change after the handover; 14.3 per cent had no opinion. These findings suggest that a significant proportion of Macau's populace are not very optimistic about the economic and social prospects in post-1999 Macau. Indeed, a majority of respondents were most worried about either continuing economic recession (42.4 per cent) or deteriorating law and order (15.8 per cent), while only a small proportion were worried about political instability or losing the freedom of speech and publication previously guaranteed by the Portuguese Constitution (see Table 4.9). It should be noted, however, that the above findings do not suggest that the Macau people are optimistic about democratic development in post-1999 Macau, they merely reflect the fact that a significant proportion of Macau citizens are apathetic to politics or, in comparison to their concerns about the economy

Table 4.8 Confidence of post-1999 development in Macau (percentages)

Q: How will Macau's overall situations change after its return to China?

Getting better	30.6
Getting worse	9.5
About the same	45.6
Don't know/no opinion	14.3

Table 4.9 Most worrying post-1999 problems (percentages)

Q: What do you worry about most after 1999?

1. Continuing economic recession	42.4
2. Political instability	4.3
3. Deteriorating law and order	15.8
4. Corruption	3.7
5. Afraid of losing freedoms of speech and publication	5.8
6. Nothing to worry about	21.1
7. Others	4.9
8. Don't know/no opinion	1.9

and public order, are less concerned about the enclave's political development. Moreover, only 21 per cent of respondents expressed no worry about the economic and social situations (as commonly described by the pro-China mass media) in post-1999 Macau. In sum, the Macau people are far from optimistic about the prospects for post-1999 Macau.

Another hotly debated topic during the transition is the population issue. Since the collapse of the real estate market in 1994, Macau has accumulated more than 30 000 unsold flats, accommodation which could house a quarter of the enclave's population. Some property developers and business people have advocated a large increase of permanent residents in the enclave to absorb the vacant flats. Some local scholars also believe that only by increasing the territory's population to about one million, the size of a middle-size city, and by importing a large number of professionals or technicians, can Macau significantly enlarge its small economy of scale and become more competitive.[7] What is the mass public's view towards the population issue? In the 1998 survey, over 70 per cent of respondents felt that Macau's current population is 'just right' or opposed any policy measure to increase the enclave's population (see Table 4.10). Only 16 per cent of respondents felt that Macau should increase its population while 12 per cent had no opinion. Clearly, a majority of Macau citizens are opposed to increasing the intake of immigrants from mainland China. They are afraid of losing their jobs to the new immigrants as well as of losing education opportunities for their children. Understandably, in contrast to politicians or scholars, the mass

Table 4.10 Should Macau increase its population? (percentages)

Q: Is Macau's population adequate?

1. Just right	43.5
2. Should increase to 500 000	4.8
3. Should increase to 600 000	5.8
4. Should increase to 700 000–800 000	2.7
5. Should increase to 900 000–1 000 000	2.6
6. Should not increase the population	28.6
7. Don't know/no opinion	12.1

public is more concerned about the short-term effects rather than the long-term implications of an immigration policy.

The problem of identity

Identifying with China or Macau?

Over 96 per cent of Macau's population are ethnic Chinese, including about 45 per cent locally-born, immigrants from the neighbouring Guangdong and Fujian provinces as well as returned overseas Chinese. Do they identify themselves with China or with Macau? Are they proud of being a Chinese or a Macau citizen? Table 4.11 shows that 74.1 per cent of respondents were proud to be Chinese while 15 per cent did not feel so. By contrast, only 38.8 per cent of respondents were proud to be Macau citizens while 45.9 per cent did not feel so. This is very different from the situation of Hong-Kongers who tend to identify themselves more with Hong Kong than with China.[8] It is also worthy of note that the proportion of Macau citizens who tend to identify themselves with Macau declined during the 1990s. A survey conducted in 1991 by the present writer and his colleagues at the University of Macau indicated that 53.6 per cent of respondents were proud to be Macau citizens.[9]

Many local Chinese are proud of China's history, culture, and moral and ethic traditions. They are also proud of China's economic achievements and rising international status since the PRC adopted its open policy in the late 1970s. This partly explains their inclination to identify themselves with China. Yet few (only 0.5 per cent of respondents) are proud of the PRC's socialist political system. This suggests that the local residents' identification with China is of a cultural rather than a political nature. By comparison, only about a quarter of respondents were proud of Macau's cultural diversity, its

Table 4.11 Identifying with China and Macau (percentages)

	Yes	*No*	*Don't know/ no opinion*
1. Are you proud of being a Macau citizen?	38.8	45.9	15.3
2. Are you proud of being Chinese?	74.1	15.0	10.9

mixture of Oriental and Western culture and its Southern European style buildings, while about 40 per cent of respondents felt that there is simply nothing to be proud of. In the early 1990s, many Macau people were proud of Macau's economic prosperity, yet more recently Macau recorded negative economic growth for three consecutive years. Many people worry about the depressed state of the economy, the rising unemployment rate, as well as the erosion of law and order. This largely explains the declining trend towards identification with Macau and Macau citizens' weakening sense of belonging to Macau will, in the long-run, cause a brain-drain of local talents and hence problems for the territory's economic development and social stability.

Fortunately, most Macau citizens do not find the present situation hopeless. Table 4.12 shows that a majority (62 per cent) of respondents had a good overall impression of Macau, only slightly lower than the proportion of those who had a good overall impression of Hong Kong (71 per cent) but higher than that of mainland China (57 per cent) and Taiwan (43.7 per cent). Clearly, despite economic recession and problems of law and order, most Macau citizens still find the enclave a reasonably decent place to live. The image of Macau could be further improved by raising its international status and preserving its unique cultural heritage.

Table 4.12 Overall impression of mainland China, Hong Kong, Taiwan and Macau (percentages)

Q: What is your overall impression of mainland China/Hong Kong/ Taiwan/Macau?

	Very good	*Good*	*Bad*	*Very bad*	*Don't know/ no opinion*
1. Overall impression of mainland China	1.9	56.6	34.8	1.7	5.1
2. Overall impression of Hong Kong	3.1	68.7	22.1	1.4	4.8
3. Overall impression of Taiwan	1.5	42.2	22.5	2.2	31.5
4. Overall impression of Macau	2.7	59.3	32.2	2.2	3.7

Problems of cultural identity

Due to geographic proximity, Macau's lifestyle and popular culture are greatly influenced by the mainland and Hong Kong – particularly the latter which has a similar political and economic system and where people speak the same Cantonese dialect. According to the survey, about half of Macau's citizens read only local newspapers; about 40 per cent read both local and Hong Kong newspapers; and about 10 per cent read only Hong Kong newspapers. One respondent remarked: 'I enjoy reading Hong Kong newspapers which are more colourful and of higher quality than the local press. But in order to follow the local events I have to read the local newspapers; yet very often I only read the headlines'. The situation is even more lopsided when it comes to choosing television stations. Over 80 per cent of the Macau people only watch programmes from Hong Kong television stations while less than 20 per cent occasionally switch to the local television station watching the broadcasting of local news. If this trend continues, Macau will, in the long-run, risk losing its cultural identity. The SAR government has an urgent task to financially assist the development of local press and other mass media into greater diversity. It needs to have a specific cultural policy to preserve and further develop Macau's unique cultural heritage which includes the local Chinese, Portuguese and Macanese cultures. When Macau retains its distinctive cultural features and becomes a noted city of culture the local people will find it easier to identify themselves with the territory and feel proud to be its citizens.

Qualifications for the Macau SAR's chief executive

According to the demands of Macau Basic Law, the SAR's first chief executive was elected by a 200-member special election committee.[10] The mass public's political right was denied; they had no say in the choice of their political leader. In order to find out the people's choice for their chief executive, the survey had the following question inserted: 'What kind of person is best qualified for the post of Macau SAR's chief executive?' Table 4.13 shows that public opinion was divided on this issue. About 21.5 per cent of the respondents felt that the chief executive should be one who is patriotic towards China and Macau; yet about 27 per cent felt that whoever happened to be competent, regardless of his or her attitudes towards China or Macau, was

Table 4.13 Qualifications for the Macau SAR's chief executive (percentages)

1. Those who are trusted by the Chinese government	6.6
2. Those who love China and Macau	21.5
3. Those who are willing to fight for Macau's interests even at the expense of offending the Chinese government	17.5
4. Whoever is competent	26.9
5. It doesn't really matter	5.1
6. Other	9.7
7. Don't know/no opinion	12.6

Table 4.14 Self-assessment of concerns about China and Macau (mean)

1. Are you concerned about China's future?	68.7
2. Are you concerned about Macau's future?	71.5
3. Do you love your country?	72.7

qualified for the post. It is worthy of note that only 6.6 per cent of the respondents felt that it was necessary that the chief executive be one who was trusted by the Chinese government. Clearly, the majority of Macau citizens would not accept candidates who merely listen to or take orders from Beijing. In fact, 17.5 per cent of respondents felt that a good chief executive should be willing to fight for Macau's interests even at the expense of offending the Chinese government. The message from the mass public is clear: they want a competent leader who puts Macau's interests ahead of national interests.

The above findings do not suggest that Macau citizens have a strong anti-China feeling. In fact, this survey indicates that many local Chinese, including both the locally-born and new immigrants, have a strong emotional attachment to China. When asked to give a self-assessment of their concerns about China and Macau, ranging from 0 to 100 marks, the mean scores for concerns about China's and Macau's future, as well as patriotic feeling towards China are, respectively, 68.7, 71.5 and 72.7 (see Table 4.14). Although some respondents might well have given 'desirable' answers to the above apparently 'sensitive' questions and had perhaps over-rated themselves, the findings adequately reflect the local citizens' calm and accommodating attitude towards Macau's return to the motherland.

Background variables

One outstanding feature of Macau citizens' attitudes towards the transition is the lack of statistically significant disagreements across different gender and occupation groups. This reflects the conformity of a generally conservative society to the prevailing mood of the time. The lack of an opposition or counterculture may also have contributed to the uniformity of attitudes across groups.[11] Yet some background variables do account for the variation in our respondents' responses to some questions.

One dominating factor affecting attitudes towards the transition is a respondent's emotional attachment to China. Our findings indicate that new immigrants from the mainland are more patriotic about China than the locally-born Chinese: 35 per cent of those respondents who have lived in Macau for less than 10 years had given themselves 80 or above marks for their patriotic feeling towards China while only 17 per cent of those locally-born respondents did so. Age also plays a part in patriotism: 41 per cent of those respondents who are 50 years of age or above had given themselves high marks (80 or above) for their Chinese patriotism while only 16 per cent of those younger than 30 did so. It is understandable that new immigrants who still have strong family or personal links with people in the mainland tend to have a stronger emotional attachment to China than the locally-born Chinese. It is more difficult to explain the age factor. One possible explanation is that older people, who are generally concerned about Macau's political and social stability and were disappointed with the incompetent Portuguese administration, tend to look forward to a strong SAR government backed by Beijing. Another possible explanation is simply that older people tend to be more cautious in answering sensitive questions and hence had given 'desirable' responses.

Education is another important variable that accounts for the variation in responses to some questions. The better-educated tend to be more critical of government performance: 55 per cent of university-educated respondents were dissatisfied with the Portuguese administration's overall performance while only 37 per cent of those with primary school-education or no formal education were dissatisfied. The better-educated were particularly harsh about the slow pace of localization: 57 per cent, 54 per cent and 60 per cent, respectively, of those university-educated respondents expressed dissatisfaction over the pace of localization of civil service, localization of law and legalization of Chinese as an official language, while the corresponding figures for those with primary school-education or no formal education were 25 per cent, 22 per cent and 23 per cent. Clearly, the university-educated local Chinese, who are qualified for the government posts left vacant by the Portuguese expatriates, were unhappy with the slow pace of localization.

It is interesting to note that poorer people are less confident of the prospects for political autonomy and democratization in post-1999 Macau. While only 17.8 per cent of those respondents who had earned more than 10000 patacas (or 1250 US dollars) a month did not believe in the 'one country, two systems' concept, 38.5 per cent of those who had earned 5000 patacas or less did not believe the above. Furthermore, only 26.6 per cent of the lower income group felt that the Macau Basic Law had provided sufficient safeguard for the enclave's democracy, while 43 per cent of the higher income group felt so. The reason for the confidence gap between the income groups is not very clear. One probable explanation is that many poor people are new immigrants who tend to be sceptical of mainland China's policies.[12] Another probable explanation is that poorer people normally feel alienated from politics and hence have less confidence in promises made by any government. In any event, our findings suggest that in order to increase citizen confidence and trust in the new administration the SAR government must open its decision-making process to the Macau people, especially poorer people at the grassroots level.

As is to be expected, poorer people who are worrying about losing their jobs to the new immigrants are strongly opposed to any increase in Macau's population: of our respondents, only 10 per cent of the lower income group were in favour of population increase; by comparison, about one-third of the higher income group were in favour. Clearly, a rapid population increase will only create social conflict and instability in the territory.

Elite attitudes toward the transition

Since the December 1966 anti-government riot and the expulsion of pro-Taiwan Chinese community leaders, Macau's society has been dominated by pro-China social and political groups. Since the late 1980s the pro-China elites have replaced the Macanese as a dominant political force in the legislature and the municipal councils. The rise of the middle-class pro-democracy force since the 1980s has been proven too weak to challenge the strong pro-China political force. The *nouveau riche* business elites of the 1990s have also been co-opted by the pro-China groups. This does not mean to say Macau possesses a homogenous social and political elite. Indeed, there are conflicts of interests within the pro-China groups, especially between the labour union and the Chinese Chamber of Commerce. The analysis in this section is based on interviews with 55 local elites in 1998 and 1999, including pro-China, pro-democracy, politically independent and Macanese elites. The list is comprised of senior government officials, legislators, municipal councilors, scholars and community leaders. Most of the interviewees prefer anonymity. Although the list is not a representative sample, the following findings do reflect the general mood among the Macau elites at the handover.

Evaluation of Portuguese administration's performance

Most elites, regardless of political inclination, have blamed the Portuguese administration for Macau's economic recession. They point out that the Portuguese administration had been too conservative, bureaucratic and incompetent in wooing investments from Taiwan, Hong Kong and other countries or regions; too dependent on tourist and gambling business; and, most importantly, lacked a concrete strategic plan for Macau's long-term economic development. They also blamed the Portuguese administration for the deterioration in law and order and rampant corruption prior to the handover, which, according to the critics, was a direct result of the administration's incompetent, inefficient and bureaucratic management. Some local elites were particularly critical of the Portuguese administration's financial management. It was accused, for instance, of transferring the territory's financial sources to Portugal via the Orient Foundation.[13] The Portuguese administration's decision, a month before the handover, to extend the existing monopoly contract which remains effective until 2001 with the Telecommunication Company of Macau (CTM) for another 10 years, despite strong opposition and protest from the Macau people including pro-China legislators[14] – who normally refrained from publicly criticizing the Portuguese for ensuring a smooth handover – was particularly unpopular. The Portuguese administration was criticized for protecting the interests of Portuguese companies and not opening the local telecommunication market to competition. Indeed, 55.6 per cent of those interviewed were dissatisfied or very dissatisfied with the Portuguese administration's overall performance, about 16 percentage points higher than that of the mass public (see Table 4.2, above), while only 16.7 per cent were satisfied.

However, some local elites, especially the pro-democracy, politically independent, and Macanese elites, have given credit to the Portuguese administration for introducing a modern, Western legal and political system which, they believe, is a relatively more open and just system than the one in mainland China. Some, mainly the Macanese, regard law and protection of freedom and human rights as the best gift given to the territory by the Portuguese.[15] Most, including the pro-China elites, have praised the Portuguese administration for introducing free education (up to the ninth grade), free medical care and low-price housing to the enclave. In comparison, Macau's elites appear to be more generous than the mass public in recognizing the Portuguese contribution to the territory.

Confidence in the Chinese government

Needless to say, members of the pro-China elites have expressed confidence in the 'one country, two systems' concept. They point out that: (1) the PRC has always fulfilled its international agreements; (2) post-1997 Hong Kong is a successful case; and (3) the PRC will make sure that the 'one country, two systems' policy actually works in Hong Kong and Macau in order to set up an example for Taiwan. Pro-democracy and independent elites are less confident yet many feel that Macau is too small and insignificant for the central government to interfere at the expense of China's international image. As a senior civil servant remarks: 'China wants to maintain a good international image. Hong Kong is already a successful example. Macau is only a small place. Besides, the PRC has already fully controlled the enclave's economy through the mainland companies. Moreover, the Macau citizens are apathetic towards politics. Why does China need to interfere in Macau's affairs?' A few, however, do not trust the PRC government because of its past record of policy changes. Moreover, they argue, China is still to a certain extent ruled by man rather than ruled by law. It is thus difficult to say whether the 'one country, two systems' policy could remain unchanged for 50 years. In fact, China itself is arguably already under significant social and political transformation.

Likewise, the pro-China elites believe that the Macau Basic Law has provided sufficient safeguard for a high level of political autonomy including an independent judiciary for the Macau SAR. Pro-democracy and independent elites, however, are more sceptical. Some point out that the SAR's political autonomy and democratic development is in effect limited by the Basic Law. On paper, they argue, the Basic Law may provide sufficient safeguard for political autonomy but it all depends on the actual implementation of the 'one country, two systems' policy, especially relations between Beijing and Macau. They are afraid that Beijing may attempt to influence the SAR government through the local pro-China social groups or mass media.

Members of the pro-China elites are reluctant to discuss the issue of democratization in Macau. They insist that Macau already has democracy and that the Basic Law has provided sufficient safeguard for the enclave's democratic development. They argue that since most Macau citizens do not possess a civic or participant culture democratization should proceed slowly and cautiously in Macau; rapid democratization such as opening all seats in the legislature to universal suffrage may only result in chaos and political instability. Interestingly, many pro-democracy and independent elites share the above concerns. Yet they differ from the pro-China elites by arguing that all legislative seats as well as the SAR's chief executive should eventually be directly elected by the Macau people.

Confidence in the post-1999 SAR government

Is Macau going to be better or worse after the handover? As the findings of the reported telephone survey of Macau citizens suggests, the Macau people have some reservation about the prospect of governance under the new SAR administration. Do Macau's social and political elites have confidence in the post-1999 SAR government? The views of the pro-China elites are unanimous: 'Tomorrow's Macau will be much better!' They all point out that with the help of the motherland and governed by a new administration comprised of local talents, the post-1999 Macau society will be definitely more prosperous and harmonious than in the pre-handover era.[16] The only drawback of the new administration, the pro-China elites believe, is the lack of experience which, however, can be made up in a matter of a year or two. Some pro-democracy or independent elites share this view. They believe that Macau's economy and public order had already reached the worst possible situation under the Portuguese administration and things could only get better under the new administration. Besides, they believe, the PRC will definitely support the SAR government because China will not allow the policy of 'one country, two systems' to fail in Macau. Other pro-democracy or independent elites, however, are less optimistic. They point out that Macau lacks natural resources, capital and manpower, especially high quality manpower. Besides, the small Macau economy is highly dependent on and hence vulnerable to many uncertain outside factors.

In fact, when asked what they worry about most after the handover, about half of those interviewed, including the pro-China elites, have expressed concerns about the continuing economic recession in Macau. Some pro-democracy or independent elites, however, are more concerned about corruption and maladministration in the SAR administration as well as losing the freedom of speech and publication which had been previously guaranteed by the Portuguese Constitution. As a senior local journalist remarked: 'After the handover, the mass media will impose self-censorship and comply with Beijing's views. The dissenting voices will have little public outlet for expression. Besides, after the departure of the Portuguese, the Macau society will be more integrated with its economic, social and political groups. The Macau society will become less diversified and be united, or forced to be united, under the banner of *ai guo ai Aomen* (love China and love Macau).'

If a line could be drawn between the pro-China and pro-democracy or independent elites in terms of confidence in the Chinese government and post-1999 SAR administration, attitudes towards the population issue is clearly divided between the mass public and the elites. While our telephone survey suggests that only 16 per cent of the mass public are in favour of population increase, 60 per cent of those social and political elites interviewed by the author are in favour of increasing the territory's population in the range of 600 000 to one million. Many feel that Macau's economic development is limited by its small population and small-scale economy and suggest developing the enclave into a medium-sized international city. They feel that there is enough land and space in Coloane and Taipa islands to accommodate the increased population. Besides, as has been said, there are still about 30000 unsold flats to be filled. Nevertheless, they caution that the population should not be increased overnight but that this must be a well-planned increase together with other supporting services such as housing, education for children and medical cares. Some people, particularly labour union leaders, however, are opposed to increasing the enclave's population. They fear that the large influx of new immigrants will put high pressure on the local labour market and the education and social welfare system. They point out that Macau's population should be increased by natural growth only and that the quality rather than the quantity of the population are more important in an era of high technology.

Conclusion

Limited by the Macau Basic Law and the undemocratic nature of the PRC regime, the SAR government is not elected by the Macau people. The legitimacy of the new administration can only be sustained through policy performance. The SAR administration should conduct public opinion polls at regular intervals (for example, once every three months) on important policy-making such as population increase, management of and contracts for the local casinos, and education, culture and social welfare policies, as well as anti-corruption and anti-crime measures. Only when the new administration's policies truly reflect public opinion will it enhance its legitimacy among Macau's citizens. Unlike the Portuguese colonial administration which was accountable only to the Portuguese president and parliament, the SAR administration under the policy of 'Macau people ruling Macau' is arguably directly accountable to the Macau citizens. Its performance is thus under the close scrutiny of its citizens. Macau citizens are likely to be more critical of a SAR administration which is supposed to represent citizens' interests than of the former Portuguese administration.

In fact, as indicated by our telephone survey of the mass public and interviews of local social and political elites, there are divided views towards Macau's transition. On some issues such as whether the Macau Basic Law has provided sufficient safeguard to implement the 'one country, two systems' policy, or guarantee for the SAR's political autonomy and democratic development, opinions are divided between the pro-China and pro-democracy or independent groups. On other issues pertaining to population and economic policies opinions are divided between the better-off and the low income groups as well those between the mass public and the elites. In other words, there are potential conflicts of interest on certain important policy issues among and between social and political groups as well as between the rich and poor. If the SAR government does not handle the policy issues carefully, social discontents and industrial action may erupt which may challenge the legitimacy of the new administration. Only by opening the decision-making process for policy consultations can the new administration alleviate pressure from the public and enhance its own legitimacy.

5
Mass Political Culture in Macau: Continuity and Change

About 96 per cent of Macau's population is ethnic Chinese. Most local Chinese residents came from the neighbouring counties in Guangdong province, especially from Zhongshan. A significant minority, estimated to be around 50 000, came from the province of Fujian. Very few local residents are descendants of the original residents of Macau. When the Portuguese first landed in Macau in 1553, they found only a few hundred inhabitants. In fact, less than one-third of Macau's adult residents are local-born. To a large extent, therefore, Macau's mass political culture is a microcosm of Chinese political culture and, in particular, the culture of Guangdong and Fujian. Even locally-born Chinese are greatly influenced by their parents and grandparents who were born in China. According to the Basic Law, the Macau SAR has high political autonomy under the banner of 'one country, two systems'.

Almond and Verba define political culture as psychological orientation towards political objects.[1] They classify societies into three different political cultures according to their respective political orientations, namely, the 'parochial', 'subject', and 'participant' cultures.[2] In a 'parochial' culture, people do not separate their political orientations from their religious and social orientations. The masses in a parochial culture have little understanding of, feelings for, or expectations from the political system.[3] In a 'subject' political culture, people are primarily concerned with the political system and its output objects and pay little attention to the input objects and the self as an active political participant.[4] Citizens are merely passive subjects and rarely voice their opposition to the political system. By comparison, the 'participant' political culture is one in which members of society tend to be explicitly oriented towards the system as a whole and towards both the input and output aspects of the political system. Citizens tend to be oriented towards an 'activist' role of the self in the polity, although their feelings and evaluations of such a role may vary from acceptance to rejection.[5]

First published in the early 1960s, Almond and Verba's classic study was hailed as a landmark in political culture studies. At the same time, however, the study was severely criticized for its vague concept of political culture, the alluded to causal relationship between political culture and political structure, and lack of methodological rigour. Despite its critics, *The Civic Culture* remains one of the most frequently cited works in the field and its definition of political culture and research design has been emulated by numerous researchers, many of whom have applied Almond and Verba's theoretical framework to specific country studies. Cultural variables have often been used to explain the problems of democratic movement.[6] However, Inglehart argues, despite the renaissance of studies of political culture, we do not yet have sufficient data to sort out the causal linkage between political culture and democracy in any conclusive fashion.[7]

The author shares the assumption that political culture affects a populace's subjective orientation towards politics. In this chapter, the author partially adopts Almond and Verba's theoretical framework. Compared to *The Civic Culture*, however, which is a comparative study of political cultures in America, Britain, Germany, Italy and Mexico, this chapter merely focuses on the political culture of the Macau masses. It makes no explicit attempt to investigate the causal linkage between political culture and democracy. Our objective here is modest. We are interested in finding out whether there is a 'civic culture' among the Macau populace, which, according to Almond and Verba, is a necessary condition for a stable democracy.

The findings of a 1991 survey indicate that Macau has a mixed political culture, representing a combination of subject and participant orientations.[8] This culture is a mixture of traditional Chinese values of respect for authority, patience and tolerance with the modern, Western value of open competition.[9] What are the special features of the current mass political culture in Macau? Is it similar to or different from the culture of the early 1990s? This chapter examines continuity and change in Macau's mass political culture in the 1990s and the implications for the city-state's political development.

The data for this analysis is based on two surveys of Macau residents conducted in 1991 and 1999 respectively. The 1991 sample was a systematic selection from a full list of the addresses of all living quarters in Macau.[10] The survey was conducted during a seven-month period from April to October of 1991. Our interviewers approached people's living quarters and randomly selected one qualified person from among those living in the residence. The number of successfully completed interviews was 663. The successful response rate for the 1991 survey was 65 per cent. The 1999 survey was a telephone survey conducted in January.[11] The number of successfully completed interviews was 496. The successful response rate for the 1999 survey was 60 per cent. A change in research methodology from a face-to-face interview to a telephone survey was necessary because of insufficient research funding.

Our two samples are quite representative of the population of Macau. Table 5.1 indicates that in terms of sex distribution, the male respondents were slightly over-represented by 2–3 percentage points. In terms of age distribution, old people aged 60 and above were under-represented in the 1999 survey. More difficult is a comparison of the educational level of our sample respondents to the population as a whole because of the different ways of composing the data.[12] Nevertheless, people from different levels of education are well represented. Moreover, people from different income groups were well represented in the two samples.

Concerns about public affairs

Both the 1991 and 1999 surveys indicate that Macau residents are quite concerned with public affairs: 66.7 per cent and 71.4 per cent of the respondents in 1991 and 1999 respectively followed 'everyday' or 'often' the news on television, in the press, or on radio (see Table 5.2). Interesting to note, however, is that the Macau people have tended to engage more in discussing government affairs with their friends and relatives than before (see Table 5.3). One probable explanation is that the impending return of Macau to China had aroused public interest in and concerns about government affairs. Neverthe-

Table 5.1 Sample profiles and Macau's population profiles (1991 and 1999) (percentages)

	Sample profiles		Population profiles*	
	1991	*1999*	*1991*	*1998*
Sex				
Male	50.2	51.6	48.5	48.0
Female	49.8	48.4	51.5	52.0
Age				
18–19	4.2	–	3.7	–
20–29	26.5	28.7**	27.7	20.0
30–39	32.5	30.2	31.1	29.1
40–49	16.8	28.1	14.8	25.8
50–59	7.7	9.9	8.0	10.4
60 and above	12.3	3.0	14.7	14.6
Education				
No education	7.6	2.0	11.5	9.2
Some primary school	14.7	5.4	15.2	12.5
Finished primary school	18.0	17.3	29.4	27.4
Form 1–Form 5	27.8	20.8	26.7	27.0
Finished high school	27.1	37.7	11.1	16.1
University	4.8	16.7	6.1	7.8

* The population profile is based on the 1991 population census data and the 1998 (estimated) data, provided by the Census and Statistics Department, Government of Macau.

** This age group includes those who are 18 and 19 years old.

Table 5.2 Concerns about public affairs (percentages)

Q: *Do you follow the news on television, in the press, or on radio?*

	Every day	*Often*	*Occasionally*	*Rarely*	*No opinion*	*N*
1991 Survey	41.8	24.9	22.8	10.3	0.2	662
1999 Survey	48.6	22.8	21.8	6.8	–	496

less, discussion of public affairs among private circles are still quite uncommon: 60.9 per cent of those surveyed in 1999 'rarely' or 'never' discussed government affairs with friends and relatives. By comparison, in a survey conducted in Hong Kong in 1991, only 5.5 per cent of the respondents 'often' discussed government policies with

Table 5.3 Discussion of government affairs with friends and relatives (percentages)

Q: Do you discuss government affairs with your friends or relatives?

	Often	*Occasionally*	*Rarely*	*Never*	*No opinion*	*N*
1991 Survey	5.4	22.8	32.9	37.5	1.4	663
1999 Survey	6.3	32.9	34.7	26.2	–	496

friends or relatives; 28.1 per cent 'occasionally' did so.[13] In a nation-wide survey conducted in 1987 in mainland China, 62.4 per cent of respondents indicated that they were very cautious in discussing political issues with others.[14] There thus appears to be an inclination to avoid discussing public or political affairs among Chinese communities.

Conceptions of democracy

A correct understanding of conception of democracy among citizens is essential to a stable democracy. In the 1991 survey, high on the list of conceptions of democratic government was the traditional Chinese expectation of good government: 30 per cent of respondents believed that a democratic government is one that 'listens to public opinion and takes care of citizen interests'. Second on the list was freedom of speech, with 21.2 per cent choosing this Western concept as one of the crucial elements of democracy. Third was a government elected by the people, with only 9.6 per cent choosing this impor-tant Western concept (Table 5.4). Apparently our respondents were more concerned about the performance of a government than with the process of democracy. In the 1999 survey, however, the ranking of democratic values was almost reversed. High on the list was an elected government, something which is the hallmark of Western democracy: 32.3 per cent of respondents chose this concept. Second was the traditional Chinese value of an omnipotent government which takes care of citizen interests, with 26 per cent choosing this concept. Third was freedom of speech, with 22.9 per cent choosing this concept (Table 5.4). The new emphasis on an elected gov-ernment by the Macau residents is a big step forward in Macau's

Table 5.4 Conceptions of democracy (percentages)

*Q: What is a democratic government?**

	1991 (N = 663)	1999 (N = 496)
1. The government listens to public opinion and takes care of citizen interests	30.0	26.0
2. The people have freedom of speech	21.2	22.9
3. The government is elected by the people	9.6	32.3
4. The government is just and incorrupt	8.1	10.9
5. The government acts according to law	4.8	3.4
6. The government is efficient	4.8	0.9
7. The government is structured on the principles of 'checks and balances' between the executive, legislative and judicial branches	3.0	1.7
8. The decision-making process is open	–	10.0
9. The government is responsible	–	2.9
10. The government respects human rights	–	2.0
11. Other	13.3	18.5
12. Don't know/no opinion	39.6	34.5

* In the 1991 survey this was a close-ended question which listed nine items including 'other' and 'don't know/no opinion'; respondents were allowed to choose several items. In the 1999 survey this was an open-ended question.

democratization. After three elections of the Legislative Assembly in the 1990s,[15] which had drawn high voter turnouts,[16] the Macau residents have apparently attained a new election culture.

Nevertheless, like the earlier survey, the recent survey indicates that very few Macau citizens have realized the importance of the principles of 'checks and balances' between the executive, legislative and judicial branches in a democracy: only 1.7 per cent of the respondents chose this concept in the 1999 survey. The Macau people are probably influenced by Beijing's propaganda against the Western concept of 'separation of powers' and its blunt rejection to the idea of introducing such a concept to China and Hong Kong/Macau. Beijing continues to sell the idea to the local people that only an 'executive-led' government is suitable to Hong Kong and Macau. It is also important to note the high percentage of 'don't' knows' or 'no opinion' in both the 1991 and 1999 surveys. This partly reflects the fact that quite a significant proportion of the Macau people do not know much about democracy or that they simply do not care about democracy. Indeed, many respondents were quite reluctant to answer questions pertaining to politics. This reflects the lingering Chinese tradition of political disinvolvment. Another strong, lingering tradition is the stress on the instrumental value of governance. Like the survey of the early 1990s, over 60 per cent of the respondents in the 1999 survey agreed or strongly agreed with the statement that 'it really does not matter if a government is democratic or not as long as it can improve people's livelihood'. In short, despite an emerging election culture, the Macau people, like their parents or grandparents, are still more interested in the output or performance of the government than the process of governing.

However, one should be cautious in interpreting the data in Table 5.4. In the 1991 survey the question asked was a close-ended question which listed nine items including 'other' and 'don't know/no opinion'; respondents were allowed to choose several items. In the 1999 survey this was an open-ended question. The switch in question design is partly due to the change in research method from face-to-face interview to telephone survey and partly because the researcher wanted to minimize the effect of 'desired' or 'guided' response. For instance, 'listen to public opinion and takes care of citizen interests' was listed as the first item while 'government elected by the people' as the third item in the 1991 questionnaire. It is possible that some respondents in the 1991 survey were misled and believed that the first item in the list was the most 'desirable' answer. The change in conceptions of democracy as indicated in the 1999 survey could thus be partly a result of change in questionnaire design.[17] In any case, since the question on conceptions of democracy was asked differently in the two surveys, the problem of comparability cautions that one must treat the findings as indicative, not conclusive.

In order to probe deeper into the political psychology of the Macau populace, we had designed another set of questions in the 1999 survey to investigate the respondents' attitude towards political rights and the principles of 'checks and balances' between the executive, legislative and judicial branches within government power branches. We have adopted a framework designed by Wu Fo of the National University of Taiwan, who had conducted a Taiwan-wide survey in 1986.[18] Table 5.5 indicates that there is no consensus

Table 5.5 Positive attitude* toward political rights and the principles of 'checks and balances' between powers (percentages)

1. *The Equality right*
   We should let rich people become members of the Legislative Assembly.   79.6
   No matter what, women should not participate in politics.   84.2

2. *The right of political participation*
   We should let the central government in Beijing to directly appoint the Chief Executive for the Macau Special Administrative Region   62.7
   An ordinary citizen should not participate in politics   61.4

3. *Civil liberties*
   The government should punish immediately those criminals who have committed serious crimes without waiting for the court trial   54.9
   If there are too many different opinions regarding how to solve Macau's social problems it will only lead to chaos   38.7

4. *Pluralist politics*
   If there are too many interest or pressure groups in such a small place like Macau it will certainly affect Macau's social stability   51.1
   If Macau, like Hong Kong, has many political parties, Macau's politics would become chaotic   45.1

5. *'Checks and Balances' between the executive, legislative and judicial branches*
   The operation and efficiency of the government would be affected by the supervision of and constraints imposed by the legislature   55.1
   While dealing with a serious crime which threatens Macau's public order, the judge(s) should consult the government administration during the trial   32.2

* Positive attitude is measured by the proportion of respondents who 'disagree' or 'strongly disagree' with the listed statement.

among the Macau citizens towards various aspects of political rights, with the probable exception of the equality right. About 80 per cent of the respondents held positive attitudes towards equality rights, that is, disagreed or strongly disagreed with the listed statements pertaining to the equality right, while about 60 per cent held positive attitudes towards the right of political participation. Yet, on the average, less than 50 per cent of the respondents held positive attitudes towards civil liberties, pluralist politics and the principle of 'checks and balances' between the executive, legislative and judicial branches. The findings tend to support our observation that a participant culture has emerged in Macau since the early 1990s. It also supports our view that the Macau citizens have an incomplete understanding of democracy, paying insufficient attention to the importance of political pluralism and the supervision of political power.

Local Chinese residents are particularly sensitive to public disorder or chaos (*luan*). Table 5.5, above, shows that only 38.7 per cent of the respondents disagreed or strongly disagreed with the statement: 'If there are too many different opinions regarding how to solve Macau's social problems it will only lead to chaos'. At the same time, only 45.1 per cent of the respondents disagreed or strongly disagreed that party politics would cause chaos in Macau. Indeed, our respondents were so afraid of *luan* that a majority of them would not object to political intervention in court trials against serious crimes which threaten Macau's public order. Apparently the traditional Chinese fear of *luan* is deeply rooted among the local residents, although the enclave's deteriorating public order on the eve of Macau's return to the PRC also contributed to the *luan* scare. In any event, the resentment against different opinions and party politics, as well as the lack of alertness against political interference in court trials, is detrimental to democratization in Macau.

If we compare our findings to a survey conducted in 1986 in Taiwan,[19] we discover some interesting similarities and differences between the two regions. Table 5.6 indicates that the level of democratic consciousness of the Macau populace in the 1990s are lower than that in Taiwan in the mid-1980s. The 1986 Taiwan survey suggests that the Taiwan people had reached a consensus and held positive attitude towards the equality right and the right of political participation, about 15 per cent and 20 per cent, respectively, higher than that held by the Macau people in the above two aspects of political rights. It is interesting to note that, like the Macau people, Taiwanese in the mid-1980s did not have a consensus towards civil liberties and pluralist politics. There are obvious similarities in political and social environments between Taiwan in the mid-1980s and Macau in the 1990s: both were under an authoritarian, undemocratic government. Nevertheless, there is one distinctive difference between the two Chinese communities: the Taiwanese had appar-

Table 5.6 A comparison of Macau and Taiwan people's positive attitudes toward political rights and the principles of 'checks and balances' between power branches (percentage)

	*Macau (1999)**	*Taiwan (1986)***
The equality right	81.9	96.6
The right of political participation	62.1	84.1
Civil liberties	46.8	55.9
Pluralist politics	48.1	43.1
'Checks and balances' between the executive, legislative and judicial branches	43.7	74.5

* The percentage of positive attitude in each category is the average of the responses to the two listed statements in Table 5.5.
** From Wu Fo, *Zhengzhi wenhua yu zhengzhi shenghuo* (Political Culture and Political Life) (Taipei: Sanmin shuju, 1998), p. 86.

ently reached a consensus in the mid-1980s towards the principle of 'checks and balance' between the government power branches while the Macau people still do not have such a consensus. A probable explanation is that Taiwan had for a long time advocated and practised the so-called 'Five Power Constitution' separating, at least in theory, the executive, legislative, judicial, examination and supervision branches of power centres, while Macau residents have been under constant indoctrination from Beijing that only an 'executive-led' government is suitable to Macau.

Orientation toward political participation

The Portuguese had ruled Macau for more than 400 years. The Portuguese government, however, did not have a popular mandate to rule Macau. It derived formal and legal authority to rule from the authorities in Lisbon; the President of the Republic of Portugal appointed Macau's governor. Moreover, unlike Hong Kong, the sovereignty over the territory of Macau was never ceded to Portugal by a treaty; the Sino-Portuguese Treaty of 1887 only transferred administrative rights over the territory to the Portuguese. The exact boundary of the enclave was never demarcated. The legitimacy of the Portuguese governance of Macau was constantly challenged by the mainland Chinese authorities and local residents.[20] Partly due to the language barrier, there was little direct communication between the ruling Portuguese elite and the Chinese community. The colonial government had to rely on the Macanese (the Eurasians), who can speak both Chinese (Cantonese) and Portuguese, as the intermediary between the government and the local Chinese elite. The Chinese masses were virtually ignored and forgotten by the colonial government. However, the signing of the Sino-Portuguese Joint Declaration in 1987 had changed the relationship between the colonial government and the local Chinese residents. The process of localization had promoted young and capable local Chinese to high-ranking government positions to replace the departing Portuguese expatriates. The language barrier between the government authorities and the general public has been gradually broken. The mass public are now in a much better position to criticize government wrongdoing and to lodge complaints against government authorities.

Largely due to the inflow of capital from Hong Kong and mainland China, Macau's economy began to take off in the late 1970s. It recorded double-digit growth throughout the 1980s and early 1990s. In 1994, Macau's per capital gross domestic product (GDP) reached US\$16164,[21] ranked number five in East Asia behind only Japan, Brunei, Singapore and Hong Kong. However, the collapse of the real estate market in 1995 and the subsequent financial crisis in Hong Kong and other East Asian countries have plunged Macau into economic recession. Macau has recorded negative growth since 1996 with no recovery yet in sight. Meanwhile, partly due to the decline of tourism from Hong Kong and other Asian countries,[22] competition among local casinos is keen and severe. Underground societies which had great interest in casinos often chose to use force to settle their conflicts. Since 1996 and until the eve of handover killings and street gun-fightings between opposing triads and gangs had taken place almost every week, sometimes two or three days in a row. The colonial government appeared to be helpless in maintaining public order or in turning the economy back on track. Most Macau citizens were disappointed with the incompetent colonial government, something which affected citizen attitudes towards political participation.

One major difference in the findings between the two surveys is Macau citizens' attitudes towards the colonial government. In the 1991 survey, 55.5 per cent of respondents agreed or strongly agreed with the statement: 'We should obey the government because the government is always concerned about us'. In the 1999 survey, however, only 14 per cent of the respondents would let the colonial government have a free hand to do the job because they believed that the government was always concerned about its citizens; 73.3 per cent of the respondents thought the opposite (see Table 5.7). The finding suggests that: (1) the Macau people no longer trusted and had in effect cast a vote of no-confidence on the incompetent colonial administration; and (2) Macau citizens are no longer the traditional, obedient 'subjects' of the government. In fact, according to findings in another recent telephone survey, the Macau people were very disappointed with the colonial government's failure to develop the enclave's depressed economy and to maintain public order.[23]

Partly because of their disappointment with the Portuguese administration, the Macau people in general do not have high esteem for politicians. Table 5.7 shows that only 31 per cent of the respondents in the recent survey agreed or strongly agreed that 'political activity is a clean and noble job', a drop of 13.9 percentage points from the 1991 survey. Like their counterparts at the beginning of the decade, our recent survey indicates that a plurality of Macau citizens are still hesitant to be personally involved in political activities. Nevertheless, 61.4 per cent of respondents believed that all Macau citizens, regardless of social and economic status, should have equal right to participate in politics, while 79.5 per cent believed that a good citizen should vote in the election.

Interpersonal trust and co-operation represent the basic psychological infrastructure by which a true and lasting democracy could be established. The game of democracy can only be played by civilized people who respect and observe the rules of the game and who can trust and be trusted by others. Another noted continuity in Macau people's attitudes is their trust towards their fellow citizens, belief in competition, and tolerance of different opinions. Despite economic recession and worsening public order, Macau people's trust towards and patience with their fellow citizens have not shown any sign of significant decline. As indicated in Table 5.7, 51.1 per cent of respondents agreed and 3.8 per cent strongly agreed that most people are sincere, reliable and trustworthy. In answer to a different question, however, 36.7 per cent (a 11.7 percentage point drop from the 1991 survey) of respondents cautioned that one can easily be taken advantage of by other people in Macau society. It is possible that our respondents were referring to different societal groups while answering the two questions. Apparently, many believed that most ordinary people, or *laobaixing*, are trustworthy, while one has to be cautious in dealing with strangers. The above proportion is comparable to figures in Western democratic states: about half of the American and British respondents agreed that 'most people can be trusted'.[24] In addition, the Macau people appear to be quite tolerant of different opinion: 47.5 per cent agreed and 2.8 per cent strongly agreed that one should not quarrel with people and should always be patient and reconcilable. Yet at the same time, 70.8 per cent of respondents agreed and 8.9 per cent strongly agreed that people shall always fight for what they believe. In short, similar to the early 1990s, the Macau culture of the late 1990s is a mixture of traditional Chinese value of patience, tolerance and trustfulness with the modern, Western value of fighting for what one believes.[25]

Political efficacy

Political efficacy is an important indicator of participant political culture. Only when citizens are confident in the impact of their political actions on government policies will they incline to take such actions. Political efficacy has two aspects: civic competence and subject competence. The former refers to a citizen's capacity to influence government decision-making while the latter refers to a citizen's confidence in dealing with administrative officials according to a set of regular rules. Findings in our 1991 survey suggested that the Macau people were low in both civic and subject competence. Has political efficacy among Macau citizens increased over the last decade? Tables 5.8 and 5.9 indicate that there is little change in either civic or subject competence of Macau citizens over the last decade. Like the earlier survey, only a very small proportion (1.8 per cent) of respondents in the 1999 survey felt that they definitely or most likely could influence government policies, while 85.7 per cent felt that they had little or no influence at all. Likewise, only 12.2 per cent of respondents were confident that if they asked government departments for help the concerned departments would seriously help them to solve problems, while 41.2 per cent did not have such confidence in government departments. Apparently, the Macau people

Table 5.7 Orientation toward political participation (percentages)

Q: Do you agree with the following statements?

	Strongly agree	Agree	Disagree	Strongly disagree	No opinion	N
1. An ordinary citizen should not participate in politics						
1991 Survey	0.8	24.0	54.8	1.8	18.7	663
1999 Survey	0.2	20.0	57.4	4.0	18.4	496
2. Political activity is a clean and noble job						
1991 Survey	0.8	44.1	28.7	1.4	25.1	663
1999 Survey	1.0	30.0	37.2	1.2	30.6	496
3. A good citizen has the obligation to vote in an election						
1991 Survey	5.7	79.5	3.3	0.2	11.3	663
1999 Survey	9.5	70.0	8.1	0.2	12.3	496
4. To be involved in politics is dangerous						
1991 Survey	3.6	40.1	31.0	0.8	24.5	663
1999 Survey	2.2	37.4	29.7	0.0	30.7	496
5. We should obey the government because the government is always concerned about us						
1991 Survey	2.6	52.9	26.8	0.9	16.7	663
1999 Survey	0.4	13.6	65.8	7.5	12.8	496

6. In Macau's society, one can easily be taken advantage of by other people						
1991 Survey	1.2	47.2	31.4	0.2	20.1	663
1999 Survey	2.0	34.7	42.2	0.8	20.2	496
7. Most people in Macau are sincere, reliable and trustworthy						
1991 Survey	1.2	56.3	25.0	0.9	16.6	663
1999 Survey	3.8	51.1	24.6	1.6	18.8	496
8. We shall always fight for what we believe						
1991 Survey	5.3	77.0	7.6	0.2	10.0	663
1999 Survey	8.9	70.8	6.9	0.0	13.5	496
9. Don't quarrel with people, be patient and reconcilable whenever possible						
1991 Survey	2.4	51.0	33.9	1.2	11.5	663
1999 Survey	2.8	47.5	30.2	2.2	17.2	496

Table 5.8 Civic competence (percentages)

Q: Can you influence government policies?

	Definitely can	*Most likely*	*Occasionally*	*Rarely*	*Definitel cannot*	*No opinion*	*N*
1991 Survey	0.5	3.2	2.0	18.2	76.1	–	658
1999 Survey	0.2	1.6	3.2	17.8	67.9	9.3	496

Table 5.9 Subject competence (percentages)

Q: If you ask some government departments for help, do you think they will seriously help you to solve your problem?

	Definitely	*Most likely*	*Perhaps*	*Most unlikely*	*Definitely not*	*No opinion*	*N*
1991 Survey	1.5	12.5	32.5	19.7	11.0	22.8	661
1999 Survey	0.5	11.7	30.7	31.9	9.3	15.8	496

had little confidence in dealing with the Portuguese colonial government which, in the eyes of Macau citizens, had lost the will and capability to govern over the final years of the colonial rule. Indeed, it will be interesting to find out if the political efficacy of Macau citizens will increase after the return of Macau to China when the enclave, according to the Basic Law of the Macau Special Administrative Region, is supposed to be ruled by the Macau residents themselves.

The Macau people's disillusion with the Portuguese administration is reflected in the significant decrease in the proportion of residents who were willing to deal with the government. When asked whether they would take actions to oppose government wrongdoing that had seriously affected their personal interest, only 22.7 per cent of respondents in the 1999 survey indicated that they would definitely or most likely take action, a drop of 13 percentage points from the 1991 survey. However, interesting to note is that those who did indicate that they would take action against government wrongdoing in the 1999 survey would opt to use more channels to voice their grievances than their counterparts in 1991. Table 5.10 indicates that in the 1999 survey more than three times the respondents in the 1991

Table 5.10 Possible actions against government wrongdoing (percentages)

*Q: What possible action would you take against government wrongdoing?**

	1991	1999
1. Complain to government departments	19.0	59.7
2. Ask legislators for help	11.3	41.3
3. Write or call up the local press, television and radio stations	20.1	38.8
4. Ask social and citizen groups for help	9.1	28.1
5. Protests, demonstrations, sit-ins and strikes	13.2	11.2
6. Other actions	25.6	6.5
7. Don't know/no opinion	24.2	18.9

* This is a multiple choice question. The sum of the percentages is thus larger than 100 per cent.

survey would complain to government department and ask legislators or societal and citizen groups for help. Those who would write or call up the local press, television or radio stations were also doubled. Thus, if we divide the Macau population into two groups – those who would take action to oppose government wrongdoing (or political activists) and those who would decline to do so (often referred to as the 'silent majority'), the latter have apparently increased in proportion since the early 1990s. Yet Macau's political activists, although decreasing in proportion, are increasingly more aggressive and opt for a wider range of options to oppose government wrongdoing. Nevertheless, also important to note is that, like political activists in the early 1990s, few current political activists would opt for such radical action as protests, demonstrations, sit-ins and strikes. Compared to their counterparts in Hong Kong, Macau's political activists are far more conservative and restrained.

Background variables

In the 1991 survey, we found that women, as compared to men, have less time to read a newspaper or to watch television news. Yet women, like men, were highly critical of government policies; they also held a positive attitude towards political participation and believed that one shall always fight for what one believes. The 1991 data clearly indicated that Macau's women were no longer passive or apathetic towards political participation.[26] The 1999 survey tends to confirm the trend of increasing women participation in politics. There is still a gap between men and women regarding concerns about public affairs, but this gap has considerably narrowed: 75 per cent of our male respondents followed the news from the radio, television or newspaper 'everyday' or 'often' (the same as in the 1991 survey), while 67.6 per cent of the female respondents did so (a 9 percentage point increase over 1991). In attitudes towards such other aspects of politics as government performance, political participation, tolerance of dissenting opinion and belief in open and fair competition, this research has found no significant difference between our male and female respondents in the most recent survey. A new generation of active, sophisticated and independent-minded women has gradually replaced the passive, naïve and dependent-minded older generation of women. Increasing active women participation in politics is an irreversible trend in Macau politics.

In our 1991 survey, we found that young people, as compared to the older generation, were more critical of government performance, more active towards political participation, more willing to fight for what they believe, yet tended not to trust others and were less tolerant of dissenting opinions.[27] In our 1999 survey, we still found a significant gap between the younger and older generations towards the traditional virtue of unlimited patience: of our respondents, 71.4 per cent of those aged 50 and above agreed or strongly agreed with the statement that 'one should not quarrel with people but be patient and reconcilable whenever possible', while only 38.3 per cent of those in the 18–19 age group did so (see Table 5.11). There is clearly a significant relationship between the two variables (gamma = 0.248, significance = 0.000). However, in attitudes towards other aspects of politics we have found no significant difference in the 1999 data across different age groups. In other words, there is a tendency towards convergence of political attitudes between the older and younger generations. One possible explanation is the impending return of Macau to China and the disappointing performance of the colonial government had generated a consensus among Macau citizens – across the age groups – towards political issues.

Our findings in the 1991 survey supported a positive relationship between education and political development. The better-educated and hence better-informed respondents were more critical of gov-

Table 5.11 Age and attitude toward patience

Q: Do you agree with the statement that 'one should not quarrel with people but be patient and reconcilable whenever possible'?

	Strongly disagree	*Disagree*	*Neutral/ no opinion*	*Agree*	*Strongly agree*	*Total*
Age: 18–29	1	56	30	52	2	141
30–39	6	43	33	63	3	148
40–49	2	39	15	77	6	139
50–59	1	10	4	33	1	49
60 and above	1	1	1	9	2	14
Total	11	149	83	234	14	491

Gamma = 0.248; significance = 0.000.

ernment performance and tended to be participant-oriented. They also tended to reject the traditional values of passivity and submissiveness to authority and social harmony, preferring instead a more open and competitive polity.[28] Our 1999 findings tend to reconfirm the 1991 findings: of the respondents, 83 per cent of university graduates followed the news from radio, television or newspaper 'everyday' or 'often', while only 55 per cent of those who received primary school or no education did so. At the same time, 50 per cent of the former and 19 per cent of the latter groups discussed government affairs with their friends and relatives. More importantly, 82 per cent of the university-educated disagreed or strongly disagreed with the statement that 'one should obey the government because the government is always concerned about its citizens', 30 per cent higher than the lowly-educated group (see Table 5.12). There is a significant relationship between the two variables (gamma = 0.349, significance = 0.000). The better-educated also tend to have a better understanding of Western democracy, a higher level of civic and subject competence, and a desire for political rights. For instance, 96.4 per cent of university-educated respondents disagreed or strongly disagreed with the statement, 'no matter what, women should not participate in politics', about 20 per cent higher than primary school-educated and illiterate respondents; 72 per cent of the former also either disagreed or strongly disagreed that 'the government should punish immediately those criminals who have committed serious crimes

Table 5.12 Education and attitude toward government

Q: Do you agree with the statement that 'one should obey the government because the government is always concerned about its citizens'?

	Strongly agree	Agree	Neutral/ no opinion	Disagree	Strongly disagree	Total
Education:						
Illiterate	0	5	1	3	1	10
Some primary school	0	10	4	13	0	27
Finished primary school	0	26	11	46	3	86
Form 1–Form 4	2	11	15	65	9	102
Finished Form 5	0	10	22	139	16	187
College/university	0	5	10	59	8	82
Total	2	67	63	325	37	494

Gamma = 0.349; significance = 0.000.

without waiting for the court trials', again about 20 per cent higher than the latter group. Table 5.1 indicates that the educational level of the Macau people has significantly increased over the last decade. It is thus quite accurate to say that Macau citizens are more politically participant-oriented and have a better understanding of democratic processes and values than a decade ago.

Another important background variable is length of residence in Macau. Our findings indicate that there is a positive relationship between the length of residence and the concerns about public and government affairs. In our 1999 survey, for example, 75 per cent of those respondents who were born and grew up in Macau followed the news from the radio, television or newspaper 'everyday' or 'often', while only 51 per cent of those who have lived in Macau less than ten years did so. At the same time, 45 per cent of the former 'often' or 'occasionally' discussed government affairs with others, while only 17 per cent of the new immigrants did so (see Table 5.13). In the 1991 population census only 40.1 per cent of the Macau residents were locally-born. This increased to 44.1 per cent in the 1996 interim population census; estimates hold that at the turn of the twenty-first century close to half of the current Macau population will be local-born.[29] The Macau SAR government will

Table 5.13 Length of residence and tendency toward discussing government affairs with others

Q: Do you discuss government affairs with your relatives and friends?

	Often	Occasionally	Rarely	Never	Total
Length of residence in Macau					
1–5 years	1	0	2	8	11
6–10 years	1	8	21	18	48
11–20 years	4	40	47	37	128
20 and more years	12	38	30	27	107
Locally born	13	75	70	39	197
Total	31	161	170	129	491

Gamma = –0.219; significance = 0.000.

likely confront an informed, concerned, critical and participant-oriented public.

Continuity and change

Almond and Verba distinguish three levels of orientation towards the political system – the cognitive, affective and evaluative orientations.[30] Findings from our 1991 and 1999 surveys suggest that Macau citizens' cognitive orientation is positively linked to education. The better-educated are normally better informed and hence more knowledgeable about the structure and functions as well as the performance of the political system. The more they know about politics, the more they are concerned about public and government affairs and tend to discuss public affairs with friends and relatives. As the overall educational level of the Macau people has significantly increased over the last decade, our findings confirm our expectation that local residents are better informed and more concerned about public affairs than a decade ago.

Evaluative orientation is also positively linked to education. The better-educated tend to be more critical of government performance. We are thus not surprised to find that Macau citizens are more critical of government policies than before. We must point out, however, that education is not the only and, in the case of Macau, not the most important variable that affects a citizen's evaluative orientation.

The incompetence of the Portuguese colonial government as indicated by the depressed economy and worsening public order had greatly disappointed Macau citizens from all walks of life. Indeed, increasing criticism against government performance in recent years was largely a result of government incompetence.

Affective orientation is more complicated. A citizen's affective orientation or feeling towards the political system is partly affected by the performance of the government. In the 1999 survey, only 35 per cent of our respondents were proud of being Macau citizens, a drop of 18 percentage points from 1991 survey. In the early 1990s, the Macau people were proud of the enclave's double-digit economic growth as well as social and public stability. In the recent survey, many of our respondents indicated that they could find nothing to be proud of. Yet many still have a strong feeling towards Macau. These include those older residents who have spent most of their life in Macau, as well as the locally-born who have an emotional attachment to their birthplace.

It is important to note that a new election culture has emerged in Macau. After experiencing three legislative elections in the 1990s, many Macau citizens have begun to realize the importance of an elected government in their conceptualization of democracy. 'An elected government' has replaced a government that 'listens to public opinion and takes care of citizen interests' as the foremost essential element of democracy in the minds of many Macau citizens. In other words, the traditional instrumental value of an omnipotent government is no longer the dominant value of the local residents. Their understanding of democracy is converging with Western democratic values.

Yet some deep-rooted traditional values remain strong among the local populace. The Macau people in general have low esteem for politicians and are inclined to believe that to be involved in political activities could be dangerous. Like their grandparents or great-grandparents in traditional Chinese society, they do not think they themselves can influence government policies. Few would thus take actual political action to oppose government wrongdoing. Moreover, the traditional virtue of unlimited patience and tolerance towards personal relations and authority is still highly respected among the local populace.

Political culture is a result of a long process of socialization. An individual's orientation towards politics is affected by the family environment, education and the political atmosphere of society. An earlier study indicates that traditional big families in Macau are fast vanishing, being replaced by small nuclear families.[31] Most nuclear families are no longer man-centred or father-dominated; family decisions are usually made by both parents after consultations with their children. Many children do feel they have some influence on family decision-making.[32] In other words, the newer generation is growing up in modern, democratic families. As they are usually better educated than their parents and grandparents, they are also better informed, more concerned about public affairs, participant-oriented and more receptive of Western democratic values. Furthermore, the global and regional wave of democratization, such as the Taiwan and Hong Kong experience, will no doubt have some degree of impact on Macau citizens' attitudes toward politics. The trend towards a participant culture among the Macau populace can therefore be expected to continue in the future.

Implications for political development in Macau

Findings from our two surveys, especially the 1999 survey, have implications for Macau's future political development as well as policy implications for the SAR government. First and foremost, our findings suggest that the Macau people were very unhappy with the colonial government: they distrusted the Portuguese government and had low esteem for government officials. Indeed, the legitimacy of the colonial government was in doubt. The foremost task of the SAR government is thus to restore the legitimacy of the government among the Macau populace by restoring law and order and leading the enclave out of economic recession.

Second, the SAR government should open the policy decision-making process to the public, hold more formal and informal consultations with citizen and societal groups on policy issues, and hold more open forums or public hearings on political and social issues. Macau is merely a small city-state with a population of less than half a million and an area of about 24 square kilometers. There is no conflict or regional interests. As the overall educational level of its citizens increases and a participant culture emerges, Macau may develop to became an ideal city-state able to practice a direct participation style of democracy. Due to restraints imposed by the Macau Basic Law, the SAR government is not popularly elected and is hence weak in legitimacy. To encourage Macau citizens to directly participate in politics is one way to increase the legitimacy of the SAR government.

Third, in 2009 the year for reviewing, the SAR government should, according to the Basic Law, greatly increase the proportion of directly elected seats from the current one-third to two-thirds of the total seats in the Legislative Assembly and abolish the appointed seats. In the 1999 survey, 94 per cent of respondents indicated that their ideal political system is democracy and 75 per cent believed that a democratic political system is suitable to Macau. To increase the proportion of directly elected seats or, indeed, to make all legislative seats to be elected through universal suffrage, is the only way to meet the political aspirations of Macau citizens.

Last but not least, the traditional 'consensus politics' in the Chinese community which is based on compromises between the Chinese Chamber of Commerce, labour unions, neighbourhood or *kaifong* associations, and other professional, citizen, societal and religious groups may no longer be viable in the post-1999 Macau SAR. Politically aspired citizens and the emerging election culture will challenge the traditional institutions that mediate between the mass public and the government. The Macau people may no longer be satisfied with a passive political role. They may increasingly prefer to deal directly with the government. Moreover, they would like to elect their own leaders who are accountable to them. In any event, traditional community leaders are losing their influence in an increasingly pluralistic society. Hong Kong style party politics may be introduced to the enclave in one or two decades. The days when one or two community leaders can change the course of Macau's politics are gone for ever.

6
Money Politics and Political Mobilization: the 1996 Legislative Assembly Elections

The 1996 Legislative Assembly elections are important for several reasons. First, this new body was set up to sit for five years, until 2001. Thus, the legislators who were elected in 1996 would ride the 'through train' to become members of the first Legislative Assembly in the Macau Special Administrative Region (SAR). Second, an unprecedented number of political groups (12) were formed and candidates (62) registered for elections. Third, voter turnout on election day was one of the highest in Macau's history. Last but not least, there is the prominent role that money politics played in Macau politics and the elections.

The Fifth Legislative Assembly (1992–96) approved 28 private bills introduced by the legislators and 35 law proposals drafted by government.[1] As in other colonial political systems, however, Macau politics was dominated by the executive branch. The governor and his seven under-secretaries were appointed by Portugal's president and thus were not held accountable to the Legislative Assembly nor to the people of Macau. In addition, the Macau government could make laws by administrative decrees that did not require legislative approval. But while the Legislative Assembly had little influence over government policies, only it and the Municipal Council (*Leal Senado*) have directly and indirectly elected members who can claim to represent the interests of Macau citizens. Thus, Legislative Assembly elections are important events in Macau politics.

The evolution of the Legislative Assembly elections in Macau

Unlike Western democracies, where elections have become a normal feature of the political system, elections in Macau have only a short history. Portugal had ruled Macau for more than 400 years, but this modern from of political participation was not brought to the colony until after the Portuguese revolution in 1974. As a result, electoral laws and systems are far from being institutionalized, and voters may not be acquainted with the meaning and rules of the game. To put the following analysis in context, it is necessary first to look at the existing political system of Macau in some detail.

In 1976, the Portuguese parliament ratified the Organic Statute of Macau under which the Legislative Assembly has the constitutional power to make laws, scrutinize public expenditure, and amend the Organic Statute. It consists of 17 members, of which six are elected directly, six indirectly by designated interest groups, and five appointed by the governor. In contrast, the pre-Organic Statute Legislative Assembly had been composed mainly of appointed members, the majority of whom were Portuguese and Macanese (Macau-born residents with mixed Portuguese–Chinese blood).[2] The colonial administration, however, did always feel obliged to include some Chinese voices in this law-making body. In 1974, for example, three of the 15-appointed members were Chinese. In 1976, when only one Chinese candidate was directly elected to the Legislative Assembly, and in 1980 when none were, the governor appointed two Chinese legislators to each assembly.

Introducing direct elections to the Legislative Assembly did not substantially increase political participation among Macau's Chinese citizens. One reason is that the franchise was restricted. Macau electoral law at the time required that Chinese nationals live in the colony for five years and nationals other than Chinese and Portuguese seven years to establish the residency needed to acquire voting rights, while no such requirements were imposed on Portuguese nationals.[3] The native Macanese had voting rights by birth. This residence requirement meant that a large proportion of the Macau population could not vote, namely, new immigrants from mainland China. It was not until 1984 that a new electoral law conferred equal voting rights for all Macau residents regardless of length of residence,[4] and by the early 1990s, the majority of registered voters were Chinese nationals. Indeed, the 1991 revisions of the electoral law, aimed at barring the participation of Portuguese expatriates in elections by restoring the residence requirement,[5] were initiated by a Legislative Assembly dominated by Chinese and Macanese.

The 1976 and 1980 Legislative Assemblies were often at odds with the administration, a corpus dominated by Portuguese nationals from Lisbon. In 1980, the chairman of the Legislative Assembly, Carlos d'Assumpcao, and three other Macanese legislators put forward a proposal to amend the Organic Statute. They proposed a 24-member elected legislature with the power to cast no-confidence votes against government officials. Governor Egidio rejected the proposal. The row reached its height when both the Macanese legislators and Governor Egidio went to Portugal to lobby members of Portugal's parliament for their respective positions. China finally intervened, with China's leaders explicitly rejecting any change in Macau's Organic Statute.[6] This prompted pro-Beijing, Macau Chinese legislators, together with some Portuguese legislators,[7] to take action to block the Macanese foursome's proposal. As a result, the Legislative Assembly did not submit the proposed Organic Statute amendment to the Portuguese parliament.

This did not bring to an end the power struggle between Macanese legislators and the governor. In 1984, Governor Costa's decree that the administration of the Municipal Council be centralized precipitated the resignation of two Macanese municipal councillors.[8] Macanese legislators retaliated by revising Governor Costa's administrative decrees without his approval. The governor was infuriated and asked Portugal's president to dissolve the Legislative Assembly. He also introduced an electoral reform in the Legislative Assembly to counterbalance the influence of Macanese legislators there. Anticipating that the Macanese would capture most of the directly elected seats in the forthcoming 1984 election, he altered the electoral law to allow economic interest groups to vote on legislators for two more of the indirectly elected seats, giving them the power to choose five of the six available seats.[9] Only representatives from government-registered business organizations such as the Chinese Chamber of Commerce, the Construction and Real Estates Association, the Factory Employers' Association, the Exports and Imports Association and a few smaller business associations were allowed to cast votes in the elections for these five seats that had been designated for the economic constituency. Since local business sectors were controlled by Chinese, this would result in more Chinese representatives being elected to the legislature.

Costa's reform was opposed by Macanese legislative leaders, including d'Assumpcao, who threatened to boycott the 1984 Legislative Assembly elections. The conflict eventually drew intervention from Beijing, and pro-Beijing leaders agreed to support the d'Assumpcao-led Macanese elites in the direct elections in return for their support in the indirect elections.[10] D'Assumpcao formed the Electoral Union, which had the support of pro-Beijing forces, and won four of the six directly elected seats in the 1984 elections. Meanwhile, Costa's extension of the franchise for direct elections was accompanied by the emergence of a new political force: locally born, young, middle-class, Chinese elites outside the pro-Beijing coalition. They launched a political group, the Flower of Friendship and Development of Macau, and its leader, Alexandre Ho, was elected. The group gained two more seats in the 1988 elections, but the Chinese community was and still is dominated by the pro-Beijing forces.

In fact, since 1988 the Macanese influence in Macau politics has significantly declined. In the 1988 elections, only two Macanese, Carlos D'Assumpcao, the chairman of the Legislative Assembly, and Leonel Alberto Alves, a young lawyer, won their seats through direct ballot. The Macanese won only one directly elected seat in the 1992 election and none in 1996. The Macanese, however, won two indirectly elected seats in the expanded 1992 and 1996 legislature with, ironically, the tactical support of the pro-Beijing Chinese community leaders.[11] The end of the Macanese era signalled the beginning of Chinese domination. Indeed, Governor Carlos Melancia had to appoint four Macanese to the 1988 legislature to counterbalance the influence of the local Chinese legislators. Likewise, Governor Vasco Rocha Vieira appointed Macanese or Portuguese legislators to counterbalance the Chinese influence in the 1992 and 1996 legislature. Table 6.1 shows the changing political scene of the Macau legislature since 1976.

Another significant trend in the enclave's political scene in the last two decades is the increase in the number of registered voters and the increasing voter turnout. Table 6.2 indicates that, partly due to the strict residency requirements for Chinese nationals, there were

Table 6.1 The proportion of Chinese and Portuguese* legislators (1976–2001)

	Directly elected seats		Indirectly elected seats		Appointed seats		Total	
	Chinese	Portuguese	Chinese	Portuguese	Chinese	Portuguese	Chinese	Portuguese
1976–80	1	5	4	2	2	3	7	10
1980–84	0	6	4	2	2	3	6	11
1984–88	2	4	6	0	1	4	9	8
1988–92	6	2	7	1	0	7	13	10
1992–96	7	1	6	2	0	7	13	10
1996–2001**	8	0	6	2	0	7	14	9

* Including the Macanese (Eurasians).
** The Sixth Legislative Assembly has a tenure of 5 years.

Table 6.2 Voter turnout rate in legislature
elections (1976–96)*

Year	Registered voters	Turnout rate (%)
1976	3 674	78.04
1980	4 195	61.98
1984	51 454	56.30
1988	67 492	29.71
1991	97 648	18.64
1992	48 139	59.25
1996	116 441	64.49

* The statistics are provided by the Division of Technical
Support for Elections, Office of Administration and Public
Service, the Government of Macau.

only several thousand registered voters, largely Macanese and Portuguese nationals, in the 1976 and 1980 legislature elections. The Macanese were highly motivated voters whose objective was to dominate the legislature. This partly explained the high voter turnout in the two elections. Under the active mobilization of Governor Costa, with the apparent approval of the mainland Chinese authorities,[12] more than 45 000 local Chinese residents registered as voters in 1984 and slightly more than half of them actually cast their ballots in the election. Voter turnout, however, dropped significantly in the 1988 election and 1991 by-election. The drop in voter turnout was partly a result of insufficient mobilization or propaganda from the government authorities when both Governor Melancia's and Vieira's administrations were largely indifferent to the elections, and partly due to the emigration or death of those registered voters who registered in the 1970s and 1980s. Despite the fact that they were no longer in Macau (by emigration or death), their registration remained valid until 1991. In other words, the actual number of registered voters in 1988 and 1991 was considerably smaller than the figures indicated in Table 6.2. When re-registration was required for all voters in 1992, the turnout rate increased significantly in the 1992 and 1996 elections (again see Table 6.2). The number of registered voters doubled in 1996 against 1992 partly because the pro-Beijing political and social groups as well as the *nouveau riche* business groups had actively mobilized and assisted the grassroots populace to register as voters.

Of course, rapid economic development and social change in Macau in the 1980s and early 1990s had also contributed to the rise in citizen participation and hence the increase of registered voters and higher voter turnout in the last two elections.

The pro-Beijing Chinese Chamber of Commerce has assumed a leading role in Macau's Chinese community. Its leaders act as the backbone of the Macau economy, as the representatives of the colony's Chinese elites, as mediators between the Chinese and Portuguese governments, and sometimes as the spokespeople of the Chinese government. Ho Yin (or He Xian), who chaired the Chamber from 1950 until his death in 1983, had been widely accepted as the leader of the Chinese community in Macau. He had a very close relationship with Beijing and assumed an important leading role at crucial points in the territory's recent history.[13] Ho was succeeded as chairman by Ma Man Kei (or Ma Wanqi), who is a standing committee member of the Chinese National People's Congress (NPC) and was a member of the Macau Legislative Assembly from 1980 to August 1996.[14] Other members of the Chamber, such as Edmund Ho Hau Wah (or He Houhua, son of the late Ho Yin), and Victor Ng, are also deputies of the NPC and also served as indirectly elected Legislative Assembly members. Because of the Chamber's mediating role, candidates standing for indirect elections through an economic constituency often run unopposed. In any case, the majority of the Macau people are excluded from participation in indirect elections because votes are accorded not to individual voters but rather to member organizations.

Direct elections thus became the only way most of Macau's citizens could participate in the political process. The 1987 Joint Declaration would turn Macau into a SAR with a high level of autonomy and self-government, and one part of this transition had been an increase in the number of elected seats in the Legislative Assembly. In March 1991, by-elections were held for four additional seats of which two were directly elected and two indirectly elected. The current 23-member Assembly comprised eight directly elected seats, eight indirectly elected seats chosen through functional constituencies, and seven officially appointed seats. It should be noted, however, that the proportion of elected seats *vis-à-vis* appointed seats remains basically the same as it was in the 17-seat body.

Money politics and political mobilization

As a seasoned observer of Macau politics noted a few days before the 22 September 1996 Legislative Assembly elections, the event was a litmus test for Macau's political culture whose results would indicate whether Macau possesses a mature or democratic culture.[15] An earlier study has reported that Macau's mass political culture was high on subject orientation, which reflects the influence of traditional culture, and low on participant orientation. It argued that the majority of Macau's citizens were indifferent to the processes and instruments of democracy, such as elections. Most tended to agree that a good citizen should participate in politics and hold high regard for those actually involved in politics, yet in practice they preferred to stay away from politics and let others do the job.[16] In short, according to the study, Macau citizens were passive, if not apathetic, toward political participation.[17] The results of the 1992 and 1996 Legislative Assembly elections tend to support such observations.

Following the Portuguese example, Macau's direct elections adopt the d'Hondt rule, also known as the 'list system' or 'proportional representation by the highest average'. Each political group formed to participate in the Legislative Assembly direct elections has to put up a list of at least four candidates in consecutive order.[18] Macau is treated as one big electoral district in the election, and each voter is requested to choose *one* political group (not individual candidate) during the ballot. The election's outcome is decided by the number of votes each group receives. According to the new d'Hondt rule that came into force in the 1992 elections, the first candidate in each group receives all of the votes his or her groups receives, the second candidate half, the third a quarter, the fourth one-eighth, the fifth one-sixteenth, and so on. This version of the d'Hondt rule tends to favour smaller and weaker political groups.[19] Partly encouraged by the new rule, an unprecedented nine political groups participated in the 1992 Legislative Assembly elections.

The 1992 elections would see pro-Beijing forces mobilize Macau citizens in a bid to consolidate their dominance of Macau politics.[20] Macau's Chinese community has been dominated by pro-Beijing forces ever since the anti-government demonstrations and riots of December 1966 forced the Portuguese government to surrender to Chinese demands and bar all pro-Taiwan associations from the colony.[21] The pro-Beijing Chinese Chamber of Commerce and its affiliated economic groups have monopolized almost all of the legislature's indirectly elected seats, while the pro-Beijing Federation of Kaifong (Neighbourhood) Associations and the Federation of Labour Unions have attempted to dominate the direct elections. These forces put up two political groups for the 1992 elections, the Federation of Kaifong Association-backed Union for the Promotion of Progress (UNIPRO) and the Federation of Labour Unions-backed Development Union (UPD). During the voters' registration period, the two federations mobilized pro-Beijing organization staff members and their relatives, organizations that included schools, banks, unions, and *kaifong* associations.

Their efforts focused on getting people who had previously registered as voters to 'reconfirm' their voter status and encouraging unregistered voters to register and they set up 'service stations' in various districts to help citizens register or reconfirm.[22] The pro-Beijing groups also took advantage of social functions during the campaign period such as the Teachers' Festival, and the meetings and dinners that marked the PRC's national day on October 1. Finally, the pro-Beijing *Macau Daily News* (*MDN*), by far Macau's most popular newspaper, frequently reported on the activities and political platform of pro-Beijing candidates, while playing down those of their opponents, particularly pro-democracy candidates Wong Cheong Nam (or Wang Changnan) and Ng Kuok Cheong (or Wu Guochang).[23] On election day, the newspaper reiterated its position that voters should elect candidates who could communicate with Portugal and the PRC.[24] The labour union and *kaifong* association federations mobilized staff members and supporters of their affiliated organizations to ensure high voter turnout, activities that included transporting the elderly and women in particular by school bus to voting stations. As a result, the UNIPRO and UPD captured four of the eight directly elected seats. Wong Cheong Nam was defeated and Alexandre Ho, another independent (i.e. not pro-Beijing) incumbent, was elected with the least votes of any candidate.

The success of pro-Beijing groups in capturing half of the directly elected seats in the 1992 elections demonstrated that most Macau voters were politically passive and susceptible to mobilization. This success was fostered in part by the consistent failure of Portuguese authorities to narrow the communication gap between ordinary citizens and the government. Lacking knowledge of the Portuguese language and the proper channels through which they could contact government authorities, Macau's ordinary citizens must often rely on interest groups to serve as intermediaries to voice their grievances. The well-organized and numerically much larger Beijing-backed labour unions and *kaifong* associations easily out-performed other political groups in the elections.

The UNIPRO and UPD conducted intensive lobbying activities of their own in the 1996 Legislative Assembly elections, hoping to repeat their victories of 1992. They were, however, faced with a very different economic and social environment and with new challengers. In all, 12 political groups participated in the 1996 elections: two pro-Beijing groups; five formed by independent business people unaffiliated with the pro-Beijing mainstream; one made up of staff and workers from the local casinos; another comprised primarily of Macanese; two pro-democracy groups; and one independent group (see Table 6.3). Each of the 12 political groups registered four to six candidates, resulting in a total of 62 candidates contesting for the eight directly elected seats. The 12 groups represented various interests in Macau society, but only the pro-Beijing groups had support from broadly based associations. The other groups relied either on their associated business or ethnic groups, or simply on a maverick candidate, as was the case with the pro-democracy groups headed by Ng and Wong.

Although there were variations in emphasis and priorities, the groups' political platforms contained more similarities than differences. This is not too difficult to explain. To appeal to all voters in a single electoral district that is, in fact, a small city where variations in regional interests are minimal, the issues and policy recommendations in the competitors' political platforms tend to overlap. In the light of the sluggish economic growth in recent years, all groups advocated some concrete steps to boost the economy. The five pro-business groups in particular emphasized the need both to speed up Macau's transition from a labour-intensive economy to a capital intensive and technologically advanced one, and to improve the enclave's investment environment. They emphasized the need to streamline an inefficient government bureaucracy and complete such essential infrastructure projects as advanced communication and transportation networks to link Macau physically and otherwise with

Table 6.3 Political groups in the 1996 Legislative Assembly's direct elections and results

List	Name	Background	First candidates*	Seats
A	Association for the Promotion of Macau's Economy and Livelihood (APPEM)	Independent/pro-business	Choi Ho Cheong (Chan Kai Kit)	2
B	Association in Promotion of Democracy and Livelihood (ADBSM)	Pro-democracy	Wong Cheong Nam	0
C	Development Union (UPD)	Pro-Beijing	Tong Chi Kin	1
D	Alliance for a Prosperous Macau (CODEM)	Independent/pro-business	Chow Kam Fai	1
E	Union for the Construction of Macau (UDM)	Independent/pro-business	Fong Chi Keong	1
F	Union for the Promotion of Progress (UNIPRO)	Pro-Beijing	Leong Heng Teng	2
G	Alliance for Entertainment Associations (AEA)	Independent (casinos)	Cheung Kong Lok	0
H	Alliance for Economic Construction (ADE)	Independent/pro-business	Chan Tse Mu	0
I	New Democratic Macau (ANMD)	Pro-democracy	Ng Kwok Cheong	1
J	Amity Association (AMI)	Independent	Alexandre Ho	0
L	Association for Fujian Residents in Macau (FM)	Independent/pro-business	Ngan Yin Ling	0
M	'Root in Macau' (SEMPRE)	Independent (Macanese)	Carlos Marreiros	0

* Chinese names are spelled using the Wade-Giles system heretofore commonly used in Hong Kong and Macau.

mainland China, other Asia–Pacific states, Europe and Latinate language-speaking regions.[25] Only Wong Cheong Nam's Association in Promotion of Democracy and Livelihood (ADBSM) and Ng Kuok Cheong's New Democratic Macau (ANMD) advocated democracy and political reform.[26] The two pro-Beijing groups, UNIPRO and UPD, on the other hand, appealed to the grassroots by emphasizing the need to improve both the existing social welfare system and extant housing, medical and educational policies.[27] Indeed, only the political platform of SEMPRE (a Macanese political group), which appealed to the voters to support its efforts to keep Portuguese language and culture in post-1999 Macau SAR,[28] was significantly different from other groups. It is doubtful, however, that political platforms played a significant role in influencing the voters' decisions. In an exit poll conducted by the author, only 30 per cent of the 200 respondents indicated that they had voted for a particular group because they were happy with its platform, while another 36 per cent voted based on the candidates' past performance.

In fact, campaign strategies adopted by the competing political groups determined the final outcome of the elections. Three main tactics were used: (1) invite movie stars, popular singers and other celebrities to perform at campaign gatherings; (2) mobilize staff and supporters in affiliated associations; and (3) use money or gifts to buy votes. Only four groups – Wong's ADBSM, Ng's ANMD, Alexandre Ho's Amity Association (AMI), and Carlos Marreiros's 'Root in Macau' (SEMPRE) – did not use any of these tactics, and most used two or three. The four that didn't lacked the financial resources, manpower or supportive associations needed to engage in such tactics. Ng, for example, had only one small campaign car; by contrast, some business groups had 50 or more cars or vans available for campaign activities.[29] Ng concentrated his campaign efforts on middle-class intellectuals and professionals, who in general resent mainland Chinese interference in Macau affairs and appeared sympathetic to Ng's commitment to maintain a pro-democracy and independent voice in the legislature. Ng also emphasized his record of active participation in the legislature and particularly his frequently sharp criticisms of government policies.

The UPD and UNIPRO used campaign strategies similar to those that had proved successful in the 1992 Legislative Assembly elections. They mobilized staff and supporters in the same sorts of affiliated, pro-Beijing associations. With the help of the pro-Beijing *MDN*, the campaigns of UPD and UNIPRO candidates again enjoyed full press coverage, while those of such candidates as Ng Kuok Cheong, Wong Cheong Nam, and Alexandre Ho were rarely reported.[30] But the pro-Beijing groups underestimated their opponents and appeared too complacent. They limited their mobilization efforts to their traditional supporters and did not extend an appeal to other sectors, despite the urging of younger members to do so.[31] In fact, some members of the Federation of Labour Unions were unhappy with the government's policy of continuing to import workers from mainland China. The government had approved a request by employers to import 5008 foreign workers primarily from mainland China in the first nine months of 1996, even though Macau's economy had slowed down. Its 1992 annual growth rate of 13.4 per cent had slipped to a mere 3.9 per cent in 1995, and the unemployment rate had increased from an insignificant 2.2 per cent in 1992 to 4.5 per cent in 1995.[32] On the eve of the 1996 elections, Macau had 30 180 imported workers, or about 15 per cent of the total labour population.[33] Many felt the federation had not done enough to persuade the government not to import workers.

The five political groups headed by non-mainstream local business people were alleged to have used cash or gifts to buy votes at a rate of 500 patacas to 1000 patacas (US$62–$125) per vote.[34] It was also alleged that the APPEM, CODEM and UDM had attempted to buy votes from recently registered voters. There were 48 137 registered voters for the 1992 Legislative Assembly elections, but by the 1996 elections the number of voters registered stood at 116 445, a more than twofold increase – 10 008, 6225, 34 595, and 17 480 citizens were registered as voters in 1993, 1994, 1995 and 1996, respectively.[35] It was reported that the APPEM, CODEM and UDM conducted voter registration drives among their employees and the staff and supporters of affiliated associations. New registrants allegedly received 100 to 500 patacas as a 'down payment' and were promised more on election day. Their voter registration cards were withheld (or registration and telephone numbers were written down) by the respective political groups alleged in vote buying.[36]

It was further alleged during the election campaign that the Alliance for Economic Construction and the Association for Fujian Residents in Macau, the other two business groups, had also joined the race to buy the votes of registered voters.[37] However, these five groups were not the only ones that had been involved in improper campaign activities. Virtually all of the groups, including the pro-Beijing groups but notably excluding Ng Kuok Cheong's ANMD and Wong Cheong Nam's ADBSM, gave such petty gifts as pens, notebooks, towels and 'moon cakes'[38] to woo voter support. Political groups also treated supporters and their friends to free meals. Macau's electoral laws do not spell out clearly whether such activities violate the laws, and in any event, the Election Committee, which was comprised of seven senior government officials, did not take any action to stop them. Despite warnings from the government authorities,[39] money politics dominated the campaign.

On election day, long queues had already formed at some polling stations even before the stations opened at nine o'clock. The pro-Beijing groups transported supporters, particularly women and the elderly, to polling stations by school bus. The five independent pro-business groups rented public buses and used taxis and private cars to take their supporters to the polls. The major candidates from pro-business groups treated their supporters to free breakfasts or lunches in restaurants the candidates owned. At a restaurant owned by Fong Chi Keong (or Feng Zhiqiang), first candidate on the UDM list, supporters were seated at tables labelled with the names and locations of specific polling stations. After eating, the guests were ushered to buses and cars that took them to their designated polling stations.[40] They were greeted at the polling stations by Fong's campaign workers identically dressed in red and white T-shirts, who reminded them to vote for UDM.

Chan Kai Kit's (or Chen Jijie) APPEM, Chow Kam Fai's (Zhou Jinhui) CODEM, and Chan Tse Mu's (Chen Zewu) ADE also escorted supporters to the polling stations. Campaign workers from all four groups wore readily identifiable T-shirts. Although the electoral law stipulates that no campaign activities are permitted within 100 metres of the polling stations, no police officer or Election Committee members interfered with the campaigning that did take place. Ironically, the same law also forbids the police officer from going within 100 metres of the polling stations on the grounds of preventing interference with the polls.[41] Indeed, of the ten polling stations (out of a total of 14) visited by the author, only one checked each voter's identification and allowed only voters to enter the polling stations. The author was able to walk in unchallenged at the other nine. He also witnessed a group of voters receiving cash from a campaign aide of an unidentified political group in a small shop opposite the entrance of one polling station. As for the presence of campaign workers at the polling stations, it posed a psychological, if not physical, threat to the voters, as many such workers were allegedly members of triad or other gangs.

The 1996 election results

The outcome of the direct elections was a surprise to many observers of Macau politics, including pro-Beijing legislators,[42] for the pro-Beijing forces captured only three of the eight directly elected seats. Chui Sai On (or Cui Shian), an incumbent legislator and second on the UPD list, lost his seat. To everyone's surprise, the independent, pro-business APPEM won the most votes and by the d'Hondt rule captured two seats in the legislature. The remaining three went to Fong Chi Keong (UDM), Chow Kam Fai (CODEM), and Ng Kuok Cheong (ANMD). Pro-democracy candidate Wong Cheong Nam and independent Alexandre Ho were defeated. The Macanese SEMPRE group also failed to win a seat through direct elections in the legislature.

A total of 75 093 voters cast their ballots in the 1996 legislature elections, a turnout rate of 64.49 per cent and about 5 higher than the 1992 turnout (see Table 6.2, above). Deducting the 2218 invalid ballots and the 467 left blank, there were 72 498 valid votes. The five, independent, pro-business groups (Lists A, D, E, H, and L in Table 6.3) won 36 740 votes, or 50.7 per cent of the valid votes. The two pro-Beijing groups, UPD and UNIPRO, won 21 547 votes (29.7 per cent). Clearly, the pro-business groups were the big winners in the 1996 elections. Compared to their 1992 performance, when the UPD and UNIPRO won four seats and 49 per cent of the valid votes, the pro-Beijing groups did poorly this time. The big losers in 1996 were the pro-democracy groups. The two pro-democracy groups, combined with Alexandre Ho's group, won only 8781 (12.4 per cent) of the votes. Indeed, even the top pro-democracy candidate Ng Kuok Cheong lost some ground, winning only 8.7 per cent of the valid votes in the current elections versus the 12.4 per cent he captured in the 1992 elections.

Why did independent pro-business groups do so well in the 1996 elections? The mechanics of the electoral system and the strategies these organizations adopted suggest an answer. Voters were assigned specific ballot boxes in which to place their ballots at each of the polling stations based on their voter registration numbers. The registration numbers identify the specific year in which each voter registered. The results from each ballot box were made available to the public, and a close examination indicates that the majority of those who voted for the independent, pro-business groups had registered as voters in recent years. Chow Kam Fai (List D), Chan Kai Kit (List A), and Fong Chi Keong (List E) relied mainly on the support of voters registered respectively in 1994, 1995 and 1996.[43] This tends to confirm the alleged vote buying activities of the pro-business groups that focused on newly registered electors. In short, money politics worked, playing a crucial role in the 1996 legislature elections.

Four factors explain the success of money politics. First, economics and politics combined to induce people with money but without political connections into the political arena. The sluggish economy had helped the pro-business groups, and these groups stressed more than other groups the need to improve the investment environment and the infrastructure in their political platform. Non-mainstream, independent business people in particular were concerned that the pro-Beijing Chamber of Commerce had done little to push the government to take concrete steps to boost the sluggish economy. Moreover, independent business people recognized that they were unlikely to get a seat in the legislature through indirect elections monopolized by the pro-Beijing business groups. They were thus left with no choice but to concentrate their efforts on the direct elections. Leaders of independent business groups, such as Chow, Fong and Chan Kai Kit, were in their 40s and had earned their fortunes in the 1980s and early 1990s when Macau enjoyed unprecedented economic growth.[44] Reliable estimates[45] put their family fortunes on a par with those of Edmund Ho Hau Wah, Ma Man Kei and Chui Tak Kei (or Cui Deqi), three men whose families have dominated Macau's Chinese community over the past three decades. Understandably, the *nouveau riche* have not been happy with being excluded from the leadership of mainstream business organizations and money politics is the only means they can use to challenge the well established, Beijing-backed, traditional political forces.

Secondly, those pro-Beijing forces had apparently underestimated the challenges from the newly wealthy. They used old campaign strategies that had worked so well in the 1992 elections and, as a result, a majority of the newly registered voters was won over by the money politics of the independent pro-business groups. Internal conflicts also weakened the pro-Beijing groups and led some 1992 supporters to cast their lot with the independent business groups. Disagreements over the policy of importing foreign workers split the pro-Beijing forces by pitting wealthy employers against relatively deprived workers. Some workers and the unemployed disregarded their Federation of Labour Unions directives and voted for the independent, pro-business groups. A sum of 500 or 1000 patacas was quite appealing to these people.

Thirdly, there are loopholes in the electoral laws and the government authorities did not rigorously enforce the laws and failed to charge those suspected of buying votes. Unlike Hong Kong's Independent Commission Against Corruption (ICAC), Macau's Anticorruption Commission prior to 1997 had no power to investigate or prosecute bribery activities in elections. Before 1996, the law did not punish those who had tampered with a voter's registration card.[46] The Election Committee is responsible for co-ordinating and supervising the election process but has no power to investigate improper activities. In any event, the Election Committee is not a permanent organization which can regularly oversee the process of elections and voter registrations. Its members were appointed by the governor 15 days before the election day and the Committee was to be dissolved 90 days after the election. Only the police can investigate acts of bribery, yet even they cannot patrol within 100 metres of the polling stations unless called upon to maintain order by the Election Committee. As mentioned above, the government workers at the polling stations had failed to stop illegal gatherings in front of the entrance and that the author was able to walk into nine stations without a registration card. Arguably, the government needs to establish a multidepartmental co-ordinating body to supervise and investigate bribery and other improper activities during the campaign and on election day. Electoral laws also do not provide adequate protection to those who might come out to testify against bribery and other wrongdoings. Moreover, the law has set no upper limit on political campaign expenditures, which apparently gave the green light to bribery activities in the 1996 elections. In the end, none of the suspected bribery cases have been prosecuted.[47]

Lastly, many voters were apparently not aware of the confidentiality of the vote despite repeated assurances from the Election Committee. Some feared that they might be punished if they did not vote for the candidates from whom they had received cash or gifts. The presence of triad members and gangsters during campaigning and on the election day also scared many voters. There were also many local Chinese, especially the elderly, who were influenced heavily by the obligation in traditional Chinese culture of having to repay a favour. Moreover, the overall educational level of Macau's citizens is low – about 46 per cent of the populace have only primary school education and about 10 per cent are illiterate.[48] This low educational standard is reflected in the high rate of invalid votes in the 1996 elections: 2218 (2.83 per cent) were invalidated for failing to indicate clearly the choice of political groups.[49] This generally low educational level may also explain in part why many were ignorant of the vote's confidentiality and thus vulnerable to vote-buying pressures. Clearly, many Macau citizens do not yet possess a mature or democratic political culture.

Implications for Macau's political development

The pro-Beijing forces monopolized the indirectly elected seats as they had in previous elections, capturing the four seats representing employer interests and the two representing worker interests. In a gesture of political goodwill, the pro-Beijing groups had nominated two Macanese candidates, the incumbent legislator Leonel Alberto Alves and the incumbent Legislative Assembly Chairperson Anabela Fatima Ritchi, to represent, respectively, professional interests and the interests of charitable, cultural, educational and sports organizations. All candidates nominated for indirect seats were elected unopposed.[50] Governor Vieira filled the legislature's seven remaining seats on 8 October 1996, appointing three incumbent Portuguese legislators and four Macanese legislators. His appointments suggest that he intended to balance the Chinese-dominated legislature with Portuguese and Macanese legislators, mirroring Governor Costa's ethnic juggling in the early 1980s when Chinese had fared less well in the polls. The fully seated Legislative Assembly thus comprised nine pro-

Beijing members, nine pro-government or pro-Portugal members, including three Portuguese and six Macanese, four independent pro-business members, and one pro-democracy member. The Macanese were not necessarily pro-government; in fact, at times they had been quite critical of government policies. They were, however, often pro-Portugal or sympathetic to Lisbon's efforts to preserve Portuguese interests in Macau in the run-up to 1999 and beyond. On 19 October 1996, the legislators elected Anabela Fatima Ritchi and Edmund Ho Hau Wah as the new legislature's chairperson and vice-chairperson, respectively, an indication of the roughly even distribution of seats between the pro-Beijing and pro-Portugal forces. The four, newly elected, independent, pro-business legislators could thus play a crucial role in balancing Chinese and Portuguese interests in the legislature.

Chan Kai Kit, the top vote carrier in the elections, was reported to have made overtures to Ng Kuok Cheong, the lone pro-democracy member of the legislature.[51] Fong Chi Keong, Macau's leading real estate tycoon, clearly leans towards the pro-Beijing group, despite the stance he took during the campaign. A director of the Chinese Chamber of Commerce and board member for pro-Beijing charitable organizations, Fong's challenges to the pro-Beijing forces were more a protest against the mainstream business people than a deviation from the coalition. It is reasonable to expect the four independents, who are all local business people with enormous economic interests with mainland China, to co-operate with the pro-Beijing bloc. It is also in the interest of this pro-Beijing bloc to co-opt the independent, pro-business legislators. So far there is no sign of any major confrontations between these two groups in the legislature.

The 1996 election results did signal a likely change in the composition of the pro-Beijing forces. Traditionally, influential families, such as those of Edmund Ho Hau Wah, Ma Man Kei and Chiu Tak Kei, can no longer dominate the pro-Beijing coalition. Ho Hau Wah is still highly respected in the Chinese community and in May 1999 was elected first chief executive of the Macau SAR. The children, nephews and nieces of Ma Man Kei and Chiu Tak Kei are far less respected in the Chinese community, however. Once the senior Ma and Chiu retired from active political life in recent years, the influence of their families dropped significantly. Indeed, this decline of traditional forces partly explained the ascendancy of the independent, pro-business groups in the 1996 elections.

The pro-Portugal legislators were expected to continue to balance the pro-Beijing bloc and maintain the viability of the Portuguese government in the run-up to 1999. But the defeat of the Macanese SEMPRE group in the direct elections and the election of the two Chinese-backed, Macanese candidates in the indirect elections indicate that pro-Portuguese forces were facing an uphill battle to maintain Portuguese interests in the territory. Clearly, the Macanese's future political role is determined by the pro-Beijing faction. This is not very encouraging to the Macanese since many local Chinese residents still remember the days when they were dominated and exploited by the Portuguese and the Macanese. The local Chinese are thus not likely to share political power with the Macanese in post-1999 Macau.

The democrats were the big losers in the 1996 elections, and their prospects in the post-1999 Macau SAR are dim. There is no indication that the current sluggish economy will improve greatly in the near future. Macau's relatively small economy is subject to political influence from China. In fact, mainland Chinese capital already dominates the financial and real estate markets. Macau does not have and is unlikely to develop an independent middle-class similar to the one which is the backbone of the democratic forces that have propelled democratization in Hong Kong. The generally low educational level of Macau's citizens and the lack of a democratic culture further handicaps the territory's democratization process. Macau is already a territory 'half-liberated' by mainland China.[52] And it is likely to remain so in the post-1999 SAR. Though the pro-Beijing groups suffered a serious setback in the 1996 elections, they are likely to reorganize to come back strongly in the 2001 legislature elections.

On 29 August 1999, the Macau SAR Preparation Committee re-confirmed and approved the 'through-train' to post-1999 Macau for the seven directly elected and eight indirectly elected members of the 1996–2001 legislature.[53] Ironically, Chan Kai Kit, the top winner in the 1996 election, failed to show up for re-confirmation. He was allegedly involved in commercial fraudulence activities and was sought by the Hong Kong ICAC.[54] Chan also had the lowest attendance rate (38 per cent) in the 1998–99 legislature.[55] In their first three years in the legislature, the performance of Chan and the other three pro-business legislators elected in 1996 was described by their fellow legislators as at best mediocre (partly because they were inexperienced) or as having a lack of political commitment or both.[56] Money politics creates unfair competition between contending political groups and hence possibly excludes capable candidates who do not have the resources for winning seats in the legislature. On 24 September 1999, Edmund Ho Hau Wah, the chief executive designate, appointed 7 legislators for the Macau SAR's first legislature.[57] All but one member are newly appointed; the only appointed legislator from the former Portuguese administration is Jose Manuel de Oliveira Rodrigues, a Macanese lawyer. There are only four Macanese in the new legislature, two indirectly elected and two officially appointed. The new legislature is overwhelmingly pro-Beijing.[58] The only democratic voice in the legislature is Ng Kuok Cheong. A new era, for better or worse, has begun in Macau's political scene. Yet, it is unclear whether money politics will vanish altogether under the new post-1999 administration.

7
The Eurasians (Macanese) in Macau: the Neglected Minority

It is hard to explain in a few words what it means to be Macanese. We have our own way of life here. We have memories and traditions lasting hundreds of years, even our own cuisine. We are part of the city and we always will be. You need to spend time in Macau to understand why we are in love with this city. I could go to Portugal any time, I've got plenty of resources. I've got two houses in Portugal, but I stay here because I was born here, all my ancestors and my children are linked to this city. It's a very strong attachment and it would be terribly difficult to put all that aside and begin a new life . . . To consider this place a part of Portugal, and then suddenly to realize that the sovereignty will be changed and Macau will become a pure Chinese city is really sad.

Henrique de Senna Fernandes[1]

I see myself as Macanese – but then one has to ask: what does that mean? We could debate that all day. I see the Macanese as people brought up here, who identify with this way of life. Macau is small, but I'm very proud of its heritage, not only its architectural traditions. I'm proud of the bureaucratic tradition, the attitude of tolerance. The Macanese are a unique cocktail of ethnic backgrounds and this means we can fit in and survive anywhere.

Carlos Marreiros[2]

In the run-up to the 1997 reversion of Hong Kong to the People's Republic of China (PRC), the status of Eurasian residents was not an issue in Sino-British negotiations. It was a major issue, however, in Sino-Portuguese negotiations over the reversion of Macau to the PRC in 1999. Unlike the British colonists, who generally did not encourage intermarriage with the indigenous populace, many Portuguese colonists were married to indigenous women. The outcome of the Beijing–Lisbon negotiations would thus affect the political and social status of the Eurasians in the future Macau Special Administrative Region (SAR). Indeed, the very existence of the Eurasians (or 'Macanese', *tusheng Puren*, as they are commonly called in Macau) as a viable ethnic group in the Macau SAR was at stake.

In the Sino-Portuguese Joint Declaration of 1987 regarding the reversion of Macau to the PRC on 20 December 1999, Beijing and Lisbon agreed that 'interests of Macau residents of Portuguese descent will be maintained'. Portuguese is designated to be the second official language (behind Chinese) in the Macau SAR. However, Lisbon and Beijing disagreed over the issue of nationality. The Portuguese memorandum attached to the Joint Declaration states that Portugal, which accepts dual nationality, will continue to recognize Macau citizens holding Portuguese passports after 1999, while the Chinese memorandum states that the PRC, which does not recognize dual nationality, will treat the Portuguese passports held by Macau citizens of Chinese descent as travelling documents only, that is, without the privilege of Portuguese consular protection. The Chinese Nationality Law stipulates that all China-born citizens of Chinese descent possess the qualifications for Chinese citizenship. Since most Macanese have some Chinese blood and are locally-born, they will be treated as Chinese citizens in the SAR if no special measures are taken to protect their Portuguese nationality. The scenario of becoming a national minority in a Chinese-dominated society shocked the Macanese community, leading many to consider leaving the colony for good.

This chapter studies the changing Macanese community and the issues it confronts during the transition to 1999 and beyond. Can the Macanese survive what has been called the 'typhoon of 1999'[3] and retain their Eurasian cultural features in post-1999 Macau?

A profile of the Macanese

Macau has a population of approximately 437 000 residents.[4] About 96 per cent of the population are ethnic Chinese. The Eurasians or Macanese, who are mostly Macau-born people of mixed Portuguese–Chinese blood, constitute about 2–3 per cent of the population; about 1 per cent of the population are Portuguese from Portugal, Angola, Mozambique and Goa, as well as people from other countries. The Macanese, however, are not merely of mixed Portuguese and Chinese blood; many are descendants of inter-racial marriages between Portuguese soldiers and indigenous women in former Portuguese colonies in Africa and South and Southeast Asia.[5]

There is no accurate figure for the population of Macanese living in Macau. Estimates range from 5000 to 10 000 depending on the definition of 'Macanese'. João de Pina Cabral, a Portuguese anthropologist, uses four criteria to identify the Macanese: (1) language, that is, whether the individual or his family members have definite links to the Portuguese language; (2) religion, or whether the individual or his family members are Catholic; (3) race, or whether the individual or his family members are Eurasians; and (4) individuals who identify themselves as Macanese.[6] According to Pina Cabral, any Macau-born resident who fulfills all the above criteria (and in some special cases where he or she does not possess one or two of the criteria) can be considered Macanese. Yet, those who possess all of the above characteristics make up the core membership of the Macanese community. Pina Cabral has thus come up with a figure of approximately 7000 Macanese currently living in Macau.[7]

The Macanese vary widely in terms of their physical appearance. Some possess outstanding Caucasian features, especially the older generation Macanese. However, many younger generation Macanese possess clear Mongoloid features, due to the increase in intermarriages between Macanese and local Chinese.[8] Most Macanese are bilingual or trilingual. In a 1995 survey conducted among the Macanese, 50.2 per cent of the respondents were found to speak Cantonese, while 46.4 per cent spoke Portuguese at home.[9] Yet, when it comes to writing, an overwhelming majority (87 per cent) used Portuguese as the written language, while only 4.8 and 5.8 per cent, respectively, often wrote in Chinese and English.[10] Moreover, 66.7

per cent of respondents read Portuguese newspapers, while only 13 and 11 per cent chose to read Chinese and English newspapers.[11] Use of the Portuguese language thus distinguishes the Macanese from the ethnic Chinese. Yet, there are clear signs that indicate that the Portuguese language and culture are losing their grip among the new generation Macanese and proficiency in Portuguese among the younger and teenage Macanese has declined conspicuously in recent years, with many speaking only Cantonese.[12]

Due to their language capabilities, the Macanese often acted as intermediaries between Portuguese from Lisbon and local Chinese residents. A majority of Macanese worked for the government and enjoyed a higher social status than local Chinese residents. They monopolized middle-ranking positions in the civil service as well as professions that required Portuguese language proficiency such as law, architecture and accountancy. However, after the signing of the Sino-Portuguese Joint Declaration and the subsequent localization process that had emphasized the recruitment and promotion of local Chinese to higher-ranking positions in the civil service, Macanese domination in the civil service has declined. As indicated in Table 7.1, the proportion of those civil servants who can speak Chinese

Table 7.1 Proficiency in Chinese language among civil servants

Year	(A) Speak (Cantonese)	(B) Write	(A)–(B) (%)	Total*
1985	6 042	3 574	2468 (29.3)	8 433
1986	5 417	3 190	2227 (24.9)	8 956
1987	7 354	4 602	2752 (27.3)	10 064
1988	8 455	5 561	2894 (27.3)	11 499
1989	8 927	6 171	2756 (21.0)	13 125
1990	10 335	6 378	3957 (27.0)	14 664
1991	9 773	6 691	3082 (20.1)	15 371
1992	10 283	7 543	2740 (18.1)	15 111
1993	12 950	9 577	3373 (21.5)	15 679
1994	13 452	10 493	2959 (18.0)	16 415
1995	13 551	12 272	1279 (7.7)	16 574
1996**	14 578	14 302	276 (1.6)	16 992

* Since those who can speak or write Portuguese and/or English are not included in the table, the total number of civil servants is not equal to (A).
** Since 1996 the assessment of language proficiency is based on the capability of using functional language related to the job, hence the sharp increase in language proficiency particularly in written Chinese.
Source: 'Documentary', *Administracao* (Macau), no. 44 (June 1999), p. 462.

Table 7.2 Proficiency in Chinese language among directors/chief executives

Year	(A) Speak (Cantonese)	(B) Write	(A)–(B) (%)	Total*
1985	62	10	52 (26.7)	195
1986	85	12	73 (28.7)	254
1987	119	14	105 (34.8)	302
1988	131	15	116 (31.6)	367
1989	143	17	126 (32.3)	390
1990	185	44	141 (28.5)	495
1991	240	72	168 (27.4)	613
1992	257	94	163 (26.2)	621
1993	305	124	181 (29.6)	611
1994	343	194	149 (23.7)	629
1995	348	252	96 (14.5)	660

* Since those who can speak or write Portuguese and/or English are not included in the table, the total number of director/chiefs is not equal to (A).
Source: as for Table 7.1, pp. 463–73.

(Cantonese) but can not write Chinese (i.e. the Macanese)[13] dropped from 29.3 per cent in 1985, the year prior to the start of the Sino-Portuguese negotiation on the reversion of Macau to China, to 7.7 per cent in 1995. Over the same period of time, the proportion of Macanese occupying the positions of director/chief in the civil service also dropped from 26.7 per cent to 14.5 per cent (see Table 7.2). Nevertheless, the Macanese still outnumbered the ethnic Chinese (those who can write Chinese) by a large margin in occupying director/chief positions in the 1980s and early 1990s. The trend, however, was reversed in 1994 when the ethnic Chinese for the first time outnumbered the Macanese in holding director/chief executive ranks (see Table 7.2). Clearly, the local Chinese will have an edge over the Macanese after the handover when Chinese becomes the first official language if the Macanese do not learn written Chinese.

The Macanese community

At the crossroads of Portuguese and Chinese cultures and peoples, with a mixture of both but belonging to none completely, Macanese ethnic identity has always been ambivalent.[14] In the past, noted and wealthy Chinese families looked down upon the Macanese and refused to let their children marry a Portuguese or Macanese. It was only the lower-class Chinese or prostitutes who would marry a soldier or sailor from Portugal or its African colonies. It was also very rare for a respectable Chinese man to marry a Macanese.[15] Conversely, marriages were often held between Macanese families and between Macanese and Portuguese military officers or soldiers. A link to Portuguese blood or culture was often regarded as an asset in attaining government jobs. Many Macanese were conscious of maintaining their Caucasian outlook,[16] even though it became increasingly difficult after the withdrawal of Portuguese soldiers from the territory in 1975. The new arrivals from Portugal in the 1980s were often administrators or bureaucrats accompanied by their families. The rise of a relatively wealthy middle class of Chinese professionals and businessmen in the 1970s and 1980s also posed new challenges to the Macanese community.

The relationship between the Macanese and the local Chinese community has never been easy. As mentioned above, the Macanese were ahead of the Chinese in attaining government positions and enjoyed relatively higher social status than the average Chinese, often prompting feelings of superiority and even mistreatment or exploitation of the local Chinese.[17] In fact racial conflict among the Chinese, Portuguese and Macanese exploded in a December 1966 riot, when eight Chinese were killed and many more were injured in a clash between local Chinese residents and Portuguese soldiers and policemen.[18] The incident resulted in the exodus of Macanese families to the United States, Portugal, Canada, Australia, Brazil and elsewhere, since people lost faith in the colony's political stability due to the increasing influence of Chinese political forces. For those who chose to stay in Macau after the riot, their social status was found to be considerably lowered in comparison with the local Chinese.

With few exceptions, the Macanese have been relatively unengaged in trade or other businesses. They thus missed the opportunity to enhance their family fortunes when Macau enjoyed double-digit economic growth in the 1980s and early 1990s. The rise of a Chinese middle class has also been accompanied by rising Chinese aspirations to participate in local politics, such as elections for the Legislative Assembly and the Municipal Councils.

A survey in the mid-1990s indicated that the Macanese in general are more participant-oriented than the Chinese.[19] They do not hesitate to become involved in politics if their interests are affected by government policies. They do not believe in letting the government, regardless of whether it is a benign and good government or not, to control their destiny. Indeed, the Macanese had traditionally played a dominant role in local politics. The newly-arrived governors, knowing little about the culture and people of the colony, had to rely on the Macanese, particularly their ability to communicate with the local Chinese community. Macanese political influence was even more pronounced when the community was united behind a commonly accepted leader, examples being the legendary Pedro José Lobo in the 1940s and 1950s[20] and Carlos d'Assumpcao in the 1970s and 1980s.[21] Power struggles between the Macanese and Portuguese from Lisbon were sometimes very severe, as the former were resentful of the latter occupying high-ranking positions in the government. Portuguese from Lisbon, on the other hand, often felt a cultural superiority over the indigenous Macanese. Power struggles eventually led to an open conflict between d'Assumpcao and Governor Vasco Costa that resulted in the dissolution of the legislature in 1984.[22] In order to balance the Macanese influence, Governor Costa increased the recruitment of Portuguese expatriates into the civil service. Moreover, he changed the election law to allow more Chinese to participate in politics to counterbalance the Macanese influence.

However, the rapid change of social and economic environment in the 1980s indicated that the rise of local Chinese in the political domain was inevitable. In the first two legislative elections held in 1976 and 1980, the Macanese dominated the elections partly due to the election law that restricted suffrage to Chinese residents who had lived in the territory for five consecutive years but exempted the Portuguese nationals from any such requirements.[23] In fact, only one Chinese won a seat in the legislature through direct elections in 1976 and not a single seat in 1980.[24] After Governor Costa lifted the residence requirements for Chinese residents in the 1984 elections, Chinese participation in politics increased sharply. D'Assumpcao and his supporters were persuaded by the Chinese government to form an Electoral Union with local pro-Beijing Chinese forces to participate in the 1984 elections;[25] as a result, the Electoral Union won four of the six directly elected seats. It was the first political coalition between Macanese and Chinese, and also signalled the rise of Chinese political forces. In the 1984 legislative elections, the Chinese captured two directly elected seats, six indirectly elected seats, and one officially appointed seat in the 17-member legislature.

In the 1988 legislative elections, the Chinese again monopolized all indirectly elected seats and won four of the six directly elected seats. Only two Macanese, d'Assumpcao and his close associate Leonel Alberto Alves, won seats in the legislature through direct elections. These results clearly signalled the political decline of the Macanese and consolidated the domination of the Chinese in local elections. The results of the 1992 and 1996 legislative elections witnessed the further erosion of the Macanese as a force in local politics: only one Macanese won a directly elected seat in 1992 and no Macanese was returned in the 1996 elections. In both the 1992 and 1996 elections, the Macanese retained, with the help of pro-Beijing Chinese forces, two indirectly elected seats in the legislature. In retrospect, the death of d'Assumpcao in early 1992 was more than a loss of an important Macanese leader; it meant the end of an era in which d'Assumpcao and his Macanese associates played a predominant role in local politics.

Accompanying the Macanese political decline has been the deepening crisis of the ethnic identity. Common Portuguese blood, language and culture and Catholic religion had long served as powerful integrative forces that held the Macanese community together. These common heritages, however, have undergone substantial changes in the last three decades, as 'Sinicization' has weakened the integrative functions of the Macanese community. Trends and developments in the following five aspects of the Macanese community have contributed to the quickening pace of Sinicization.

First, the proportion of Portuguese blood, or 'Portugueseness', among the Macanese stock has declined steadily over the years while the proportion of Chinese blood, or 'Chineseness', has increased. According to a recent study, integration between the Macanese and the local Chinese has increased significantly in the last few decades. During the period 1961–74, intra-Macanese marriages constituted 44 per cent of all Macanese marriages, but the figure declined to 30 per cent during 1975–90; during the same periods, the per centage of Chinese brides or bridegrooms in Macanese marriages increased from 42 per cent to 64 per cent. Intermarriages between Macanese and Portuguese also declined during these periods from 14 per cent to 6 per cent.[26] The above findings suggest that the Macanese community has increasingly been exposed to Chinese culture while the Portuguese influence has diminished.

Secondly, the grip of Catholicism on the Macanese community is loosening. Until the 1970s, in intermarriages between Macanese and Chinese, the Macanese family always requested the Chinese bride or bridegroom to be baptized before the marriage ceremony.[27] Today this request is rarely mentioned. Indeed, intermarriages between Catholics and non-Catholics involving Macanese have increased substantially in recent years. During the period 1975–81, 20 per cent of Macanese marriages were between a Catholic Macanese and a non-Catholic Chinese; this ratio increased to 49 per cent during the period 1987–90.[28] In a recent survey, it was reported that 82 per cent of the Macanese are Catholic.[29] This is clearly a significant drop from the decade of the 1950s to the 1960s when virtually all Macanese were Catholic. Perhaps more importantly, non-Catholics have become even more common among the younger and teenage Macanese.[30] It is likely that in another generation, Catholicism may no longer be the common feature of the Macanese community.

Thirdly, the Macanese no longer live in identifiable districts. The Macanese community previously lived in regions near the churches and in Nam Wan (Nanwan or South Bay), where government offices were located.[31] However, the economic and construction boom in the 1980s drew many Macanese families to new residential areas. Moreover, many government offices have expanded and moved to newly developed districts in recent years, and now find themselves surrounded by ethnic Chinese. Gatherings among and between Macanese families have thus decreased. A Portuguese language environment no longer exists, as many Macanese families have found it increasingly difficult to persuade their children to speak Portuguese at home. As a rule, teenage Macanese are more proficient in speaking Chinese (Cantonese) than Portuguese, and have been particularly reluctant to speak Portuguese with a Lisbon native.[32]

Fourthly, there are serious generational gaps among the Macanese due to very different socialization experiences.[33] Macanese who are in their 60s and 70s were born or grew up during the Lobo era, when the Macanese monopolized government positions and enjoyed a much higher social status than the local ethnic Chinese. Due to their importance as intermediaries between the Portuguese government and the Macau citizens who could not speak Portuguese, they developed feelings of superiority over the Chinese. Yet all this changed after the December 1966 riot, as many Macanese were humiliated by the Chinese in the months after the riot, and, as has been said, many traditional Macanese families emigrated to the United States, Portugal, Australia and elsewhere.

Macanese who are in their 40s and early 50s occupied the middle- and high-ranking positions in the government bureaucracy. Following the shock of the 1966 riot they were sent by their parents to study in Portugal in the 1960s and 1970s and came back to Macau during the boom years of the 1980s. Like their parents, they can speak good Portuguese. Yet, unlike their parents, they must live and fraternize with the rising numbers of middle-class Chinese. Their interests also clash with the Portuguese coming from Lisbon, those who were recruited by Governor Costa and his successors to counterbalance the influence of the Macanese and occupy high-ranking positions in the civil service.

Macanese who are in their 20s and 30s were born after the 1966 riot. Unlike their parents or grandparents, they did not experience humiliation under the Chinese. Since the signing of the Sino-Portuguese Joint Declaration in 1987, they have not enjoyed any clear advantage over the local Chinese in attaining government positions. In fact, many from this group feel that they are being discriminated against by both the Chinese and the Lisbon Portuguese. Many have begun to realize that the future lies in their adaptation to the Chinese-dominated society and Chinese culture. Unlike their parents or grandparents, who previously looked down upon the local Chinese and were unwilling to mingle with them, the young Macanese have experienced no problems in integrating with the Chinese community. Some have already started to learn Mandarin and written Chinese. For young Macanese who cannot or do not plan to leave the territory, basic education in Portuguese is a disadvantage, since it means that they are illiterate in Chinese.[34] In any case, Portuguese is not an attractive language for young people brought up in a world where the prevailing cultural references are provided by Hong Kong television channels in Cantonese.[35] Consequently, they have resisted efforts by their parents and teachers to involve them in a Portuguese-speaking culture. More recently, the children of mixed Chinese and Macanese marriages are tending to be sent to Anglo-Chinese schools.[36]

Fifthly, the Macanese community currently lacks leadership. In the past, the Macanese were usually united under a strong leader, like Lobo in the 1940s and 1950s and d'Assumpcao in the 1970s and 1980s. Since the death of d'Assumpcao in early 1992, no clear successor has been in sight. Leonel Alberto Alves, a lawyer and legislator who was a close associate of d'Assumpcao, is a possible candidate to succeed his former mentor. Alves is described by his fellow legislators as bright, capable, yet sometimes impatient and bad tempered.[37] Carlos Marreiros, an architect and the former director of the Macau Institute of Culture, is another possible candidate. Marreiros was the first candidate in a political group (SEMPRE, or 'Root in Macau'), organized by the Macanese, that participated in the 1996 legislative elections. SEMPRE, however, failed to win a seat in the legislature.[38] Indeed, the poor performance of the Macanese in the 1992 and 1996 legislative elections suggest that the Macanese community without d'Assumpcao has become both disunited and weak. Some Macanese speculate that a strong Macanese leader may not emerge until well after the 1999 handover.[39] Even with a strong community leader, however, it is increasingly clear that the Macanese can play a meaningful political role in the territory only with the co-operation and approval of the Chinese community.

Macanese attitudes toward the localization of the civil service

The issue of localization of the civil service was a highly controversial one in Macau politics.[40] Understandably, the Macanese, who spoke Portuguese and Cantonese and occupied most of the middle-ranking posts in the civil service, wished to be promoted to higher ranks after the withdrawal of the Portuguese expatriates. The Chinese government tended to side with the 'Sinicization' interpretation of localization, although it realized the important role of the Macanese in a smooth transition to the post-1999 administration. The Chinese have often complained about the slow pace of localization, particularly the lukewarm efforts of the Portuguese administration in promoting local Chinese to the higher ranks. They insisted that only patriotic Chinese could become the backbone of Macau's civil service.[41]

The Macau government, however, preferred to promote Portuguese-speaking Macanese and a few local Chinese who hold Portuguese passports and were educated or trained in Portuguese. The government also continued to recruit people from Portugal for legal and other key positions. As of 31 December 1995, 81 or 75.7 per cent, of directors and deputy directors were Portuguese expatriates or from former Portuguese colonies; the rest were Macanese or local Chinese with Portuguese passports. As indicated in Table 7.3, although the locally-born Macanese or Chinese occupied most of the middle-ranking positions such as division chiefs, sector chiefs and section chiefs, Portuguese expatriates still dominated the higher-ranking posts. It is thus not surprising that in a survey conducted in 1995 among the Macanese, only 9.6 per cent of the respondents indicated that they were 'satisfied' or 'very satisfied' with the pace of civil service localization, while 39.1 per cent were 'unsatisfied' or 'very unsatisfied'; the rest were either 'neutral' or 'didn't know'.[42] Apparently, the Macanese did not feel that they had benefited from the government's localization policy. In fact, many respondents (42 per cent) in the survey believed that the localization policy was meant to promote local ethnic Chinese with or without Portuguese passports; only 20.3 per cent believed that the localization policy was meant to promote the Macanese.[43]

On 21 February 1994, the Macau government issued a decree detailing the plan for integrating qualified personnel from Macau's civil service into Portugal's civil service.[44] The integration plan allowed those who were permanent employees of the Macau government – Portuguese nationals, and those proficient in Portuguese – to choose to stay in Macau's civil service or join Portugal's civil service after 1999. Since few local Chinese are proficient in Portuguese, the integration plan was clearly aimed at offering the Macanese a choice in the run-up to 1999. Yet, not every Macanese was happy with the choice. When asked if they felt the Portuguese government had given sufficient protection to their interests in the transition to 1999, only 14.5 per cent of the Macanese respondents indicated that they felt the protection was 'sufficient' or 'very sufficient'; in contrast, about 48.3 per cent felt the protection was

Table 7.3 Distribution of Macau's high-ranking civil servants according to place of birth (1995)

	Place of birth								
	Macau	%	Portugal	%	PRC/HK	%	Other	%	Total	%
Director	9	15.8	43	75.4	0	0.0	5	8.8	57	8.6
Deputy director	16	32.0	28	56.0	1	2.0	5	10.0	50	7.6
Department chief	29	29.6	49	50.0	2	2.0	18	18.4	98	14.8
Division chief	77	55.4	45	32.1	7	5.0	10	7.2	139	21.1
Sector chief	160	72.7	29	13.2	17	7.7	14	6.4	220	33.3
Subsector chief	2	100.0	0	0.0	0	0.0	0	0.0	2	0.3
Section chief	74	83.2	7	7.9	1	1.1	7	7.9	89	13.5
Other	4	80.0	1	20.0	0	0.0	0	0.0	5	0.8
Total	371	56.2	202	30.6	28	4.2	59	8.9	660	100.0

Source: Office of Administration and Civil Service, Government of Macau.

'insufficient' or 'very insufficient'.[45] Apparently, many Macanese were unhappy with some aspects of the integration scheme. First, the Portuguese government did not guarantee those who chose to join Portugal's civil service a job in Portugal. Such people had to wait for job assignments and other arrangements made by the Personnel Department in Portugal's civil service. If no job assignments could be arranged within three years in Portugal, the person who chose to join Portugal's civil service would have to find his/her own job. Second, it is well known that the salary and social status of civil servants in Portugal are lower than those in Macau.[46] Third, some Macanese would find it difficult to integrate themselves into Portuguese society. They were afraid that they might be discriminated against by indigenous Portuguese people and become 'second class' citizens in Portugal. Some indicated that they would prefer to immigrate to Brazil, Australia or elsewhere rather than to Portugal.

As of 1 January 1999, among the 6400 civil servants who were qualified for the integration scheme, only 386 persons, or 6 per cent, had chosen to join Portugal's civil service after 1999; 516 persons, or 8.1 per cent, had chosen early retirement; 583 persons, or 9.1 per cent, had chosen to leave the civil service; and 4915 persons, or 76.8 per cent, had chosen to stay in the future SAR civil service after 1999.[47] Those who chose to join Portugal's civil service gave the following reasons: (1) distrust of the Chinese government and the fear that their salaries and other benefits would be lowered or lost in post-1999 Macau; (2) discomfort with the idea of living under a communist state; (3) not wishing to become a 'national minority' in a Chinese community; and (4) feeling handicapped in a post-1999 SAR government where Chinese is the first official language.[48] In short, Macanese chose to join the integration plan not because they found Portugal a better place than Macau, but because they were afraid of facing political uncertainties in post-1999 Macau.

An uncertain future

On 31 March 1993 the PRC's National People's Congress (NPC) approved the 'Basic Law for the Macau Special Administrative Region', which would become effective on 20 December 1999. The document also includes a chapter on the basic rights and duties of the citizens of the SAR. 'Citizens' or 'permanent residents of the Macau SAR' are defined in Article 24, Chapter 3, as those who, regardless of nationalities, have lived continuously in Macau for seven years as well as Chinese and Portuguese nationals who were born in Macau. The term 'Macanese' is not specifically mentioned in the Basic Law. Article 42 of Chapter 3 states: 'The interests of Macau residents of Portuguese descent are protected by the laws of the Macau Special Administrative Region; their customs, culture, and tradition shall be respected'.[49]

However, the Basic Law does not specifically spell out how the SAR can protect the interests of those 'Macau residents of Portuguese descent'. Presumably the Macanese can retain their Portuguese nationality after 1999 because the Basic Law does not say they can not. It is not clear in the Basic Law, however, whether a Macanese can choose to become a Chinese national. It is apparent that a Macanese cannot hold Portuguese and Chinese nationality at the same time, because China's Nationality Law does not recognize dual nationality. Here lies the dilemma for the Macanese: retaining a Portuguese nationality will be jeopardized by the Basic Law, which reserves important government positions for Chinese nationals; opting for a Chinese nationality, however, means that the Macanese will become a 'national minority' in a community dominated by ethnic Chinese. The real concern of the Macanese was that Beijing would not let them choose their nationality after 1999 and would treat their Portuguese passports merely as travelling documents without consular protection.[50] In the run-up to the handover, Portugal, which recognizes dual nationality, had urged the Chinese government to adopt flexible policy towards the Macanese nationality issue. Beijing had promised to take a more accommodating stand on the issue.[51] To the Macanese, the best possible solution is that they will be recognized as Portuguese nationals by both Portugal and China but treated as Chinese (albeit not as a 'national minority') in the Macau SAR. If they were forced to make a choice, most would no doubt choose Portuguese nationality.[52] Many Macanese have an emotional attachment to Portugal and Portuguese culture. As Jorge Rangel, a Macanese and the Under-Secretary for Administration, Education and Youth Affairs until the handover, remarked in an interview with a Western journalist: 'I feel I belong here, but culturally I am, of course, Portuguese; we've been Portuguese for generations. My values, my way of life, the way I feel, the way I look at things – they're all a product of my European education'.[53]

It is thus not a surprise that, when asked whether they felt the Basic Law gives sufficient protection to Macanese interests, only 3.4 per cent of Macanese respondents felt the protection was 'sufficient' or 'very sufficient'; in contrast, 37.2 per cent indicated that the protection was 'insufficient' or 'very insufficient'; and 43.5 per cent were reluctant to indicate their opinions on the Basic Law (Table 7.4). The main Macanese complaints regarding the Basic Law include: (1) it does not offer a choice of nationality and of dual citizenship in particular; (2) it does not guarantee sufficient retirement funds for civil servants who are qualified for retirement benefits after 1999; (3) it limits recruitment and promotion opportunities for the Macanese; and (4) it is generally vague about giving specific protection to the rights of the Macanese. Few Macanese believed that the Chinese government was sincere in its intention to carry out the 'Macau people ruling Macau' policy after 1999, as promised in the Sino-Portuguese Joint Declaration.[54] As a Macanese remarked: 'I have no confidence in the Chinese government. The Chinese authorities will continue to intrude in the affairs of Macau after 1999 as they are actually doing now. At best, the Chinese authorities will only let those pro-Beijing local political forces rule Macau'.[55]

The Macanese had to make a very difficult decision regarding whether to leave or stay in Macau after 1999. An overwhelming

Table 7.4 Macanese attitudes toward the Basic Law

Q: Does the Basic Law give sufficient protection to Macanese interests?

	%	N
1. Very sufficient	0.5	1
2. Sufficient	2.9	6
3. Neutral	15.9	33
4. Insufficient	32.4	67
5. Very insufficient	4.8	10
6. Don't know/no opinion	43.5	90

Source: Herbert S. Yee, 'The Macanese Political Subculture' (A research report submitted to the Macau Institute of Culture, December 1995).

majority of the Macanese are locally-born, and it is difficult for anyone to leave his/her birthplace, a feeling well expressed in the quotations by Henrique Fernandes and Carlos Marreiros at the beginning of the chapter. In general, the Macanese are happy with their present lives in Macau.[56] We have already mentioned the Macanese worries and reservations about life in Portugal, in particular the fear of losing what they have possessed in Macau, such as a good salary and a relatively high social status. In a survey conducted in the spring of 1995, 31 per cent of the Macanese respondents indicated that they would certainly or most likely leave Macau after 1999, while 24.2 per cent would certainly or most likely stay in Macau (Table 7.5).[57] Hence, there is no clear majority opinion among the Macanese regarding the issue of immigration. It is important to note, however, that 39.6 per cent of the respondents were undecided. This suggests that a majority (i.e. those who were undecided or had decided to stay after 1999) of the Macanese are reluctant to leave Macau and to face uncertainties in Portugal or other foreign countries. Most were taking the wait-and-see attitude.

There is a strong link between Macanese trust of the Chinese government and the decision to leave Macau after 1999. For example, 84.2 per cent of those respondents who indicated that they would 'certainly leave Macau' after 1999 also did not believe Beijing would let the Macau people rule Macau after 1999; likewise, 69.2 per cent of those who would 'most likely leave Macau' also indicated their distrust of the Chinese government.[58] Yet, on closer examination, we

Table 7.5 The Macanese decision to leave or to stay in Macau after 1999

Q: Do you plan to leave Macau after 1999?

	%	N
1. Will certainly leave Macau	18.4	38
2. Will most likely leave Macau	12.6	26
3. It all depends/undecided	39.6	82
4. Most likely will not leave Macau	12.1	25
5. Certainly will not leave Macau	12.1	25
6. Don't know/no opinion	5.3	11

Source: as for Table 7.4.

also found that even those who had decided not to leave Macau did not necessarily trust Beijing. Only one-third of those who had decided to stay in Macau after 1999 believed the Chinese government was sincere in letting the Macau people rule Macau. Clearly, distrust or lack of confidence in the Chinese government was important factor that had contributed to the decision to leave Macau after 1999, but trust or confidence in China was not necessarily a crucial factor in the Macanese decision not to leave Macau. Fear of facing possible greater uncertainties in Portugal and elsewhere had apparently persuaded many Macanese to stay in Macau after 1999.

The above conclusion is further supported by the linkage between Macanese attitudes towards the Basic Law and their decisions to leave Macau. A majority of those who had decided to leave Macau after 1999 had also indicated that the Basic Law did not give sufficient protection to Macanese interests.[59] Yet even those who had decided to stay after 1999 were not very happy with the Basic Law. Indeed, less than one-tenth of respondents who had decided to stay were inclined to accept the promises and protection given to the Macanese in the Basic Law.[60] Obviously, distrust or lack of confidence in Beijing prevailed among the Macanese community. Some Macanese have sold their properties in Macau and bought houses and other properties in Portugal.[61] Indeed, even the 400-year old Santa Casa Da Miscricordia (*Rencitang*), a charity organization established in 1569 by the Portuguese settlers that has been since run by the Macanese, had sold most of its properties before the handover.[62] The Chinese authorities have a considerable amount of work to do if they wish to convince the Macanese of their sincerity in protecting Macanese interests post-1999.

Conclusions

In a conference entitled 'The Macau Society and the Eastern and Western Culture' held in Macau, none of the papers presented mentioned the role of the Macanese as the intermediary between the East and the West.[63] Some local Chinese participants pointed out the importance of maintaining Portuguese language and culture in post-1999 Macau, yet none suggested specific measures to ensure this. It seems that in post-1999 Macau, the Chinese government and local Chinese residents are more eager to restore Chinese as the first official language than they are to maintain Portuguese as a viable language. The Basic Law stipulates that the Macau SAR will make the policies regarding Portuguese language education. However, the prospects for Portuguese language education are not bright. Local Chinese schools are reluctant to include Portuguese as a second language in their curriculum. Indeed, few Chinese parents would let their children study Portuguese, a language which many regard as having no future in the Macau SAR.[64] Although the Basic Law stipulates that Portuguese will also be used as an official language in the SAR, many expect Chinese to become the working language in government offices. In fact, newly promoted directors of Chinese descent have already notified their staff that they must write their reports or memos in Chinese. It is possible, however, that the Chinese-dominated SAR government may, partly for political reasons, agree to maintain a Portuguese culture in post-1999 Macau.[65]

The Chinese community is divided in its attitude towards Portuguese culture and the Macanese as an ethnic group. Western-educated professionals and younger generation Chinese, who have experienced no maltreatment or discrimination by the Macanese and are more open and liberal in outlook, wish to preserve Portuguese culture and the Macanese ethnic group as a distinctive feature of Macau that is different from that of other Chinese cities.[66] However, the older generation of Chinese who had endured the pre-1966 era of racial inequality between the ruling Portuguese/Macanese and Chinese subjects, especially the leftists who had participated in the 1966 riot, are reluctant to accommodate the Macanese in a new era. They have complied with Beijing's instruction to appease the Macanese to ensure a smooth transition such as efforts to co-opt Macanese into the Macau SAR Preparatory Committee and the Election Committee for the selection of the chief executive of the Macau SAR, yet they pay only lip service to preserving Portuguese culture. Indeed, some leftists even have suggested that Chinese should be the only official language in the Macau SAR.[67]

The Portuguese government in Macau, on the other hand, had either been unwilling or unable to pressure the Chinese authorities to take concrete steps to preserve Portuguese language and culture in post-1999 Macau. The Portuguese government's efforts to establish monuments as a means to preserve Portuguese cultural heritage in post-1999 Macau had been severely criticized by local pro-Beijing political forces in the legislature as waste of public funds.[68] Indeed, the 'lame-duck' colonial government's authority in governing the territory was gradually eroding, as witnessed by the rapid increase in social crimes and disorder in local casinos.[69] The underground societies (i.e. triads and gangsters) that had controlled the local casinos had begun to make their way to the legislature. Money politics and bribery dominated the 1996 legislative elections, and a number of political groups that won the elections were reported to have strong linkages with the underground societies.[70] In fact, the deteriorating political and social order had directly led some Macanese to decide to leave Macau after 1999.[71] Many Macanese felt that they had been neglected by both the Chinese and Portuguese governments and had become a political 'orphan'[72] facing a harsh and uncertain future.

In a 1995 survey, less than one-third of Macanese respondents indicated that they would certainly or most likely leave Macau after 1999, while about 40 per cent were undecided.[73] In other words, if the political and social environment did not deteriorate in the run-up to 1999, approximately two-thirds of the ethnic Macanese were likely to stay in Macau after 1999. That is to say, about 5000 Macanese would stay after 1999 to fight for their political and other interests. This is certainly a small minority in an overwhelming Chinese population. Yet, taking into consideration that this small ethnic group is politically participant-oriented[74] and that, according to the Macau Basic Law, Portuguese will remain one of the two official languages in post-1999 Macau, their future political role should not be underestimated. The real danger is that as the Macanese community does not have a strong ethnic or group identity,[75] and integration trends with the Chinese community such as intermarriage and cultural assimilation are accelerating, the Macanese may lose their distinctive cultural heritage in the not-too-distant future. Indeed, many noted Macanese community leaders have expressed their concerns that the Macanese culture will, given the accelerating cultural integration with the Chinese community and the bleak outlook of Portuguese language education, eventually be assimilated by the dominant Chinese culture after 1999.[76] Some regard the process of Sinicization as inevitable, but believe that as long as the Macanese exist as an ethnic group, their distinctive culture will not disappear.[77]

The Macanese had successfully lobbied the Portuguese government and the Chinese authorities before the handover to maintain a Portuguese school in post-1999 Macau. However, they were less successful in convincing the Chinese authorities to adopt a genuinely bilingual policy, that is to treat Portuguese language on a par with the Chinese language, when the Chinese authorities were more interested in establishing Chinese as the first official language as a symbol of restoring Chinese sovereignty in the enclave. Macanese who have chosen to stay in Macau after the handover try to adapt themselves to the new political and social environment. Yet, paradoxically, those who believe that there is a place for the Macanese and Portuguese culture in post-1999 Macau also urge their fellow Macanese to learn the Chinese language, both spoken (Putonghua) and written, and to integrate themselves into the Chinese community which, in the long-run, will quicken the pace of cultural assimilation and the eventual extinction of Macanese as a viable ethnic group.

In the first Macau SAR government, the Macanese are barred from high-ranking government posts and the powerful 10-member Executive Council due to the Chinese nationality requirement as stipulated in the Basic Law. There are only four Macanese (two appointed and two indirectly elected) in the 23-member Legislative Assembly. In short, the Macanese have become merely a marginal political force in post-1999 Macau, a far cry from the heydays of the 1970s and early 1980s when the Macanese dominated the legislature and the civil service. The Macanese have often been proud of their adaptability to the changing political and social environment. Carlos Marreiros believes the Macanese are 'a unique cocktail of ethnic backgrounds' and this means they 'can fit in and survive anywhere'.[78] Another noted Macanese said: 'We are not like iron bars that can easily be broken. We are more like bamboo stems that can be bent. When a typhoon comes we may be blown down on the ground; yet after the typhoon we will be up and flourish again'.[79] The Macanese, however, have yet to prove that they can survive the 'typhoon of 1999'.

8
Conclusion and Prospects for Democratization

The implementation of the concept of 'one country, two systems' in Hong Kong and Macau has played and will continue to play an important exemplary role for eventual settlement of the Taiwan question. . . . Macau inhabitants, irrespective of race or belief, will all be masters of this land, enjoying, as equals, the rights and freedoms guaranteed by law.

Jiang Zemin[1]

Portugal will continue to express its solidarity with Macau, and will remain committed to its future in the conviction that here, too, democracy and freedom are an irreplaceable reality.

Jorge Sampaio[2]

The rhythm of the town is very slow, like that of a man fairly dropping from fatigue. The boredom stems from a feeling in Macau of a complete lack of energy and of any need for change. . . . The people here don't care about anything, even important things, even things that concern their future. Before, if we wanted to do something, give our opinions, the government would ignore us. Now it acts as though it wants to hear our opinions, what we want for our future, but no one knows if it'll actually listen.

Frank Lei[3]

> I want to be free to criticize the government, to carry on
> with demonstrations to remember June 4, and to create a
> positive image for democracy.
>
> Ng Kuok Cheong[4]

Macau's transition from a Portuguese autonomous territory to a
Chinese special administrative region (SAR) was relatively smooth, in
sharp contrast to the far less smooth Hong Kong transition. Explanations for the differences in the two transitions are, first and foremost, the power asymmetry between the PRC and Portugal. Unlike
the United Kingdom, which is a major power and had negotiated
hard with the PRC on Hong Kong's political reform and democratization during the transitional period, Portugal, a small and relatively
undeveloped European state, had complied with Beijing's wishes for
a smooth transition. Beijing had used friendly Sino-Portuguese relations as a model, or bargaining chip, in its negotiations with London
over Hong Kong's transition. Second, Macau is relatively unimpor-
tant to Beijing and Lisbon, in comparison to Hong Kong's importance to Beijing and London. Both Beijing and Lisbon were therefore
unwilling to bargain hard on the subject of Macau's future at the
expense of Sino-Portuguese relations. Third, unlike Hongkongers
who were by and large unenthusiastic about the territory's reversion
to China (many sided with London in its row with Beijing over the
transition), the Macau people were generally pro-Beijing and were
yearning for Macau's return to China. Lastly, while Hong Kong's
handover was the centre of international attention, Macau's handover was relatively ignored by the international community. Many
assume that Macau is not much different from Hong Kong and that
if the formula 'one country, two systems' works in Hong Kong it
should also work in Macau. In any event there was little international
pressure on Beijing or Lisbon on taking concrete steps to conduct
political reform in Macau during the transition. In short, international and local factors accounted for the different processes of
transition in Hong Kong and Macau.

Macau's decolonization process is also very different from that of
Portugal's ex-colonies in Africa and Asia. First, Lisbon would return
Macau's sovereignty to Beijing, not to the people of Macau, nor to
the Macau SAR government. In fact, like Hongkongers who had been

excluded in Sino-British negotiations over Hong Kong's transition, the Macau people were also deprived of a say in Macau's future. Second, unlike in its ex-colonies in Africa where the Portuguese had arguably controlled the rhythm of decolonization, the process of Macau's transition was largely controlled by Beijing, partly as a result of power asymmetry between Beijing and Lisbon. The future of Macau and the SAR government was also in the hands of the PRC. Third, unlike the eruption of riots, tribal wars or guerrilla warfare that often plagued Portugal's former colonies during the process of decolonization, Macau's process of transition was marked by the absence of serious open conflicts between the local societal forces as well as between the Portuguese Macau administration and the local residents. The local societal forces were either directly controlled or co-opted by the PRC, or too weak to challenge the Chinese central government, and Beijing had made it clear that it wanted a smooth transition, partly as an example for the eventual settlement of the Taiwan question.

Yet there are also similarities between the process of Macau's transition and the decolonization processes of Portugal's ex-colonies in Africa and Asia. Like any decolonizing process elsewhere, the Portuguese administration had suffered a sense of eroding legitimacy of governance and Macau society was plagued by deteriorating law and order in the final years of the transition. As is often the case, the old colonial order had been in disarray before a new political order could be established. Furthermore, similar to their former disengagements in Africa, the Portuguese were more concerned about the short-term political and economic gains than the long-term interests of Macau. Understandably, the Portuguese were also interested in preserving their culture and language in post-1999 Macau as they had done to their former colonies.

The dynamics of transition

Many actors were involved in the process of Macau's transition. Beijing was no doubt the main actor during the whole process of transition. From the economic and political viewpoint, Macau may not be important, especially in comparison to Hong Kong, to Zhongnanhai. To the Beijing leaders, however, the reversion of

Macau before the end of the twentieth century had both symbolic and practical values: it signalled the end of China's 100 years of humiliating history caused by the expansion of European imperialists and colonialists as well as the beginning of a new PRC offensive for the eventual reunification of Taiwan. Beijing, of course, is not so naïve to believe that Taipei will accept terms for reunification that are identical to the 'one country, two systems' formula applying to Hong Kong and Macau. Nonetheless, there is little doubt that Beijing is toying with the idea along similar lines for eventual settlement of the Taiwan question. The Beijing leaders were thus determined to put up a good political show – especially after the rough Hong Kong transition – at the Macau handover. That largely explains Beijing's accommodating attitude toward Lisbon and the Portuguese Macau administration during the transition period. Beijing's overt concerns with a stable and smooth transition partly explains its unilateral decision to station PLA troops in Macau SAR. By and large Beijing had taken the initiative and controlled the agenda of Sino-Portuguese negotiations over the transition. It also closely monitored the Portuguese Macau administration as well as Macau's political and social development through its local New China News Agency (NCNA or *Xinhua*) branch.

Lisbon was the other main actor in the process of Macau's transition. Macau's future was to a large extent determined by negotiations between Lisbon and Beijing through exchange of visits between the two countries' leaders as well as at meetings of the Sino-Portuguese Joint Liaison Group. Taking advantage of Beijing's overt concern with a smooth handover and using Portugal's membership in and relations with European Union as leverage, Lisbon often had been able to press Beijing for concessions and co-operation on areas of interests to Portugal such as big construction projects as well as the nationality, language and localization issues. Interestingly, as a weaker player in the Beijing–Lisbon power game, Portugal had several times skilfully adopted the tactics of threatening to abandon Macau or of being unco-operative as a bargaining leverage against the powerful PRC. Indeed, President Jorge Sampaio refused to confirm whether he would attend the handover ceremony until Jiang Zemin's visit to Lisbon two months before the handover and Jiang's promise not to send armed PLA troops to Macau before the midnight of 19 December 1999.

The Portuguese Macau administration, although officially representing Lisbon's interests in Macau, was an important actor in its
own right during the transition process. The local Portuguese administration was responsible for implementing the agreements reached
between Lisbon and Beijing. Needless to say, the attitude and co-
operation of the Portuguese administration, especially the governor's
attitude, is extremely important for a smooth transition. The personal style of governors did make a difference. Governor Vasco Rocha
Vieira, unlike his outspoken predecessor Carlos Melancia, appeared
to be more co-operative in complying with Beijing's wishes. Vieira,
however, was apparently more interested in maintaining a viable Portuguese rule than in facilitating the process of localization and preparations for the handover. He retained his seven under-secretaries and
Portuguese expatriates who had occupied key government positions
until the handover. Furthermore, arrangements for the handover,
including the venue for the ceremony, were not ready until the last
minute. Vieira was also involved in a scandal of allegedly transferring 50 million patacas (or 6.25 million US dollars) from a local foundation fund to a newly established foundation fund registered in
Lisbon and chaired by himself.[5]

Unlike the Portuguese administration's lukewarm efforts in facilitating the process of Macau's transition, Beijing's official representation in Macau, the New China News Agency, was actively involved
in monitoring the process of transition. Unlike Hong Kong, Xinhua's
Zhou Nan who had chosen a strategy of confrontation and openly
criticized Chris Patten's political reform, in Macau, Xinhua's Guo
Dongpo and later Wang Qiren had kept a low profile and refrained
from criticizing the Portuguese Macau administration, reflecting
Beijing's accommodating attitude toward Lisbon. However, the
Macau Xinhua occasionally did openly press the Vieira administration to quicken the pace of localization, especially the promotion of
local Chinese residents to senior government positions and the use
of Chinese as a working language in government offices and departments. Xinhua was also instrumental in co-ordinating the pro-
Beijing local political and social forces for the handover preparations.
Through Xinhua's organization, information and personal networks,
Beijing has a strong grip on Macau society and succeeded to place
pro-Beijing local Chinese, particularly those who were brought up
or educated in the mainland, in important government positions.

Xinhua has also successfully co-opted the independent elites into the local legislature or municipal councils as well as people's congresses or political consultative committees of the PRC.

In contrast to Hong Kong's pluralist and diversified society and the presence of a strong pro-democracy force, Macau society was and is dominated by pro-Beijing political and social groups. Macau's small economy provides little surviving space for the democrats. Unlike pre-1997 Hong Kong elites who were divided into pro-Beijing and pro-British groups in the row over Hong Kong's political reform and other issues related to the transition, the Macau elites, including the pro-democracy and independent ones, had supported Beijing on all disputes with Lisbon or with the Portuguese Macau administration. Thanks to the inefficient and incompetent sunset Portuguese administration, all societal forces in Macau were united and looking forward to the new SAR government.

Likewise, Macau's mass public were also disappointed by the Portuguese administration's failure to curb the deteriorating law and order or to boost the enclave's depressed economy. In contrast to Hongkongers' largely indifferent mood at Hong Kong's handover, a majority of Macau citizens were happy and optimistic about Macau's future at the time of handover. A clear majority of the Macau citizens also believe Beijing's promise that Macau will practice 'one country, two systems' and 'Macau people ruling Macau' for 50 years. The contrasting performances of the two respective colonial governments partly explains the local residents' different attitudes towards the handover in Hong Kong and Macau. Furthermore, about 40 per cent of the Macau residents are new immigrants from mainland China since the late 1970s, who still have strong personal or emotional links with the mainland. In any event, the prevailing pro-China mood among the Macau citizens had greatly facilitated and almost ensured a smooth transition to post-1999 Macau.

The largely forgotten actor during the process of Macau's transition was the locally-born Eurasians (or Macanese). The Cantonese-speaking Macanese had played an important role in Macau's politics and served as the intermediary between the Portuguese administration and the mass public until the mid-1980s. The Macanese political and social roles, however, have since been marginalized by the increasing Chinese domination. Macanese interests and concerns were largely neglected by both Beijing and Lisbon. Although the former had made concessions in letting the Macanese choose their own nationality, it only paid lip service to making Portuguese a viable official language equal in status to the Chinese language in the Macau SAR. Losing the language advantage, the Macanese will be further marginalized in post-1999 Macau. Lisbon and the sunset Portuguese administration were also half-hearted in protecting the Macanese interests. The former was apparently more interested in using the nationality issue as a bargaining tool, pressing Beijing to make concessions on other issues during the negotiations while the Vieira administration was more interested in retaining its own team of Portuguese expatriates than in promoting the local Macanese to senior positions. In the end, many Macanese chose to leave Macau after the handover.

Another neglected voice during Macau's transition is the enclave's democrats. Unlike Chris Patten who had tried to introduce a more democratic political system to Hong Kong by opening the government's decision-making process to public scrutiny and expanding the suffrage of the electoral system, Vieira had done neither of the above. Indeed, Vieira had complied with Beijing's wishes to isolate the Macau democrats by blocking the promotion chances of civil servants who were associated with Macau's Democratic Development Union (*Aomen minzhu fazhan lianhui*) or the New Macau Learned Society (*Xin Aomen xueshe*).[6] On the one hand, the Macau democrats who had often criticized the Vieira administration's policies were regarded by the Portuguese as a nuisance. On the other hand, Beijing, which had attempted to co-opt the Hong Kong democrats during Hong Kong's transition, had simply ignored the insignificant and relatively moderate (in comparison to Hong Kong's more radical democrats) democratic force in Macau.

In sum, the above actors had, in different degrees, all played a role in shaping the process of Macau's transition. Largely due to different interests and viewpoints, there were inevitable conflicts and misunderstanding among and between actors. Nonetheless, the course of transition was largely shaped by interactions between Beijing and Lisbon. However, human weakness and the dynamics of interactions often resulted in unintended consequences neither Beijing nor Lisbon wanted. For example, in the name of Sino-Portuguese friendship and Beijing's preoccupation with a smooth transition, the PRC had given concessions to the Portuguese that often contradicted

Macau's long-term interests. On the other hand, Vieira's preoccupation with retaining a viable Portuguese-dominated administration in the final years of Portuguese rule had resulted in a failure to promote the bilingual and pro-Portuguese Macanese to senior and key government positions before the handover. As a result, the Macanese have become politically marginalized and Portugal has lost its strongest supporter in its effort to preserve Portuguese culture and language in post-1999 Macau. In the end, Macau's citizens are the losers and Macau's long-term interests are sacrificed in the power game between the PRC and Portugal.

Prospects for democratization[7]

The introduction of direct elections to the legislature in 1976 no doubt contributed to the 'democratic opening' in Macau's long journey towards democracy by providing a forum for citizen participation. The success in the 1992 election of democrat Ng Kuok Cheong, who presented the only democratic voice highly critical of government performance, was also an important landmark in the enclave's process of democratization. Yet Macau's political and social environment has constrained the scope and pace of democratization. Since the December 1966 anti-government riots, the pro-Beijing social and political groups have dominated the Chinese community. These groups made their political debut in the 1984 legislature elections by taking one directly elected seat and all six indirectly elected seats. Despite the temporary setback to the trio of Alexandre Ho, Leong Kam Chuen (or Liang Jinquan) and Wong Cheong Nam (Wang Zhangnan) who won seats in the 1988 legislature direct elections under the banner of 'improving people's livelihood', the pro-Beijing groups came back strongly in the 1991 by-election taking the two newly created seats in the direct elections. The pro-Beijing groups consolidated their domination in the legislature in 1992 by winning half of the eight directly elected seats and all indirectly elected seats.[8] Partly due to the split within the 'livelihood group', Leong Kam Chuen and Wong Cheong Nam lost their seats while Alexandre Ho had a narrow win in the 1992 elections. The *nouveau riches*, a product of the boom years in the 1980s and early 1990s, were big winners in the 1996 legislature elections, winning four directly elected seats.[9] However, partly due to the enclave's poor economic performance in the last three years, especially with the collapse of the real estate market since 1995,[10] the *nouveau riche* legislators have found their fortunes greatly reduced. They eventually all joined or were co-opted by the mainstream pro-Beijing political force.

On the eve of Macau's return to the PRC, the enclave appears to be dominated by what is commonly referred to as 'social group politics' (*shetuan zhengzhi*). After the signing of the Sino-Portuguese Joint Declaration in 1987, pro-Beijing groups and organizations have gradually replaced the Macanese as the intermediary between the government and the people. The pro-Beijing labour union and neighbourhood (*kaifong*) associations have proved themselves very effective in mobilizing grass-roots supports in the elections. The above two organizations together won four and three directly elected seats in the 1992 and 1996 elections respectively. Pro-Beijing groups and organizations typically resist political reform and tend towards maintaining the status quo, thus creating the major obstacle to Macau's democratization process.

Although voter turnout in the last two legislature elections was high,[11] one may argue that this was the result of rigorous election campaigns by the contending political groups, in particular the mobilization of pro-Beijing labour unions and *kaifong* associations rather than the rise of political aspirations among the local citizens. Vote-buying and other irregularities were rampant in the 1996 elections.[12] Local Chinese voters were generally regarded as passive participants who could be easily manipulated by powerful and organized political groups.[13] However, a recent survey which was conducted in January 1999 indicated that Macau's citizens are no longer submissive subjects apathetic to politics.[14] Indeed, a participatory political culture is emerging in the enclave.

Findings from the 1999 survey indicate that Macau residents are concerned about public affairs: 71.4 per cent of the respondents followed the news on television, in the press or on the radio 'every day' or 'often', a slight increase over a 1991 survey.[15] It is interesting to note that the people of Macau have tended to engage more in discussing government affairs with their friends and relatives than before. One probable explanation is that the impending return of Macau to China had aroused public interest in and concerns about government affairs.

More importantly, perhaps, the introduction of direct elections in the legislature has significantly changed Macau people's conception or understanding of democracy. In the 1991 survey, high on the list of conceptions of democratic government is the traditional Chinese expectation of good government, second and third on the list are freedom of speech and a government elected by the people (see Table 5.4, above). Apparently the respondents of our survey in 1991 were more concerned about the performance of a government than in the process of democracy. In the 1999 survey, however, the ranking of democratic values was almost reversed. High on the list is an elected government, something which is the bulwark of Western democracy. The new emphasis on an elected government by Macau residents is a big step forward in Macau's democratization process. After two Legislative Assembly elections in the 1990s, which drew high voter turnouts, Macau residents have apparently attained a new election culture.

Nonetheless, few Macau citizens have realized the importance of the principle of 'checks and balances' between the executive, legislative and judicial branches in a democracy and that a significant proportion of the Macau populace does not know much about or simply does not care about democracy. Indeed, many respondents were reluctant to answer questions pertaining to politics. This reflects the lingering Chinese tradition of not becoming involved in politics. Another strong, lingering tradition is the stress on the instrumental value of governance. Many Macau people are still more interested in the output or performance of the government than in the process of governing.

It is important to note that both our 1991 and 1999 surveys indicate a positive relationship between education and political participation. The better-educated and hence better-informed respondents are more critical of government performance and are more participation-oriented. They tend to reject the traditional values of passivity and submissiveness to authority and to opt for a more open and competitive society. They also tend to have a better understanding of Western democracy and a desire for political rights. According to the figures provided by the Macau government's Census and Statistics Department, the proportion of university-educated people among the total population (aged 20 and above) had increased from 6.1 per cent in 1991 to 7.8 per cent in 1998, and it is projected to reach or exceed 10 per cent in another decade. In fact, according to government statistics, more than 70 per cent of Macau's high school graduates are now going on to university,[16] a very high rate even by world standards. It is thus quite accurate to forecast that as the overall education level of Macau's citizens increases they will have greater political aspirations, will be more participation-oriented and will have a better understanding of democratic processes and values.

Another important background variable was length of residence in Macau. Our findings indicate that there is a positive relationship between length of residence and concerns about public and government affairs. In addition, those who were born and grew up in Macau are more inclined to discuss government affairs with friends and relatives than the new immigrants by a ratio of 3 to 1. As the proportion of Macau's locally-born population has increased from 40 per cent in 1991 to the current estimated 50 per cent and, unless with a drastic increase of new immigrants, is likely to increase in the future, the Macau SAR government will face an informed, concerned, critical and participation-oriented public.

In the 1999 survey, 94 per cent of respondents indicated that their ideal political system would be democratic and 75 per cent believed that a democratic political system would suit Macau. Clearly, there is a gap between the political aspirations of Macau's citizens and the existing authoritarian political system or, in Almond and Verba's terminology,[17] there is an incongruence between Macau's political culture and the enclave's political structure. One may simply argue that to increase the proportion of directly elected seats or, indeed, to make all legislature seats open to election through universal suffrage, is the only way to meet the rising political aspirations of Macau's citizens. Yet the real political and social situations in Macau are more complicated than that. There is no short-cut to democracy for the future Macau SAR.

A look toward a brighter future?

Looking on the bright side, however, the democratic consciousness of Macau's citizens has been increasing over the last decade. A majority of local residents realize the importance of the democratic process such as elections, and yearn for open, fair, just, clean and democratic government, although, as has been said, many do not realize the importance of 'checks and balances' between government power branches, especially in the supervision of executive power and the independence of court trials.[18] However, this incomplete or inaccurate understanding of democracy is likely to be corrected under a new and better-educated generation. The new better-educated generation which will undoubtedly become a dominant political and social force in a decade or two are likely to be more open, more politically aware and more participation-oriented than their parents and grandparents. At the same time, a growing middle and professional class is likely to push the democratization process forward. Lastly, the return of Macau to the PRC at the turn of the twenty-first century provides a unique opportunity to the people of Macau to voice their opinions concerning public and government policies. Beijing's promises of 'one country, two systems' and letting 'Macau people rule Macau' have motivated and encouraged some local residents to engage actively in public affairs. Indeed, a number of research centres or learning societies such as the 'Macau Development Strategy Research Centre', 'Institute of Macau Policy Studies' and the 'Ninety-nine Learning Society' have been established in the last few years. These organizations have published journals and written up policy reports on various aspects of Macua's economic, social and political developments.[19] They may or may not have a direct impact on the policy-makers of the Macau SAR government. Yet they have created a new, unprecedented participant political atmosphere or culture in the territory. The people of Macau are urged to escape from the 'vicious circle of silence' and speak out against government wrongdoing.[20]

One hopeful aspect of Macau's democratization, according to Ng Kuok Cheong, the enclave's prominent democrat, is the change in social mobility of Macau's educated and professional groups.[21] Ng points out that in the process of localization since the late 1980s the Portuguese Macau administration had recruited or co-opted new university graduates and young professionals to the ever-expanding civil service and to replace the departing Portuguese expatriates. As a result, this better-educated social group which is normally most concerned and outspoken about public affairs, have been refrained from criticizing the Portuguese administration. In the post-1999 SAR, however, new recruits to the already over-expanded civil service will be decreased or frozen. New university graduates or young professionals have to join the private sector. As tax payers, and as a social force outside the government establishment, Ng argues, this educated group is likely to be highly critical of the SAR government.[22] By 2010, Ng predicts, a new locally-born, better-educated and pro-democracy generation will change Macau's political scene.

On the darker side, the scope and pace of democratization in Macau are inhibited by both internal and external factors. Unlike Hong Kong which is an economically highly developed, cosmopolitan city with a population exceeding six million people, Macau is a small city with less than half a million inhabitants and an area of 24 square kilometres. Macau's GDP is merely 5 per cent that of Hong Kong's. The Portuguese had long regarded this Far East outpost as an exclusive Portuguese territory and kept it away from interference by other European powers. In fact, the Portuguese government had made little effort to attract American, British, Japanese or other foreign capital. The lack of international exposure and the inefficient as well as ineffective governance by the Portuguese had contributed to the conservative outlook of the small enclave. After the signing of the Sino-Portuguese Joint Declaration on the future status of Macau in 1987, the pro-Beijing local Chinese community leaders and social groups have replaced the Cantonese-speaking Macanese as the intermediary between the Portuguese government and the public. Relying on their effective grass-roots mobilization strategies, the pro-Beijing groups have won handsomely in the legislative and city assembly elections and have dominated Macau's political scene.

The pro-Beijing groups, which are composed of traditional Chinese trading and social groups and organizations such as the Chinese Chamber of Commerce, labour unions and neighbourhood or *kaifong* associations, tend to have a conservative outlook. They wish to maintain their present political and social status and are hence resistant to political or social reform. They stress political and social stability and objected to any attempt to quicken the pace of democratization during the period of transition. In fact, they rarely mention democratization in their election campaigns. They spread the idea that Macau does not have the political and social conditions for a democratic government and that Western democracy is not suitable for Macau. The most commonly cited reason is that the overall level of education among Macau's populace is low[23] and democracy and party politics will thus only bring chaos or *luan* to the territory.

It is interesting to note that even the pro-democracy or independent political or social elites tend to agree with the idea that rapid democratization is not suitable in Macau because of the low level of education among its citizens[24] or because Macau is not a sovereign city-state.[25] Unlike Hong Kong, few pro-democracy groups in Macau advocate direct elections for all legislature seats or direct elections for the chief executive of the SAR. In Macau's present political and social environment, the pro-Beijing traditional social groups are likely winners in both the direct or indirect elections. The defeat of 'livelihood' groups in the last two elections and the election of only one democrat into the legislature indicate clearly that the new, progressive social groups are still no match for the traditional, conservative groups and organizations.

Edmund Ho Hau Wah, the SAR's first chief executive, points out that there are three major political and social forces in Macau: (1) the traditional pro-Beijing social forces; (2) people who are directly or indirectly associated with casino tycoon Stanley Ho's So-ciedade de Turismo e Diversoes de Macau (STDM); and (3) mainland cadres or entrepreneurs who came to Macau in the late 1980s and early 1990s and worked for mainland companies or established a business in Macau and later became residents.[26] The last two groups in particular, according to Edmund Ho, are only interested in profiteering while caring little about Macau's stability. The two groups are very wealthy and hence extremely influential in a period of economic recession. Rapid democratization, Ho argued, is thus not a reasonable option in Macau's present political and social environment; to open all legislature seats to direct elections would benefit only the wealthy and powerful social forces but and not necessarily the well-being of Macau. Educated in the West,[27] Ho is apparently sympathetic to Macau's democratization.[28] Yet like his counterpart Tung Cheehwa (Dong Jianhua), Hong Kong SAR's first chief executive, Ho, in order for him to be trusted by Beijing, has to be politically correct.[29] Like Tung, Ho must also watch his back against sniping from extreme local leftists.[30] Thus, if Ho shows any sign of association with Macau's democratization course it would politically be very risky for him.

Besides the internal societal constraints, the small size of the enclave's economy and geographic area has made it extremely vulnerable to external influences, particularly from mainland China. As a undemocratic, authoritarian socialist state it is understandable that the PRC does not want to see a democracy established in a Chinese community adjacent to the mainland. Democrats in Hong Kong have already caused the Chinese authorities a number of headaches by advocating and assisting the democratic movement in the mainland. Indeed, silent revolution of grass-roots political participation is already taking place in South China especially in the Pearl River Delta area, which is becoming increasingly permeated by Hong Kong's political values.[31] As in Hong Kong, the scope and pace of democratization in Macau is constrained by the region's Basic Law. In fact, unlike the Hong Kong SAR Basic Law, which was largely drafted before the 1989 Tiananmen Square Incident and was hence politically more liberal, the Macau Basic Law, which was drafted in the early 1990s imposed more constraints on the enclave's democratic development. Appointed seats, which were abolished in the Hong Kong SAR's first legislature, are retained in the Macau SAR's legislature. Moreover, an annex to the Hong Kong Basic Law stipulates that after 2007 the election procedure for the SAR's chief executive is subject to review by the Legislative Assembly which may, with the endorsement of a two-thirds majority, recommend direct or universal suffrage. The above stipulation was notably absent in the Macau Basis Law.

Through the local branch of the New China News Agency, which established an office in Macau in 1987 after the signing of the Sino-Portuguese Joint Declaration, Beijing controls or co-ordinates the local pro-Beijing groups and organizations and the local press. Regular meetings are held between NCNA cadres and lcoal pro-Beijing community leaders. The pro-Beijing groups often speak with one voice about public and political issues. The *Macau Daily* (*Aomen ribao*), which is by far Macau's largest newspaper by circulation[32] acts as Beijing's official mouthpiece in the enclave. In short, Beijing's influence is pervasive and present in all levels of Macau society.

However, the mainland's most effective control over Macau is through its domination of the enclave's economy. According to a recent study, Macau's capital structure is composed of 20 per cent of local capital, 25 per cent of Hong Kong capital, 45 per cent of mainland Chinese capital, 5 per cent of Portuguese capital and less than 5 per cent from other countries.[33] Considering that local and Hong Kong capital is concentrated in banking or manufacturing sectors, which are highly dependant on mainland connections, Chinese capital is actually higher than the 45 per cent figure suggested. The Chinese domination of the enclave's economy has effectively silenced the dissenting voices among the local press through the manipulation of advertising in that press.[34]

More importantly, this domination of the economy has severely limited the potential for survival of Macau's democrats. Ng Kuok Cheong and Au Kam San (or Ao Jinxin), the two noted local democrats, were dismissed by their respective employers after winning seats in the Legislative Assembly and the Municipal Assembly respectively. Afraid of similar treatment from their employers, supporters of Ng and Au have kept a low profile and a distance from the two democrats. Ng even expressed the opinion that he would not form a political party because he does not want his friends and supporters to suffer economic hardship.[35] *The Spiral of Silence*, a short film produced in Macau and shown in early 1999, is a collection of interviews of local residents who share the view that there is little room for freedom of speech in Macau because of mainland China's domination in almost all aspects of Macau's society. The present author encountered enormous problems when soliciting articles for a collected volume on Macau's policy issues. Many people declined the invitation to contribute an article or were willing to write only under a fictitious name because they were afraid that their writing might irritate some influential people in some circles in Macau.[36] It was estimated that about 70000 people attended in Hong Kong Victoria Park the candlelit vigil for the Tenth Anniversary of the June Fourth Tiananmen Square Incident.[37] By contrast, fewer than 200 Macau citizens attended a similar gathering in the Leal Senado Square.[38] Many Macau citizens, though supportive of democratic development in the mainland and Macau, are afraid of identifying themselves with the democrats. Moreover, some social groups or organizations choose to use force to silence dissenting voices. Victor Ng, an outspoken legislator who had criticized Stanley Ho's STDM and other irregularities in local casinos as well as government policies, was beaten by a gang of seven in front of Macau's NCNA building.[39] Seen in this light, the prospect for democratization in the enclave is very gloomy indeed.

The problem encountered by the democrats in post-1997 Hong Kong SAR may give a hint to the future direction of Macau's democratization process. According to Lau Siukai, a professor from the

Chinese University of Hong Kong, since the chief executive is not popularly elected and will not be in the foreseeable future, the political opposition (i.e. the democrats) in the legislature is – and is widely seen to be – a permanent opposition.[40] Being dyed-in-the-wool political pragmatists, Lau argues, Hongkongers are losing interest in an opposition that is becoming permanent. A permanent opposition also encounters tremendous difficulties in finding new recruits and replenishing its leadership.[41] Meanwhile the diminishing international attention to Hong Kong in general and to the political opposition in particular after the handover is a further blow to Hong Kong's democratization process.[42] Lo Shiu-hing, another noted local academic on Hong Kong politics, argues that the ability of Hong Kong's Democratic Party (DP) to increase its representation in the legislature is undermined by the new proportional representation electoral system.[43] The DP also faced being squeezed between the pro-Beijing parties on one hand and hard- and soft-line democrats on the other, as well as facing internal divisions.[44] In short, the democrats are in the danger of being increasingly marginalized in Hong Kong's politics. In the November 1999 District Council elections, the pro-Beijing Democratic Alliance for the Betterment of Hong Kong (DAB), which was far behind the DP in the 1991, 1995 and 1998 Legislative Council elections, had almost caught up with the latter in both the popularity vote and the number of seats.[45] The DP leadership has apparently realized the imminent crisis of the party and considered a switch of strategy from stressing democratic political values to effectively responding to citizen demands and grievances.[46] Paradoxically, however, such a switch in strategy will gradually lose the DP's distinctive identity as a pro-democratic force and will in the long-run be detrimental to Hong Kong's democratic development.

Likewise, Macau's pro-democratic force is in danger of being marginalized by the ever increasing pro-Beijing force. Even Ng Kuok Cheong and Au Kam San admit that they are facing an uphill fight in spreading their democratic ideas in the enclave.[47] Ng's objective is modest: to possess the right to criticize the Macau SAR government and the PRC government, and to create a positive image for democracy.[48] Au believes that it may take several generations for Macau to be fully democratized. He also believes that Macau will become a democratic polity only after mainland China itself has liberalized.

However, despite the gloomy outlook of the enclave's process of democratization, both Ng and Au are optimistic about winning the next local elections. They believe that there is a space for democracy in Macau. They are prepared to take their campaign to the streets if all public channels for dissenting views are closed. Perhaps, then, the hope of Macau's democratization lies in the unswerving belief of a few democrats.

Notes

Introduction

1. Austin Coates, *A Macau Narrative* (New York: Oxford University Press, 1978), p. 135.
2. Wu Zhiliang and Ieong Wan Chong (Yang Yunzhong) (eds), *Aomen baike quanshu* (Encyclopedia of Macau) (Macau: Macau Foundation, 1999), p. 628.
3. For the full text of the Joint Declaration, see the *Joint Declaration of the Government of the People's Republic of China and the Government of the Republic of Portugal on the Question of Macau* (Macau: Macau Foundation, 1997).
4. This is a revised section of an earlier article by the author entitled 'Prospects of Democratization: An open-ended game?' *China Perspectives*, no. 26 (November–December 1999), 28–38.
5. For a concise Chinese interpretation of the history of Macau, see Fei Chengkang, *Aomen 400 nian* (Four Hundred Years of Macau) (Shanghai: Remin chubanshe, 1988). For a recent history in English, see Jonathan Porter, *Macau: the Imaginery City* (Boulder, Colorado: Westview, 1996); and Geoffrey C. Gunn, *Encountering Macau: a Portuguese City-State on the Periphery of China, 1557–1999* (Boulder, Colorado: Westview, 1996).
6. Wu Zhiliang, *Shengcun zhidao: lun Aomen zhengzhi zhidu yu zhengzhi fazhan* (The Path of Surviving: an Analysis of Macau's Political System and Political Development) (Macau: The Macau Adult Education Society, 1988), p. 87.
7. In the 1976 Election Law, the six indirectly elected seats consisted of three seats representing economic interests groups and three seats representing, respectively, interests of moral, cultural and charitable organizations. The revised 1991 Election Law expanded the number of indirectly elected seats to eight consisting of four seats representing employer interests, two seats representing worker interests and one seat each representing, respectively, professional interests and the interests of charitable, cultural, educational and sports organizations.
8. For a detailed account of political power struggle between Governor Costa and the Macanese legislators, see Li Bingshi, *Aomen zongdu yu lifahui* (The Governor and the Legislative Assembly in Macau) (Macau: The Macau Foundation, 1994), pp. 54–81.
9. Richard Louis Edmonds and Herbert S. Yee, 'Macau: From Portuguese Autonomous Territory to Chinese Special Administration Region', *The China Quarterly*, no. 160 (December 1999), p. 813.

10. There is a rumour that some Chinese extremists plan to abolish the Portuguese language as an official language in the SAR by revising the Macau Basic Law. Some are thinking of replacing Macau's current Portuguese-based legal system with a Chinese legal system. Interview with Gary Ngai Mei Cheong, former deputy director of the Institute of Culture of Macau, 8 October 1998.
11. The survey was conducted by the Social Science Research Centre of the University of Hong Kong in 1997. *Aomen ribao* (Macau Daily News), 3 January 2000, p. B2.
12. The survey on Macau was conducted by the author in December 1998.

1   Beijing's Attitude and Strategy toward the Transition

1. The announcement that the PLA would be stationed in the Macau SAR was made at a meeting of the Macau SAR Preparation Committee held in Beijing on 18 September 1998 by Vice-Premier Qian Qichen, *Aomen ribao* (*Macau Daily News*) (*MDN*), 19 September 1998, p. A1.
2. The idea of stationing PLA troops in Macau was raised neither in the Joint Declaration nor in the Macau Basic Law. In an interview in January 1999 with João Ramos, a member of the Portuguese delegation in negotiating with the Chinese over the reversion of Macau in 1986 and 1987, the author was told that there was an understanding that no Chinese troops would be stationed in the Macau SAR.
3. Three days after the Chinese government's announcement, Governor Rocha Vieira responded by pointing out that the Joint Declaration of 1987 did not mention that the Chinese side would station troops in Macau after 1999 and that the Portuguese government in Lisbon would discuss the issue, particularly the PRC's new interpretation of the Joint Declaration, with the Chinese government (*Huaqiao bao*, 23 September 1998, p. 1).
4. The pro-China *Macau Daily News* (*MDN*) hailed the Macau handover as a significant event ending the Portuguese 400 years rule of the enclave, 20 December 1999, p. E1.
5. Interview with João Ramos, a leading member of the Portuguese delegation in negotiating with China over Macau's reversion in 1986 and 1987, 4 January 1999.
6. According to Sonny Lo Shiu Hing, the British assertiveness towards Hong Kong's political reforms in the final years of colonial rule is ascribable to Chris Patten's personal conviction that democracy is what the British owed to the Hong Kong people. See Lo's *Political Development in Macau* (Hong Kong: Chinese University Press, 1995), p. 249.
7. For a more detailed account of Hong Kong's political reform since the 1980s, see Lo Shiu Hing, *The Politics of Democratization in Hong Kong* (London and New York: Macmillan and St. Martin's Press Crow jointly Palgrave, 1997). See also Lo's 'An Analysis of Sino-British Negotiations

Over Hong Kong's Political Reform', *Contemporary Southeast Asia*, vol. 16, no. 2 (September 1994), pp. 178–209.

8. Feng Bangyan, *Aomen gailun* (A General Introduction to Macau) (Hong Kong: Joint Publishing, 1999), p. 210.

9. Interview with Antonio de Saldanha, author of *Estudos Sobre As Relatcões Luso-Chinesas* (Macau: Instituto Cultural de Macau, 1996), on 6 January 1999.

10. Ibid.

11. For an analysis of the 1966 riot, see Anthony J. Dicks, 'Macau: Legal Fiction and Gunboat Diplomacy', in Goran Aijmer (ed.), *Leadership on the China Coast* (London and Malmo: Curzon Press, 1984); and Hu Zhiliang, *Shengcun zhidao: Lun Aomen zhengzhi zhidu yu zhengzhi fazhan* (The Path of Survival: a Study of Macau's Political System and Political Development) (Macau: Macau Adult Education Association, 1998), pp. 259–86.

12. Interview with João Ramos, 4 January 1999.

13. Moisés Silva Fernandes, 'Portuguese Behaviour Towards the Political Transition and the Regional Integration of Macau in the Pearl River Region', in Rufino Ramos, José Rocha Dinis, Rex Wilson, and D.Y. Yuan (eds), *Macau and Its Neighbours in Transition* (Macau: Macau Foundation, 1997), p. 45.

14. With China 'contained' and suffering economic sanctions imposed by the United States and its allies, Macau was extremely important as a transfer point for remittances worth millions of US dollars annually to PRC residents from overseas Chinese, as an entrepôt for mainland China for importing strategic goods which were under the US embargo and for exporting Chinese goods (with a 'made in Macau' stamp), as an entrepôt for smuggling drugs grown in the mainland to Western countries such as opium and heroin, and as a regional gold transhipment centre which provided the PRC with the hard currency. See Richard Louis Edmonds, *Macau* (Oxford: Clio Press, 1989), pp. xxiii–xxiv, and Moisés Silva Fernandes, *The Chinese Cultural Revolution and Luso-Chinese Relations* (forthcoming).

15. Interview with Autonio de Saldanha, 6 January 1999.

16. On several occasions the Chinese leaders had reiterated the importance of resolving the differences between Lisbon and Beijing over Macau from a long-term perspective. See, for example, the Chinese leader of the Joint Liaison Group Guo Jiading's speech on 17 July 1997, *MDN*, 18 July 1997, p. 10.

17. See Annex II of the Sino-Portuguese Joint Declaration.

18. However, a Portuguese scholar, Moisés Silva Fernandes, told the author that, according to his recent research, the Portuguese had sold the strategic goods to China through Macau's Nam Kwong Company, the forerunner of the Macau branch of New China New Agency. Interview, 5 January 1999.

19. *MDN*, 13 March 1980, p. 1. See also 'Aomen dashiji' (The Macau Chronology) in Wu Zhiliang and Ieong Wanchong (eds), *Aomen baike quanshu*

(Encyclopedia of Macau) (Macau: Macau Foundation, 1999), p. 626. The following account of mutual visits between Chinese and Portuguese leaders is based on the above chronology.

20. Interview with João Ramos, a member of the Portuguese delegation, 4 January 1999.
21. Ibid.
22. *Huaqiao bao*, 12 December 1999, p. A3.
23. Ibid.
24. According to a local reporter, the Chinese refused the Portuguese delegation's request to hold meetings alternatively in Beijing and Lisbon. As compensation as well as an effort to shorten the duration of negotiation, Beijing sent Zhou Nan to Lisbon as a friendly gesture and to save Portugal's 'face'. See Lin Chang, *Zhongpu guanxi yu Aomen qiantu* (Sino-Portuguese Relations and Macau's Future) (Macau: Macau Foundation, 1994), pp. 103–4.
25. President Mária Soares, however, gave Li Peng a cool reception. See Lin Chang, *Zhongpu guanxi yu Aomen qiantu*, p. 292.
26. Ibid., p. 291.
27. Macau's economy had recorded negative growth for three consecutive years since 1996.
28. The enclave's worsening law and order since 1996 was directly related to the local casino business. The 1997 financial crisis of Hong Kong and the Asian region had caused a sharp decline in the number of tourists to Macau. The shrinking gambling business had created keen competition and conflicts among the local casinos which are controlled by or connected to triad or other gangs, some of which chose to use force to resolve the conflicts. For detailed account of the enclave's casino business and its relations to crime, see Lo Shiu Hing, 'Gambling and Organized Crime: Towards the End of the Stanley Ho Connection?' *China Perspectives*, no. 26 (November–December 1999), pp. 56–65. See also Liu Pinliang, 'Bocaiye de fazhan he luxiang' (The Direction and Development of [Macau's] Gambling Business), in Herbert S. Yee, ed., *Aomen huigui qianhou de wenti yu duice* (Problems and Policies in Macau Before and After its Return [to China]) (Hong Kong: Mingliu Chubanshe, 1999), pp. 331–42.
29. For a detailed account of the localization process, see Chapter 3.
30. *Ming bao*, 28 October 1999, p. A19.
31. Interview with João Ramos, 4 January 1999. All JLG meetings were closed-door. Yet leaders of the Group often voiced their differences in the press conference held after each meeting.
32. 'Macanization' means to promote the local Eurasians (of mixed Portuguese–Asian blood), commonly referred as Macanese, to higher positions. For a detailed discussion of the Macanese question during the transition process, see Chapter 7.
33. *Huaqiao bao*, 27 November 1991.
34. Ibid.
35. For detailed discussion, see Chapter 3.

36. The maximum punishment for any crime in Macau is 25 years in jail. For the Portuguese position on the issue, see *MDN*, 15 November 1998, p. A7.
37. *MDN*, 2 November 1994, p. 3.
38. The Portuguese openly admitted that they were worried that the Portuguese language would lose its official status after 1999. *Huaqiao bao*, 18 February 1998, p. 4.
39. *MDN*, 18 February 1998, p. A3 and 14 August 1998, p. A3.
40. Ibid., 18 November 1998, p. A6.
41. The agreement, if any, on the bilingual issue has not been made public by either side.
42. *MDN*, 14 January 1999, p. A3.
43. The Portuguese complained that the Chinese had refused to include or delete agenda proposed by them. Ibid., 24 January 1998, p. 13.
44. According to a Portuguese diplomat who prefers to be anonymous, the PRC's treatment of the nationality issue is not much different from those countries such as the United States which do not recognize dual nationality. Yet Lisbon does not worry about consular protection for Portuguese nationals living in the United States or about Portuguese nationals being tried in an American court because the United States is an open, free society with an independent judicial system. By contrast, China is an authoritarian regime with an imperfect legal and judicial system. Portuguese nationals without consular protection living in Chinese territory could be easily subject to political repression. This was the real concern, according to the diplomat, behind the Portuguese position on the nationality issue.
45. Later changed to 1.6 per cent of the gross revenue of STDM. In 1988, the Foundation had a capital of 300 million patacas, or 37 million US dollars. The annual contributions from STDM exceeded 200 million patacas.
46. *Huaqiao bao*, 14 March 1993 and 18 September 1993.
47. Ibid.
48. Ibid., 29 October 1993.
49. Ibid., 14 September 1996.
50. Ibid., 30 October 1996. The new foundation, namely the Development and Co-operation Foundation of Macau, was inaugurated in May 1998.
51. *MDN*, 27 May 1998, p. A2 and 16 December 1998, p. A2.
52. Ibid., 18 November 1998, p. A6.
53. Ibid., 14 January 1999, p. A3.
54. For a detailed discussion of Macau's relations with the international community see Geoffrey Gunn, 'A Few International Ambitions', in *China Perspectives*, no. 26 (November–December 1999), pp. 43–9.
55. An example is the Chinese concession to discuss at the JLG meetings the 'Bilingual Regulations' introduced by the Portuguese and the former's promise not to send an advance team of PLA troops to Macau before midnight, 20 December 1999.
56. The cited example is the Chinese approval of the Portuguese administration's decision, a month before the handover, to extend the contract

with the Telecommunication Company of Macau (CTM) for another 10 years, despite strong opposition and protest from the Macau people.

57. Richard Louis Edmonds and William John Kyle, 'Land Use in Macau: Changes between 1972 and 1994', *Land Use Policy*, vol. 15, no. 4 (1998), pp. 280–8.
58. See Annex II of the Sino-Portuguese Joint Declaration.
59. Ibid.
60. *Huaqiao bao*, 3 January 1990, 23 October 1990 and 27 March 1991; and *MDN*, 23 March 1991.
61. *Huaqiao bao*, 8 July 1992; *MDN*, 9 July 1992, p. 2 and 10 July 1992, p. 2. The Chinese leader of the Land Group pointed out that the Portuguese administration had not complied with the proper process of leasing the reclaimed land in Praira Grande to the developer. The land, according to the Chinese side, was sold at only a quarter or one-fifth of the market price.
62. *MDN*, 17 August 1993, p. 2. The Chinese side disapproved the land reclamation project on the grounds that the Portuguese administration had not consulted with the Chinese members of the Land Group.
63. Interview with a Chinese member of the Land Group in January 1999.
64. *MDN*, 7 December 1999, p. A3.
65. Interview with Rui Afonso, former legislator, 6 January 1999.
66. Interview with Almeida e Costa, 6 January, 1999.
67. For a detailed discussion of Costa's conflict with the legislature in 1984, see Li Bingshi, *Aomen zongdu yu lifahui* (The Governor and the Legislative Assembly in Macau) (Macau: Macau Foundation, 1994). See also Chapter 6.
68. See Chapter 6.
69. Machado, the first non-military governor in post-war Macau, was in constant conflict with some of his under-secretaries who were friends of and appointed by President Mária Soares. Machado resigned after one year in office.
70. Herbert S. Yee and Sonny S. H. Lo, 'Macau in Transition: the Politics of Decolonization', *Asian Survey*, vol. 31, no. 10 (October 1991), p. 912.
71. The Chinese suggested that the name should be changed as the word 'office' implies an official or semi-official establishment of the Taiwan government. As viewed in Lisbon, the relationship between Macau and Taiwan would still be confined to bilateral trade whatever term was used for the 'office' in Macau. Beijing's objection was thus viewed in Lisbon and Macau as unnecessary, over-reactive, and a clear attempt to interfere in Macau's internal affairs. See ibid., pp. 910–11. In any event, Taiwan did not change the name of its 'office' in Macau until 27 December 1999, after the departure of the Portuguese administration. The new name became the Economic and Culture Centre of Taipei.
72. For a more detailed discussion of the privatization policy, see ibid., p. 912.
73. Ibid., p. 913.
74. Ibid., p. 915.
75. Ibid., p. 913.

76. See, for example, remarks made by Jorge Rangel, Vieira's Under-Secretary for Administration, Education and Youth Affairs. Rangel thought Vieira was the right choice and that he should have been appointed a decade earlier. Jill McGivering, *Macao Remembers* (Hong Kong: Oxford University Press, 1999), p. 16.
77. See, for example, Lin Chang, *Zhongpu guanxi yu Aomen qiantu*, pp. 287–90.
78. According to Rui Afonso, however, Vieira was not the first candidate in the list considered by President Mário Soares. He was chosen only after several candidates had turned down the offer. Vieira was retained in March 1996 as Macau's last governor because the newly elected President, Jorge Sampaio, had difficulty in finding a right person for the job. Nobody was keen to become the last governor of Macau. Interview with Rui Afonso, 6 January 1999.
79. Tong is regarded by his former colleague in the legislator, Rui Afonso, as an ambitious man. Tong was appointed by Edmund Ho Hau Hua as a member in the SAR's Executive Council.
80. *MDN*, 15 December 1999, p. B3.
81. See Chapter 3.
82. Interestingly, Melancia had told the author that if he were still the governor in the final years of the transition he would replace all under-secretaries with qualified local residents.
83. See Chapter 4.
84. For the effect of the 1966 riot on Macau's political scene, see Chapter 2.
85. For the discussion on the prospects for democratization in Macau, see Chapter 8.
86. Both Hong Kong's and Macau's NCNA are led by underground Chinese Communist Party organizations, namely the 'Hong Kong Working Committee' and the 'Macau Working Committee'.
87. The 11 departments are economic affairs, co-ordination, foreign affairs, Taiwan affairs, mass work, social work, public relations, news agency, personnel, law research, and propaganda, education, culture and sports. The three offices are general office, retirement office and the policy research centre.
88. Feng Bangyan, *Aomen gailun* (A General Introduction of Macau) (Hong Kong: Joint Publishing, 1999), p. 210.
89. According to Gary Ngai, a former deputy-director of the Institute of Culture of Macau, the CCP had used the local triads to suppress the dissident voices. Fore example, after the Tiananmen Square incident in 1989, local people who tried to speak out against the crackdown were terrorized, even physically attacked, and beaten up by the triads. See Jill McGivering, *Macao Remembers*, p. 154.
90. Interview with a worker in the Federation of Kaifong Associations, 15 December 1999. According to the informant, the NCNA had intervened in local politics by allocating votes from workers in mainland companies and members of pro-China groups to the two pro-China political groups, mainly the kaifong associations and labour unions. Interestingly, the Hong Kong NCNA had also attempted to control party politics in the

British colony. *Ming bao*, 13 January 2000, p. A5. Indeed, Hong Kong's NCNA officials have been allegedly assisting Tung Chee-hwa's SAR administration by pressuring legislators during key votes. *South China Morning Post*, 14 January 2000, p. 1.

91. For a detailed discussion of the politics of Macau's Basic Law drafting, see Lo Shiu Hing, *Political Development in Macau* (Hong Kong: Chinese University Press, 1995), pp. 197–217.
92. *MDN*, 19 May 1996, p. 1 and 5 February 1998, p. 2.
93. Ibid., 9 June 1998, p. A1.
94. Ibid., 20 November 1998, p. A1.
95. Ibid., 18 January 2000, p. 1.

2   The Colonial Heritage and the Crisis of Government Legitimacy

1. Wu Zhiliang, 'Aomen zhengzhi fazhanshi dui weilai de qishi' (The Evolution of Macau's Political System and its Implication for Future [Political Development]) in Herbert S. Yee, ed., *Aomen huigui qianhou de wenti yu duice* (Macau at the Handover: Problems and Policies) (Hong Kong: Mingliu, 1999), pp. 30–1.
2. The following account of Macau's political system is based on stipulations in the Organic Statute of Macau. See also Wu Zhiliang, *Aomen zhengzhi* (The Political System of Macau) (Macau: Macau Foundation, 1995), pp. 81–111.
3. For specific authorities and duties of the governor, see the Organic Statute of Macau, Articles 4 to 16.
4. Governor Vasco Rocha Vieira, Macau's last governor, was the notable exception. Vieira was appointed by President Mário Soares in April in 1991 and was re-appointed by the newly elected Jorge Sampaio in March 1996, apparently in the hope of maintaining administrative continuity and a smooth transition until the handover.
5. Goncalo Cabral and Joao Nataf, '1999 – a Peaceful Revolution?' *China Perspectives*, no. 26 (November–December 1999), p. 19.
6. Organic Statute of Macau, Article 17.
7. When Governor Carlos Melancia was involved in a bribery scandal he was later tried in Portugal.
8. The Under-Secretary for Administration, Education and Youth had 11 offices under him.
9. The noted exception is Jorge Rangel, a local-born Macanese, who had first served as an office director in Governor Leandro's administration and later as an under-secretary in both Costa's and Vieira's administrations. The three governors who had appointed Rangel probably needed someone who was familiar with Macau affairs and/or as a friendly gesture to the local Eurasian Macanese.
10. For the organization, responsibilities and duties of the legislature, see the Organic Statute of Macau, Articles 21 to 42.

11. Wu Zhiliang, *Aomen zhengzhi*, p. 93.
12. The 1976 Electoral Law stipulates that, of the six indirectly elected seats, three are allocated to organized business interests, one each to organized moral, cultural and charity interests.
13. The expanded eight indirectly elected seats are allocated as follows: four seats from business interests, two from labour interests, one from professional interests and one from charity, cultural, educational and sport interests. It is reported that in the 1996 election no less than 28 associations were found to be representing the professional constituency, 30 representing the business constituency, 50 representing the labour constituency and a record 168 representing the charity, cultural, educational and sport constituency. See Cabral and Nataf, '1999 – a Peaceful Revolution', p. 23.
14. For a detailed discussion of limitations on Macau's democratization, see Chapter 8.
15. For the organization, responsibilities and functioning of the Consultative Council, see Articles 43 to 50 of the Organic Statute.
16. Prior to 1990 there were three government officials in the Consultative Council, including a Under-Secretary, the Assistant General Procurator and the director of the Finance Office. Hu Zhiliang, *Aomen zhengzhi*, p. 90.
17. For the organization of Macau's judicial system, see Articles 51, 52 and 53 of the Organic Statute.
18. The Portuguese Parliament passed a resolution in March 1999 to devolve the Macau judicial system. President Jorge Sampiao announced unilaterally (without consulting the Chinese government) on 20 March 1999 that effectively from 1 June 1999 Macau would possess the power of final adjudication. *Macau Daily News*, 21 March 1999, p. A1.
19. Hu Zhiliang, *Aomen zhengzhi*, p. 133.
20. Ibid.
21. Ibid.
22. Of the five indirectly elected members, three represent charity, cultural, educational and sport interests while two represent the interests of employers, labour and professionals.
23. Of the three indirectly elected members, two represent charity, cultural, educational and sport interests, and one represents the interests of employers, labour and professionals.
24. See, for example, Yang Renfei, 'Shizheng jigou de gaige shizai bixing', (The Reform of Municipal Organs must be Implemented), in Herbert S. Yee, ed., *Aomen huigui qianhou de wenti yu duice*, pp. 87–9.
25. The term civil servant is used here as a general term referring to all those who work for the government. Strictly speaking, only permanent employees of the government are civil servants.
26. Goncalo Cabral and Joao Nataf, '1999 – a Peaceful Revolution?' p. 20.
27. Ibid. See also Ng Kuok Cheong, 'Lifahui zai Aomen zhuanbianzhong de fazhi yu zhengzhi yunzuo jiqi yu xingzhengquan de guanxi' (The Legislative Assembly's Changing Legal and Political Functions and its

Relations with the Executive Power), in Herbert S. Yee, ed., *Aomen huigui qianhou*, p. 82; and Hu Zhiliang, *Aomen zhengzhi*, p. 97.

28. Ng Kuok Cheong, ibid.
29. *Macau Daily News*, 8 June 1998, p. A6.
30. Cabral and Nataf, '1999 – a Peaceful Revolution?' p. 21.
31. Ibid.
32. For a detailed and excellent account of the confrontation between the legislature and the governor, see Li Bingshi, *Aomen zongdu yu lifahui* (The Governor and the Legislative Assembly in Macau) (Macau: Macau Foundation, 1994). See also Chapter 6 of this book.
33. See Cabral and Nataf, '1999 – a Peaceful Revolution?' p. 19; and Ye Zhijiang, 'Aomen xingzhengquan yu lifaquan jijian de zhengheng' (The Balance of Power between the Executive and Legislative Power Branches in Macau), in Herbert S. Yee, ed., *Aomen zhengzhi yu gonggong zhengce chutan* (An Exploration of Politics and Public Policies in Macau) (Macau: Macau Foundation, 1994), pp. 92–5.
34. Ye Zhijiang, ibid.
35. For an interesting discussion of Macau's informal politics, see Lo Shiu Hing, 'Macao's Political System', in J.A. Berlie, ed., *Macao 2000* (Hong Kong: Oxford University Press, 1999), pp. 53–70.
36. Cabral and Nataf, '1999 – a Peaceful Revolution?' p. 20.
37. Ng Kuok Cheong, 'Lifahui zai Aomen zhuanbianzhong de fazhi yu zhengzhi yunzuo jiqi xingzhengquan de guanxi', p. 82.
38. For an interesting account of Macau's gambling and organized crime, see Lo Shui Hing, 'Gambling and Organized Crime: Towards the end of the Stanley Ho connection?' *China Perspectives*, no. 26 (November–December 1999), pp. 56–65. See also Gaoqiao Yilang (a fictitious name), 'Tanwu zai Aomen de qiyuan he houguo' (The Origin and Effect of Corruption in Macau), *Aomen zhengce yanjiu* (A Study of Policies in Macau) (Macau), no. 1 (August 1998), pp. 85–9.
39. For a discussion on Macau citizens' political culture and participation, see Chapter 5 of this book.
40. For a discussion on Macau's political mobilization, see Chapter 6.
41. See Chapter 7.
42. Personal interview with Ng, 6 March 1999.
43. Ibid.
44. See Ian Scott, *Political Change and the Crisis of Legitimacy in Hong Kong* (Hong Kong: Oxford University Press, 1989).
45. For a concise Chinese interpretation of the history of Macau, especially the Portuguese administration's relation with China, see Fei Chengkang, *Aomen 400 nian* (Macau 400 Years) (Shenghai: Renmin chubanshe, 1988). For a systematic study and a Chinese interpretation of the question of sovereignty, see Tan Zhijiang, *Aomen zhuquan wenti shimo (1553–1993)* (The Beginning and Ending of the Macau Sovereignty Question) (Taipei: Yongye chubanshe, 1994).
46. Jonathan Porter, 'A Question of Sovereignty', *China Perspectives*, no. 26 (November–December 1999), p. 12. According to Lourenco Maria da

Conceicao, *Macau entre Dois Tratados com a China 1862–1887* (Macau: Instituto Cultural, 1988), Chapter 4, in the Treaty of 1887, the Portuguese gave in on their claims to Wanzhai Island (now part of Zhuhai) and, to a certain degree, on a Chinese fiscal post in the city, but gained sovereignty over Macau. For a concise history of Macau from a more neutral point of view, see Austin Coates, *A Macao Narrative* (New York: Oxford University Press, 1978). For a recent history in English, see Jonathan Porter, *Macau: the Imaginary City* (Boulder, Colorado: Westview Press, 1996), and Geoffrey C. Gunn, *Encountering Macau: a Portuguese City-State on the Periphery of China, 1557–1999* (Boulder, Colorado: Westview Press, 1996). For another Portuguese perspective, see Antonio da Silva Rego, *Macau: Perspectiva Historica* (Lisboa: Junta de Investigacoes do Ultramar, 1966).

47. See Fei Chengkang, *Aomen 400 nian*, pp. 175, 191–2, 194 and 379, and Wu Zhiliang, *Shengcun zhidao*, pp. 255–86.

48. Herbert S. Yee and Sonny S.H. Lo, 'Macau in Transition: the Politics of Decolonization', *Asian Survey*, vol. 31, no. 10 (October 1991), p. 907.

49. Richard Louis Edmonds and Herbert S. Yee, 'Macau: From Portuguese Autonomous Territory to Chinese Special Administrative Region', *The China Quarterly*, no. 160 (December 1999), p. 804.

50. It is estimated that there are about 10 000 Eurasians (Macanese) in Macau. See João do Pina Cabral and Nelson Lourenceo, *The Typhoon Territory: the Dynamics of Ethnic Macanese* (Macau: Macau Institute of Culture, 1994).

51. For an analysis of the 1966 riot, see Anthony Dicks, 'Macau: Legal Fiction and Gunboat Diplomacy', in *Leadership on the China Coast*, Goran Aijmer, ed. (London: Curzon Press, 1984); Wu Zhiliang, *The Path of Surviving: an Analysis of Macau's Political System and Political Development*; and Ng Kuok Cheong, 'A Political History of Macau: from the Twentieth Century to the Twenty-first Century', in *Four Regions on the Two Sides of the Strait: the Development of Chinese Communities in Mainland China, Taiwan, Hong Kong and Macau*, Penny Y.Y. Chan, ed. (Hong Kong. Wide Angle, 1997).

52. Richard Edmonds and Herbert Yee, 'Macau: From Portuguese Autonomous Territory to Chinese Special Administrative Region', *The China Quarterly*, no. 160 (December 1999), p. 805.

53. Moises Silva Fernandes, 'Portuguese Behaviour Towards the Political Transition and the Regional Integration of Macau in the Pearl River Region', in Rufino Ramos, Jose Rocha Dinis, Rex Wilson and D.Y. Yuan (eds), *Macau and Its Neighbours in Transition* (Macau: Macau Foundation, 1997), p. 52.

54. Herbert S. Yee and Sonny S.H. Lo, 'Macau in Transition', p. 908.

55. According to Lo Shiu Hing, the British assertiveness towards Hong Kong's political reform in the final years of colonial rule is ascribable to Patten's personal conviction that democracy is what the British owed to the Hong Kong people. See Lo's *Political Development in Macau* (Hong Kong: The Chinese University Press, 1995), p. 249.

56. Edmonds and Yee, p. 806.

57. Lo Shiu Hing, 'Macao's Political System', p. 59.

58. Figures are provided by the Public Service and Consultative Centre and offices of the two legislators.

59. In a survey conducted in 1991 among Macau citizens, 53.4 per cent of the respondents were proud of Macau's economic development. See Herbert S. Yee, Liu Bo-long and Ngo Tak-wing, *Aomen Huaren zhengzhi wenhua* (The Political Culture of the Macau Chinese) (Macau: The Macau Foundation, 1993), p. 57.

60. Edmonds and Yee, p. 806.

61. Arguably, the Portuguese Constitution had provided better protection than the Basic Law of the individual against the state by inserting a longer list of freedoms and fundamental rights of a civil, economic, social, cultural and political nature. For example, the right to one's own life is notably absent in the Basic Law. See Cabral and Natof, '1999 – a Peaceful Revolution?', p. 25.

62. Article 75 of the Macau Basic Law.

63. Private conversations with civil servants from the Office of Macau Identification and Office of Finance.

64. Arguably, the SAR's chief executive, being elected by a 200-member Election Committee, has a higher procedural legitimacy than the governor under the former Portuguese rule. Nonetheless, members of the first Election Committee were not popularly elected but nominated by the pro-China Preparation Committee. In fact, no democrat was included in the Election Committee.

65. As noted above, Governor Vasco Costa's row with the legislature in 1984 was an exception.

66. The SAR government has abolished offices which had been set up to handling transitional matters such as the Office for Supporting the Process of Integration [of Civil Servants], Office for the Study of Transitional Affairs and the Commission for Concerning the Language Situation in Macau, as well as offices which carried the connotation of colonial rule such as the Macau Region's Commission for the Memorial of Portuguese Discoveries.

67. For example, all security forces, including the judicial police which previously was under the supervision of Under-Secretary for Justice, are now under the new General Secretary for Security. Likewise, the territory's institutes of tertiary education, which previously were under the supervision of different under-secretaries are now under one general secretary. For an organization chart of the new administration, see *Macau Daily News*, 18 September 1999, p. A1.

3   The Politics of Localization

1. Lo Shiu Hing, *Political Development in Macau* (Hong Kong: The Chinese University Press, 1995), pp. 152–3.

2. Herbert S. Yee, Liu Bo-long, and Ngo Tak-wing, *Aomen huaren zhengzhi wenhua* (The Political Culture of the Macau Chinese) (Macau: The Foundation, 1993), pp. 50–1.

3. *Xin bao* (Macau), 14 November 1992.
4. *Macau Daily News (MDN)*, 29 April 1996, p. A1.
5. According to information provided by the Macau government, as of January 1999, about 3800 high school diplomas from non-Portuguese language regions had been recognized; 380 people had attended the Portuguese language programme in Portugal; 371 had attended the Chinese language and Chinese public administration programmes in Beijing; and 10117 and 5420 respectively had attended the Chinese language (Mandarin and Cantonese) and Portuguese language programmes offered by the Office of Administration and Public Service. Moreover, of the 140 special assistants in various government offices, 131 had been promoted to director/chief ranks by or before the end of 1998.
6. For a more detailed discussion of Macanese political role, see Chapter 8.
7. *Huaqiao bao* (Macau), 26 November 1992. See also Joao de Pina Cabral and Nelson Lourenco, *The Typhoon Territory: the Dynamics of Ethnic Macanese* (Macau: Macau Institute of Culture, 1994), pp. 94–5.
8. However, a small number of Macanese also have a good command of written Chinese, such as Joaquim Ribeiro Madeira de Carvalho, president of the Camara Muncipal das Ilhas (Municipal Council of Taipa and Coloane islands).
9. It is possible that some Macanese have learned the written Chinese language after 1987 and the figures in 1994 and 1995 could have underestimated the proportion of Macanese in senior positions of the civil service.
10. Jorge Rangel, 'Naru Puguo bianzhi: jueze de shike' (Integrating into Portugal's Civil Service: the Time for the Decision), *Administracao* (Macau), no. 26 (December 1994), pp. 811–14.
11. *Official Bulletin of Macau*, 23 February 1994, pp. 108–12.
12. He Yongan, 'Aomen gongwuyuan naru Puguo renyuan bianzhi de chengxu' (The Process of Integrating Macau's Civil Servants into Portugal's Civil Service), in Wu Zhiliang, Yang Yunzhong and Feng Shaorong (eds), *Aomen 1998* (Macau 1998) (Macau: The Macau Foundation, 1999), p. 34.
13. *Aomen gongwuyuan bendihua* (The Localization of Macau's Civil Servants), A report prepared by The Committee on the Accomplishment of Localization of Civil Servants (January 1999), p. 21.
14. *Official Bulletin of Macau*, 20 April 1998, pp. 449–53.
15. *Aomen gongwuyuan bendihua*, p. 21.
16. *Administracao* (Macau), no. 44 (June 1999), p. 447.
17. *Xin bao* (Macau), 26 November 1992.
18. Written Chinese courses designed for Macanese or Portuguese expatriates offered by the Training Centre of the Office of Administration and Civil Service were poorly attended.
19. *MDN*, 16 December 1998, p. A1.
20. *Administracao* (Macau), no. 44 (June 1999), p. 447. 1995 rather than 1998 is chosen for comparison because since 1996 the Office and Administration and Civil Service has changed the criteria for assessing

language proficiency, that is, the data for 1998, 1997 and 1996 are not comparable.

21. Before 1976, all laws in Macau were either extended from Portugal's national laws or legislated in Portugal. The Organic Statute of 1976 delegates law-making power to the local legislature and the governor.

22. *MDN*, 24 September 1998, p. 83, and Xu Chang, *Aomen guoduqi zhongyao falü wenti yanjiu* (A Study of Important Legal Issues During Macau's Transitional Period) (Beijing: Beijing University Press, 1999), pp. 2–3.

23. Interview with Ng Kuok Cheong, the noted democrat in Macau's legislature, 12 December 1998.

24. The Centre of Law Translation has four bilingual legal experts. *MDN*, 14 November 1998, p. A11. The laws or decrees are first revised, in accordance with the Basic Law, by Portuguese and Chinese legal experts before being translated. The translated laws are read by Chinese legal experts to make sure the legal terms are properly translated. Finally, the legally correct version of the translation is polished by Chinese language experts.

25. Interview with Eduardo Cabrita, head of the Law Translation Centre, 7 June 1990.

26. Translation of the 'Criminal Code' was completed and became effective in January 1996, the 'Criminal Procedure Code' in April 1997, and the other three 'Major Codes' ('Civil Code', 'Civil Procedure Code' and 'Commercial Code') were completed and became effective in November 1999. *MDN*, 1 November 1999, p. A1.

27. Philipe Xavier, or Xu Huinian, a senior lawyer and an appointed legislator in the first Macau SAR legislature, is normally regarded as a Macanese although he has no Portuguese blood.

28. *Aomen gongwuyuan bendihua*, pp. 16–17.

29. *MDN*, 13 July, p. A7.

30. For an interesting comparison of Hong Kong's and Macau's localization process, see Lo Shiu Hing, 'The Politics of Localization of the Civil Service in Hong Kong and Macau', *The Journal of Commonwealth and Comparative Politics*, vol. 33, no. 1 (March 1995), pp. 103–36.

31. That is, friends or relatives of Portuguese expatriates living in Macau.

32. For example, when University of East Asia's law programme was first installed in 1988, it was thought that simultaneous interpretation could be provided and lecture notes could be translated into Chinese. This soon proved impractical and more than half of the first class of 80 students, whose Portuguese proficiency was not good enough to attend classes taught in Portuguese, were forced to withdraw from the programme.

4 Macau Citizens' Attitudes toward the Transition

1. In December 1999 the Social Science Research Centre of the University of Hong Kong conducted a survey of Macau citizens' attitudes towards the handover. The survey had successfully interviewed 575 Macau resi-

dents with a response rate of 60 per cent. *Macau Daily News*, 3 January 2000, p. B2.

2. In 1996, there were already 200 000 telephone lines. That is, on average, every two persons have a telephone. Huang Hanjiang and Hu Zhiliang, eds, *Aomen zonglan* (A General Survey of Macau) (Macau: Macau Foundation, 1996), p. 290.

3. Hu Zhiliang argues that Macau was jointly governed by the Chinese and Portuguese prior to 1849. See his *Shengcun zhido: Lun Aomen zhengzhi zhidu yu zhengzhi fazhan* (The Path of Survival: a Study of Macau's Political System and Political Development) (Macau: Macau Adult Education Association, 1998).

4. The survey was conducted by the Social Science Research Centre of the University of Hong Kong in 1997. *Macau Daily News*, 3 January 2000, p. B2.

5. Ibid., 4 January 2000, p. B1.

6. Ibid.

7. Interview with Huang Hanjiang, deputy director of the Centre for Macau Studies, University of Macau, 16 July 1998. In fact, the pro-China *Macau Daily News* also supports population increase, 4 January 2000, p. A9.

8. It was reported in a 1991 survey that 55.7 per cent of the respondents were proud to be citizens of Hong Kong. See Jermain T.M. Lam and Jane C.Y. Lee, *Research Report on the Political Culture of the Voters in Hong Kong: Part II – a Study of the Geographical Constituencies of the Legislative Council*, Department of Public and Social Administration, City Polytechnic of Hong Kong, April 1992, pp. 41–6. In another survey conducted in 1996 among Hong Kong's university students, it was reported that 55 per cent of the respondents took pride in being citizens of Hong Kong while only 40 per cent were proud to be Chinese. See Herbert S. Yee, *The Political Culture of China's University Students: a Comparative Study of University Students in Mainland China, Hong Kong, Macau, and Taiwan* (New York: Nova Science, 1999), pp. 68–9.

9. Herbert S. Yee, Liu Bo-long, and Ngo Tak-wing, *Aomen huaren zhengzhi wenhua* (The Political Culture of the Macau Chinese) (Macau: Macau Foundation, 1993), p. 42.

10. The actual number of election committee members is 199. Edmund Ho Hau Wah and Au Chung Kit had withdrawn from the committee after their announcement to run for the post of chief executive. Only one of the two vacancies was later refilled.

11. In a recent seminar on Macau's handover, Jane C.Y. Lee, a scholar from Hong Kong, made a remark that while Hong Kong has a strong opposition culture it is clearly absent in Macau. *Macau Daily News*, 22 November 1999, p. B1.

12. Our findings indicate that 36 per cent of those locally-born respondents felt the Basic Law has provided sufficient safeguard for democracy in Macau, yet only 25 per cent of new immigrants felt so.

13. The Orient Foundation was registered in Lisbon in 1988. It aims to develop the Portuguese culture and its continuity in the Orient. The

financial source of the foundation mainly comes from the annual contributions of the local casinos (5 per cent of the net profit). In 1988, the Foundation had a capital of 300 million patacas, or 37 million US dollars. It is now Portugal's second largest foundation. See Chapter 1 for a detailed discussion of the debate over the Orient Foundation issue at the Sino-Portuguese Joint Liaison Group meetings.

14. *Macau Daily News* (*MDN*), 13 November 1999, p. A3, 16 November 1999, p. A2, and 7 December 1999, pp. A1, B1. Indeed, even China's official local newspaper *Macau Daily News*, apparently feeling the strong opposition from Macau citizens, had severely criticized the Portuguese administration. See *MDN*, 7 December 1999, p. B1. Ironically, the Chinese government had given its approval to the Portuguese decision at the Sino-Portuguese Joint Liaison Group meetings, probably as a concession for Portuguese co-operation at the handover.

15. See, for example, Under-Secretary for Administration, Education and Youth Jorge Rangel's speech at the Ninth Conference on European Studies, *MDN*, 2 April 1998, p. A6. See also interview with Joaquim Madeira de Carvalho, President of Camara Municipal das Ilhas, 2 January 1999.

16. In private, however, some pro-China interviewees have expressed their concerns about possible worsening corruption and continuing economic recession in post-1999 Macau. But they do not want to be identified.

5 Mass Political Culture in Macau: Continuity and Change

1. Gabriel A. Almond and Sidney Verba, *The Civic Culture* (Princeton, N.J.: Princeton University Press, 1963), p. 15.
2. Ibid., p. 18.
3. Ibid.
4. Ibid., p. 19.
5. Ibid.
6. Ronald Inglehart, 'The Renaissance of Political Culture', *American Political Science Review* 82, no. 4 (December 1988), pp. 1203–30; Aaron Wildavsky, 'Choosing Preferences by Constructing Institutions: a Cultural Theory of Preference Formation', ibid. 81, no. 1 (March 1987), pp. 3–21; Harry Eckstein, 'A Culturalist Theory of Political Changes', ibid. 82, no. 3 (September 1988), pp. 789–804; and Michael Thompson, Richard Ellis and Aaron Wildavsky, *Cultural Theory* (Boulder, Colorado.: Westview Press, 1990).
7. Inglehart, 'The Renaissance of Political Culture', p. 1219.
8. Herbert S. Yee, Liu Bo-long, and Ngo Tak-wing, 'Macau's Mass Political Culture', *Asian Journal of Public Administration* 15, no. 2 (December 1993), pp. 177–200.
9. Ibid.

10. Excluding squatters, who constitute less than 2 per cent of the enclave's population. For a detailed description of the sampling method used in the 1991 survey, see ibid., p. 180.

11. In 1996, there were already 200000 telephone lines. That is, on the average, every two persons have a telephone. Huang Hanjiang and Hu Zhiliang, eds, *Aomen zonglan* (A General Survey of Macau) (Macau: Macau Foundation, 1996), p. 290.

12. For example, the statistics on university education provided by the Census and Statistics Department only include those who have received formal tertiary education. It is estimated that in 1998 about 10 per cent of the adult population had received tertiary education through distance learning, including degree programmes offered by the local open learning institutes, and mainland and overseas universities. Thus the proportion of those attaining university education among Macau citizens is probably underestimated by the Census and Statistics Department.

13. Jermain T.M. Lam and Jane C.Y. Lee, *A Study of the Geographical Constituencies of the Legislative Council*, Part 2 of *Research Report on the Political Culture of the Voters in Hong Kong* (Department of Public and Social Administration, City Polytechnic of Hong Kong, April 1992), p. 54.

14. Min Qi, *Zhongguo zhengzhi wenhua: Minzhu zhengzhi nanchan de shehui xinli yinsu* (The Chinese Political Culture: Socio-Psychological Elements in the Difficult Birth of Democratic Politics) (Kunming: Yunnan renmin chubanshe, 1989), p. 122.

15. The three elections for the legislature were held in 1991 (by-election), 1992 and 1996, respectively.

16. The voter turnout rate for the 1991 by-election was 18.6 per cent. However, the 1992 and 1996 elections had drawn 59.3 per cent and 64.5 per cent registered voters to vote, respectively.

17. However, 'separation and balance of executive, legislative, and judicial branches' was listed as the second item in 1991 survey, yet it was chosen by only a few respondents. This suggests that a close-ended question may not necessarily cause 'desirable' answers.

18. Wu Fo, *Zhengzhi wenhua yu zhengzhi shenghuo* (Political Culture and Political Life) (Taipei: Sanmin shuju, 1998), pp. 80–2.

19. Wo Fo, *Zhengzhi wenhua yu zhengzhi shenghuo*, pp. 75–104. It is important to note, however, that the sets of questions used to probe the attitudes towards political rights are different in Taiwan and Macau. Strictly speaking, therefore, the two cases are not comparable. Our findings are thus indicative, not conclusive.

20. Hu Zhiliang, *Shengcun zhidao: Lun Aomen zhengzhi zhidu yu zhengzhi fazhan* (The Path of Survival: a Study of Macau's Political System and Political Development) (Macau: Macau Adult Education Association, 1998), pp. 14–16.

21. Huang and Hu, *Aomen zonglan*, p. 166.

22. In 1997, Macau recorded a 14 per cent drop in overall tourism and a 20 per cent drop in tourism from Hong Kong. Data provided by the Office of Census and Statistics, Government of Macau.

23. The telephone survey was conducted in December 1998 under the present author's supervision. The sample was systematically selected. 588 telephone interviews were successfully completed. The respondents were most worried about the worsening public order as well as the depressed economy which had shown negative growth in the last three years.
24. Almond and Verba, *The Civic Culture*, p. 367.
25. The statement that people shall fight for what they believe may imply both Chinese and Western values. Many heroes, patriots and sages in traditional China subscribed to the view that one should fight for one's beliefs, uphold one's moral integrity, and not yield to external pressure and threat. Nevertheless, Western values insist that everyone should be given the chance to fight for what one believes in fair and open competition.
26. Yee, Liu and Ngo, *'Macau's Mass Political Culture'*, pp. 194–5.
27. Ibid., pp. 196–7.
28. Ibid.
29. Data provided by the Office of Census and Statistics, Government of Macau.
30. Almond and Verba, *The Civic Culture*, p. 15.
31. Herbert S. Yee, *The Political Culture of China's University Students* (New York: Nova Science Publisher, 1999), pp. 113–20.
32. Ibid.

6   Money Politics and Political Mobilization: the 1996 Legislative Assembly Elections

1. *Macau Daily News* (*MDN*), 28 August 1996, p. 15.
2. There are currently about 10000 Macanese in Macau. Many of them speak both Chinese and Portuguese and are middle- or high-ranking civil servants in Macau's administration. For a more detailed account of Macau's ethnic Macanese group, see Chapter 8.
3. *Official Bulletin of Macau*, 24 April 1976, p. 562.
4. Ibid., 20 June 1984, p. 1345.
5. Ibid., 1 April 1991, p. 1331. The new electoral law requires seven years' residency for all nationals. This apparently was a move to comply with the Macau Basic Law which stipulates that only permanent residents, that is those who have lived in Macau for seven consecutive years, are qualified electors.
6. *Xianggang xinbao yuekan* (Hong Kong Economic Journal Monthly), no. 36 (June 1980), p. 40.
7. Portuguese legislators were distrustful of the Macanese. Some Portuguese elites openly called for rejection of the Macanese proposal. See *Far Eastern Economic Review*, 18 April 1980, p. 37.
8. *Pai-Shing Semi-Monthly*, no. 66 (16 February 1984), pp. 42–4. See also Lo Shiu Hing, *Political Development in Macau* (Hong Kong: Chinese University Press, 1995), p. 33.

9. The sixth seat was designated for charitable and cultural interest groups.
10. The deal was reported to have been made during d'Assumpcao's visit to China before the elections. See *Quarterly Economic Review of Hong Kong and Macao*, no. 3 (London: Economist Intelligence Unit, 1984), p. 23.
11. Under the banner of 'Sino-Portuguese Friendship' and to assure a smooth and stable transition of Macau, the pro-Beijing organizations nominated and elected two Macanese to the 1992 and 1996 legislature.
12. According to Governor Costa, although China did not openly give instructions on what policy the Macau government should implement, the Chinese limitation on the Portuguese administration existed. Confident that most Macau Chinese were either politically apathetic or pro-Beijing, China realized that to widen the franchise as proposed by Costa would strengthen the political power of Macau Chinese, See Sonny Lo Shiu Hing, *Political Development in Macau* (Hong Kong: The Chinese University Press, 1995), p. 44.
13. For example, Ho assumed a leading role mediating during the 1966 riots.
14. Hong Kong, Macau and Taiwan were allocated seats in the PRC's National People's Congress and the National Political Consultative Committee prior to formal reunification.
15. *Huaqiao bao* (Macau), 18 September 1996. The remark was made by Wong Hau Keong (or Huang Hanqiang), president of the Macau Association of Social Sciences and director of the Macau Research Centre at the University of Macau.
16. Herbert S. Yee, Liu Bo-long, and Ngo Tak-wing, 'Macau's Mass Political Culture', *Asian Journal of Public Administration*, 15:2 (December 1993), pp. 198, 191. The survey was conducted in 1991.
17. In the author's 1999 survey, however, the respondents were more participant-oriented and expressed more interest in elections than those in the 1991 survey. For more discussion on Macau's changing political culture, see Chapter 5.
18. *Official Bulletin of Macau*, 1 April 1991, p. 1332.
19. In the old d'Hondt rule, the first candidate of each political group obtained the total votes the group received, the second candidate acquired half, the third acquired one-third, the fourth a quarter, the fifth one-fifth, and so on. Clearly, the old d'Hondt rule favoured large and strong political groups; it helped d'Assumpcao's Electoral Union win four seats in the 1980 elections and Alexandre Ho's group win three in the 1988 elections. For the differences between the old and new d'Hondt rule and their effects on Macau's elections results, see Herbert S. Yee, 'Macau's Electoral System and the 1992 Legislative Assembly Elections', in Herbert S. Yee, ed., *Aomen chaoyue jiujiu* (Macau Beyond 1999) (Hong Kong: Wide Angle, 1993), pp. 41–5.
20. For an excellent account of the political mobilization used during the 1992 elections, see Lo Shiu Hing, *Political Development in Macau*, pp. 84–8.
21. For a more detailed account of the event, see Herbert S. Yee, Liu Bo-long and Ngo Tak-wing, *Aomen huaren zhengzhi wenhua* (Political Culture of

the Macau Chinese) (Macau: Macau Foundation, 1993), pp. 72–3; and Wu Zhiliang, *Shengcun zhidao: Lun Aomen zhengzhi zhidu yu zhengzhi fazhan* (The Path of Surviving: an Analysis of Macau's Political System and Political Development) (Macau: The Macau Adult Education Society, 1998), pp. 259–86.

22. Lo Shiu Hing, *Political Development in Macau*, p. 88.
23. Ibid., p. 89.
24. 'Xiaoxin xuanze, yongyue toupiao' (Choose carefully, vote actively), *MDN*, 20 September 1992.
25. Ibid., 8, 11, 12, and 15 September 1996.
26. Ibid., 9 and 16 September 1996.
27. Ibid., 10 and 13 September 1996.
28. Ibid., 19 September 1996.
29. Personal interview with Ng Kuok Cheong, 16 September 1996.
30. On 15 September 1996, the local television station organized a forum and invited candidates from all 12 political groups to participate. The next morning, although the *MDN* gave abstracts of the speeches and remarks made by a number of candidates from various groups, it did not mention any remarks made by Ng Kuok Cheong, Wong Cheong Nam and Alexandre Ho. See *MDN*, 16 September 1996.
31. Personal interview with Tong Chi Kin, the first candidate of UPD, 5 October 1996.
32. Office of Statistics and Census, Government of Macau, *Survey of Employment, 1995* (June 1996), p. 142, and *Revised Estimates of the Gross Domestic Product, 1982–1995* (March 1997), p. 130.
33. *Huaqiao bao* (Macau), 22 November 1996.
34. The exchange rate in September 1996 stood at 8 patacas = US$1. No candidates were charged by the Election Committee for violating the electoral laws after the elections. However, the Election Committee received 20 specific complaints against vote-buying activities from voters. (See *MDN*, 5 October 1996.) In the author's interviews with Ng Kuok Cheong, Wong Cheong Nam, Tong Chi Kin and Leung Heng Teng (first candidate on the UNIPRO list), all the interviewees pointed to vote buying by the five business groups. The author's former students at the University of Macau, who had assisted some groups during the campaign, also pointed out the prevalence of vote-buying activities among some groups. The following account of 'money politics' in the 1996 elections was based on my interviews with voters, candidates and campaign aides, reports of improper activities from the local press, and my own observations on the election day.
35. 'A Report of Electoral Registration in 1996', *Administracao*, no. 33 (September 1966), p. 724.
36. Personal interviews with voters, 22 September 1996.
37. Personal interviews with ADE and FM campaign aides, 22 September 1996.
38. The election day coincided with the Mid-Autumn Festival, an important event second only to the Lunar New Year Festival. It is the Chinese

custom to give so-called 'moon cakes' to one's superior, relatives and friends during the Mid-Autumn Festival.

39. The director of the Office of Public Service and Administration warned two days before the election day that anyone involved in briberies, either giving or taking a bribe, would be subjected to a maximum of five years in prison. See *MDN*, 20 September 1996. The Under-Secretary for Administration, Education and Youth Affairs also warned the political groups and citizens not to be involved in briberies and appealed to the electors not to vote for the groups involved in bribing. *MDN*, 21 September 1996.

40. A former student who worked as a campaign aide for a pro-business group told the author that he paid the voters cash in the bus on the ride to the polling stations.

41. Macau's electoral law of 1976 was adapted from the Portuguese electoral law of 1974, which aimed at correcting the wrongdoing of the Salazar regime. Elections held in the former dictatorship was tightly controlled by the presence of police officers at the polling stations. The new Portuguese law included a clause to prevent the police officers from interfering with the polls. Macau's electoral law has copied this clause without taking into consideration the local political situation.

42. For reports and comments on the election results, see the local press of September 23, 1996. Tong Chi Kin, the first candidate of UPD, expressed his surprise at the outcome of the election during an interview with the author on 5 October 1996.

43. For the distribution of votes in all polling stations, see *Official Bulletin of Macau*, 7 October 1996, pp. 2167–9.

44. Macau enjoyed a double digit, annual economic growth rate in the 1980s and early 1990s. The enclave's per capita GDP exceeded 10 000 US dollars in 1993 and was ranked number 5 in Asia, behind Japan, Brunei, Hong Kong and Singapore.

45. Personal interview with Wong Han Keong, director of the Centre of Macau Studies, University of Macau, on 21 October 1996.

46. The electoral laws were revised in February 1996 to include a clause forbidding illegal detention of any voter's registration card and raising fines for bribery activities. Yet the move was too late to stop vote buying in the 1996 elections. In any case, the law has never been rigorously enforced. *MDN*, 27 February 1996. See also Feng Ruoyi (Joana Maria Noronha), *Aomen huixuan xianxiang fenxin* (An Analysis of Macau's Electoral Bribery Activities), Department of Politics and Public Administration, Zhongshan University, Guangzhou (December 1997), unpublished MA thesis.

47. On election day, one elderly woman went to Wong Cheong Nam's campaign headquarters after casting her vote and asked for the remaining 400 patacas promised to her. She apparently went to the wrong place. Wong called the police, who arrested the old woman. However, the woman was not charged due to lack of evidence as Wong could not prove that a specific political group had bought the woman's vote. The above was based on Wong Cheong Nam's own account of the case during

the interview on 14 October 1996. See also *Huaqiao bao*, 23 September 1996.

48. The education figure is based on the 1991 population census data, provided by the Census and Statistics Department.
49. *Official Bulletin of Macau*, 7 October 1996, p. 2166. By comparison, the percentage for the 1995 Legislative Council elections in Hong Kong was 0.9 per cent.
50. Ibid., p. 2171.
51. As informed by a Ng Kuok Cheong campaign aide on 1 November 1996.
52. The democrats coined the phrase to imply that Macau was actually governed jointly by the Portuguese and Chinese governments.
53. *MDN*, 30 August 1999, p. A1.
54. *Huaqiao bao*, 9 June 1999.
55. Ibid., 7 September 1999, p. 1.
56. Author's private conversations with some legislators.
57. *MDN*, 25 September 1999, p. A2.
58. Two pro-Beijing legislators were elected in 1999 to replace the seats left vacant by Edmund Ho Hau Wah and Chan Kai Kit.

7   The Eurasians (Macanese) in Macau: the Neglected Minority

1. Fernandes is a lawyer and a novelist. See Jill McGivering, *Macao Remembers* (Hong Kong: Oxford University Press, 1999), pp. 97–8.
2. Marreiros is an architect and the former director of the Macau Institute of Culture. Ibid., p. 165.
3. See João de Pina Cabral and Nelson Lourenco, *The Typhoon Territory: the Dynamics of Ethnic Macanese* (Macau: Macau Institute of Culture, 1994). The book was published in Portuguese and English. A Chinese translation was published in 1995 by the Macau Institute of Culture. References to the book in this article are made to the Chinese translations. The authors use a tropical typhoon as a metaphor of the changing social and political environment that threatens the Macanese community.
4. *Aomen ribao* (*Macau Daily News*) (*MDN*), 25 November 1999, p. A11.
5. Cabral and Lourenco, *The Typhoon Territory*, pp. 14–15.
6. Ibid., pp. 15–16.
7. Ibid.
8. Ibid., pp. 91–5. See also Carlos Marreiros, 'The Future of Intermarriages in Macau', *Journal of Culture* (Macau), no. 21 (Spring 1995), pp. 49–56.
9. Herbert S. Yee, 'The Macanese Political Subculture' (A research report submitted to the Macau Institute of Culture, December 1995), p. 8. Yee and his assistants interviewed 207 Macanese during a six-month period from January to June 1995.
10. Ibid.
11. Ibid.
12. Cabral and Lourenco, *The Typhoon Territory*, pp. 128–9.

13. Unlike some British expatriates in Hong Kong, who made serious efforts to learn how to speak and write Chinese, very few Portuguese expatriates in Macau did so. However, some Macanese who have little or no Chinese blood may not speak Cantonese, although their number is quite small. It is thus possible that the proportion of Macanese as indicated in Tables 7.1 and 7.2 is slightly underestimated. Nevertheless, this is the best estimation we can make from available information.
14. Ibid., p. 40.
15. Ibid., p. 46. Until the end of the 1960s in Macau, a man of Chinese origin only married a European or Macanese woman if he had given up his Chinese ethnic identity by converting to Catholicism, adopting a European name, and speaking Portuguese as his main language.
16. Ibid., p. 43.
17. Ibid., p. 64.
18. For a more detailed account of the 1966 riot, see note 55, Chapter 2.
19. Herbert S. Yee, 'The Macanese Political Subculture', pp. 29–35.
20. Cabral and Lourenco, *The Typhoon Territory*, p. 60. Lobo was the director of the Economics Department during the Japanese War. He controlled the distribution of food during the war years. It is important to note that Stanley Ho, Ho Yin, Ma Man Kei, and other Chinese leaders who dominated the postwar Chinese community, were all helped by Lobo in the 1940s and 1950s.
21. Carlos d'Assumpcao was a lawyer and chairman of the legislature from 1976 until his death in early 1992.
22. For a detailed account of the row between the Macanese legislators and Governor Costa, see Lee Ping Shi, *Aomen zongdu yu lifahui* (The Governor and the Legislative Assembly in Macau) (Macau: Macau Foundation, 1994).
23. For a more detailed discussion of legislative elections, see Chapter 6. See also Lo Shiu Hing, *Political Development in Macau* (Hong Kong: The Chinese University Press, 1995), pp. 60–1.
24. Ibid. The legislature prior to 1991 was comprised of 17 members – six directly elected, six indirectly elected, and five officially appointed. It was expanded to 23 seats in 1991, with eight directly elected, eight indirectly elected, and seven officially appointed.
25. Lee Ping Shi, *Aomen zongdu yu lifahui*, p. 124.
26. Cabral and Lourenco, *The Typhoon Territory*, pp. 94–5.
27. Ibid., p. 97.
28. Ibid.
29. Yee, 'The Macanese Political Subculture', p. 7.
30. A Chinese priest notes: 'In the past there were many Catholic families in Macau. These Catholic families are rapidly disappearing. We now only have individual Catholics. Many newly baptized Catholics may be the only Catholic in their families'. See Cabral and Lourenco, *The Typhoon Territory*, p. 98.
31. Ng Shiu Ka, 'The Macanese Social Status and Their Attitudes Towards 1999', in *Aomen zhengzhi yu gonggong zhengce chutan* (A Exploratory Study

of Politics and Public Policy in Macau), ed. Herbert S. Yee (Macau: The Macau Foundation, 1994), p. 145.

32. Cabral and Lourenco, *The Typhoon Territory*, pp. 127–9.

33. Ibid., pp. 53–79. See also Jorge Morbey, 'Macanese: Aspects of an Ethnic Group', *Review of Culture* (Macau), no. 20 (Autumn 1994), pp. 165–73.

34. Ibid., pp. 74–5.

35. In a survey conducted in 1995, 62 per cent of Macanese respondents watched Chinese television channels from Hong Kong, and only 32 per cent watched local Portuguese television channels. See Yee, 'The Macanese Political Subculture', p. 8.

36. Cabral and Lourenco, *The Typhoon Territory*, p. 75; and personal interviews with Macanese conducted in the spring of 1995.

37. Personal interview with legislator Leong Heng Teng on 16 September 1996.

38. However, Joaquim de Carvalho, a noted Macanese and president of the Macau Camara Municipal das Ilhas, believed that SEMPRE had accomplished its objective of uniting the Macanese. Personal interview with Carvalho on 30 November 1996.

39. Ibid. Carvalho pointed out that Jorge Rangel, the Under-Secretary for Administration, Education, and Youth Affairs in the Vieira administration and Andbela Fatima Ritchie, the chairperson of the Legislative Assembly until the handover, may also emerge as leaders of the Macanese community in post-1999 Macau. In another interview, however, Carvalho suggested that the absence of a strong leader may be good for the Macanese community as a whole. According to Carvalho, the Macanese community has become more mature after the death of d'Assumpcao. It no longer relies on a single leader to make important decisions but does so collectively. Personal interview with Carvalho on 2 January 1999.

40. Herbert S. Yee, 'Macau's Civil Service in Transition: the Politics of Localization', *Hong Kong Public Administration* 2, no. 1 (March 1993): p. 58. For a more detailed account of the localization issue, see Chapter 3 in this book.

41. Guo Jiading, the Chinese group leader of the Sino-Portuguese Liaison Group which discusses matters related to Macau's transition to 1999, made these complaints. *MDN*, 20 September 1994.

42. Yee, 'The Macanese Political Subculture', p. 50.

43. Ibid.

44. *Official Bulletin of Macau*, 21 February 1994, pp. 1–2.

45. Yee, 'The Macanese Political Subculture', p. 53.

46. Salaries for equivalent ranks in Portugal are less than half of those in Macau.

47. *Aomen gongwuyuan bendihua* (The Localization of Macau's Civil Service), a report prepared by the Commission for the Accomplishment of the Localization of Macau's Civil Service (January 1999), pp. 20–1.

48. Personal interviews with Macanese civil servants during the period of January–June 1995.

49. *The Basic Law of the Special Administrative Region of Macau* (Macau: The Basic Law Consultative Committee, 1993), p. 11.
50. Personal interview with Joaquim de Carvalho on 30 November 1996.
51. Guo Jiading had reiterated that the Chinese government would allow the Macanese to choose either Chinese or Portuguese nationality. *MDN*, 15 September 1996.
52. *MDN*, 15 October 1996.
53. Jill McGivering, *Macao Remembers*, p. 18.
54. Yee, 'The Macanese Political Subculture', p. 59. Yee's 1995 survey indicated that 60 per cent of Macanese respondents did not believe the Chinese government would keep its promise to let the Macau people rule Macau after 1999; only 18 per cent believed the Chinese government would keep its promises.
55. Ibid.
56. Ibid., p. 61.
57. Ibid., pp. 61–3.
58. Ibid., p. 63.
59. Ibid., p. 65.
60. Ibid.
61. *MDN*, 7 August 1997, p. 2.
62. Ibid., 22 July 1997, p. 14.
63. The conference was held on 23–24 November 1996 and was organized by the Macau Society of Social Sciences. About 50 local scholars and Chinese scholars from the mainland participated in the conference, but no Macanese attended.
64. Personal interview with Lee Cheong Lap (Li Xiangli), the principal of a prestige local Chinese school, on 30 November 1996. Lee told the author that fewer than ten students took the Portuguese language course offered by his school.
65. *MDN*, 20 October 1996.
66. For example, José Chui, an engineer and a son of Chui Tak-kei, the powerful figure in the Chinese community, is quite open towards Portuguese culture and the Macanese; Gary Ngai, a former deputy director of the Macau Institute of Culture, has passionate views about Macau's Portuguese cultural heritage. For Chui's and Ngai's views on Portuguese culture, see Jill McGivering, *Macao Remembers*, pp. 87, 157–8.
67. The author's private conversations with some leftists who preferred anonymous. A member of the Macau SAR Preparation Committee also expressed such a view in a meeting held in Beijing on 14 January 1999. *MDN*, 16 January 1999, p. B3.
68. Ibid., 29 November 1996.
69. The deputy director of the Department of Gambling Contracts and Supervision, who is responsible for supervising the local casinos, was shot by a gangster on 25 November 1996. Ibid., 26 November 1996.
70. Personal interview with legislator Ng Kuok Cheong on 14 October 1996. For a more detailed account of the 1996 legislative elections, see Chapter 6.

71. Personal interview with Carlos Marreiros on 14 October 1996.
72. Personal interview with Joaquim de Carvalho on 30 November 1996.
73. Yee, 'The Macanese Political Subculture', p. 63.
74. Ibid., p. 35.
75. In a survey conducted in 1995, only 34 per cent of respondents were proud of being Macanese, while 49 per cent were not. Ibid., p. 26. Interestingly, Macanese who have emigrated overseas tend to have a stronger ethnic identity than their counterparts in Macau. In a survey of overseas participants to the 'Third International Conference of Macanese' held in Macau on 22–25 March 1999, 91.3 per cent of respondents (sample size 116) were proud of being Macanese. Many overseas Macanese held regular meetings in their respective 'Home of Macau' in their country of residence and maintain strong feelings towards Macau. An overwhelming majority (85 per cent) of respondents were proud of their Portuguese heritage and the fact that ethnic Macanese is a product of a mixture of Western and Oriental culture. Many still have relatives and friends in Macau and visit the enclave every two or three years. The above survey was conducted by the author.
76. *MDN*, 13 October 1996.
77. Ibid.; and personal interview with Carlos Marreiros on 14 October 1996.
78. Jill McGivering, *Macao Remembers*, p. 165.
79. Cabral and Lourenco, *The Typhoon Territory*, p. 17. The source does not identify the quoted Macanese.

8   Conclusion and Prospects for Democratization

1. Jiang's speech at the handover ceremony. *South China Morning Post*, 20 December 1999, p. 1.
2. Sampaio's speech at the same occasion. Ibid.
3. Frank Lei is a local-born Macanese artist. Gerard Henry, 'Frank Lei: the Sleeping City', *China Perspectives*, no. 26 (November–December, 1999), p. 66.
4. *South China Morning Post*, 21 December 1999, p. 9.
5. *Huaqiao bao*, 15 January 2000, p. A4.
6. Personal interview with Ng Kuok Cheong, 29 January 2000.
7. Part of this section is derived from a previously published article in *China Perspectives*, no. 26 (November–December 199), pp. 28–38.
8. The eight indirectly elected seats in the 1992 election were won by the pro-Beijing political force, including two Chinese-supported Macanese, Anabela Fatima Ritchie and Leonel Alberto Alves.
9. For a detailed discussion of the 1996 elections, see Chapter 6.
10. Macau has experienced an unprecedented negative economic growth since 1996. A –6.8 per cent growth rate was recorded in 1998 and an estimated –4.4 per cent for 1999. See *Xunbao* (Information Journal), 7 August 1999, p. 1 and 14 August 1999, p. 8.
11. See Chapter 6, Table 6.2.

12. Herbert S. Yee, 'Money Politics and Political Mobilization in Macau: the 1996 Legislative Assembly Elections', *Asian Survey*, vol. 37, no. 10 (October 1997), pp. 944–60.
13. Ng Kuok Cheong, the noted democrat, expressed his disappointment with Macau's voters in a personal interview with the author on 6 March 1999.
14. For a detailed description of the research method of the 1999 survey, see Herbert S. Yee, 'Mass Political Culture in Macau: Continuity and Change', *Issues & Studies*, vol. 35, no. 2 (March–April 1999), pp. 177–9.
15. Ibid.
16. *South China Morning Post*, 19 December 1999, p. 9.
17. Gabriel A. Almond and Sidney Verba, *The Civic Culture*, Princeton, New Jersey, Princeton University Press, 1963, pp. 20–1.
18. For a more detailed discussion, see Chapter 5.
19. The Institute of Macau Policy Studies has published a bimonthly journal entitled *Aomen zhengce yanjiu* (Policy Studies of Macau) since August 1998.
20. 'The Spiral of Silence' was the name of a short film which was produced and shown in Macau in February 1999.
21. Personal interview with Ng Kuok Cheong, 29 January 2000.
22. Ibid.
23. In fact, compared to Hong Kong, the proportion of the Macau population who have attended higher education is not that low. In 1998, 7.8 per cent of the Macau population aged 20 and over attended higher education compared with 10.3 per cent of the Hong Kong population aged 15 and over. The Hong Kong figure is provided by the statistics section, University Grants Committee, the Government of Hong Kong.
24. Personal interview with Ng Kuok Cheong, 6 March 1999.
25. Leng Xia, 'Eryuan zhengzhi de keguan cunzai yu chongxin zhenghe' (The Objective Existence of a Binary Politics and its Restructuring [in Macau]), *Aomen zhengce yanjiu* (Policy Studies of Macau), Macau, February 1999, pp. 21–9.
26. Personal interview with Edmund Ho Hau Wah, 11 August 1999.
27. Ho has obtained a degree in business at Canada's York University.
28. According to Ng Kuok Cheong, Ho had sometimes held discussions with him on social issues and government policies before Ho was elected as chief executive-designate. Yet Ho has since distanced himself from Ng or any Macau democrats.
29. The remark about Tung Chee-hwa was made by Lau Siu-kai, a professor at the Chinese University of Hong Kong. See *South China Morning Post*, 15 October 1999, p. 25.
30. Ibid. Also personal interview with Au Kam San, a noted Macau democrat and a directly elected municipal councilor since 1993, 3 February 2000.
31. Lo Shiu-hing, 'Democracy Movement in Hong Kong and Its Implications for South China', *Journal of Contemporary Asia*, vol. 27, no. 2, 1997, pp. 198–215.

32. It is estimated that *Aomen ribao* has a circulation of about 80 000 while *Huaqiao bao*, Macau's second largest Chinese daily, has a circulation of about 10 000.

33. Feng Bangyan, *Aomen gailun* (A General Introduction to Macau) (Hong Kong: Sanlian Shudian, 1999), p. 210.

34. With the exception of the weekly *Xunbao*, which is financially supported by the Taiwan government, the entire local Chinese press has to depend on advertising customers.

35. Personal interview with Ng Kuok Cheong, 6 March 1999.

36. The volume entitled *Aomen huigui qianhou de wenti yu duice* (Macau at the Handover: Problems and Policies) (Hong Kong: Mingliu chubanshe 1999)

37. *South China Morning Post*, 5 June 1999, p. 1.

38. *Huaqiao bao*, 5 June 1999, p. 1.

39. Ibid., 19 August 1999, p. 1.

40. Lau Siu-kai, 'Political opposition in the doldrums', *South China Morning Post*, 24 October 1999, p. 11.

41. Ibid.

42. Ibid.

43. Lo Shiu-hing, 'The Democratic Party in the Hong Kong Special Administrative Region', *The Round Table*, no. 352 (1999), pp. 635–58.

44. Ibid.

45. *Ming bao*, 1 December 1999, p. B15.

46. Ibid., 10 February 2000, p. C7.

47. Personal interview with Ng on 29 January 2000 and Au on 3 February 2000.

48. Ibid.

Select Bibliography

Afonso, Rui and Francisco Goncalves Pereira, 'The Political Status and Government Institutions of Macao', *Hong Kong Law Journal*, vol. 16, Part I (January 1986), pp. 28–57.

Almond, Gabriel A. and Sidney Verba, *The Civic Culture* (Princeton, N.J.: Princeton University Press, 1963).

Bender, Gerald J., *Angola under the Portuguese: the Myth and the Reality* (Berkeley and Los Angeles: University of California Press, 1978).

Berlie, J.A. (ed.), *Macao 2000* (Hong Kong: Oxford University Press, 1999).

Bray, Mark and Ramsey Koo (eds), *Education and Society in Hong Kong and Macau: Comparative Perspectives on Continuity and Change* (Hong Kong: Comparative Education Research Centre, University of Hong Kong, 1999).

Bruce, Neil, *Portugal: the Last Empire* (North Romfret, Vermout: David & Charles, 1975).

Cabral, Goncalo and Joao Nataf, '1999 – a Peaceful Revolution?' *China Perspectives*, no. 26 (November–December 1999), pp. 18–27.

Cabral, João do Pina and Nelson Lourenco, *The Typhoon Territory: the Dynamics of Ethnic Macanese* (Macau: Macau Institute of Culture, 1994).

Chan, Penny Y.Y. (ed.), *Aomen shehui wenti* (Macau's Social Problems) (Hong Kong: Wide Angle, 1995).

—— (ed.), *Liang'an sidi: Zhongguo, Taiwan, Xianggang, Aomen sige huaren shehui de fazhan* (Four Regions on the Two Sides of the Strait: the Development of Chinese Communities in Mainland China, Taiwan, Hong Kong and Macau) (Hong Kong: Wide Angle, 1997).

Chang, Joanne Jaw-ling, 'Settlement of the Macao Issue: Distinctive Features of Beijing's Negotiating Behaviour', occasional paper no. 4 (Baltimore: School of Law, University of Maryland, 1988).

Cheng, Christina Miu-bing, *Macau: a Cultural Janus* (Hong Kong: Hong Kong University Press, 1999).

Conceicao, Lourenco Maria da, *Macau entre Dois Tratados com a China 1962–1887* (Macau: Instituto Cultural, 1988).

Coates, Austin, *A Macao Narrative* (New York: Oxford University Press, 1978).

Cremer, R.D. (ed.), *Macau: City of Commerce and Culture* (Hong Kong: UEA Press, 1987).

——, 'Hong Kong, Macau, and the People's Republic of China: a David and Goliath Relationship?' *Asian Affairs*, vol. 18 no. 3 (Fall 1991), pp. 153–66.

—— (ed.), *Macau: City of Commerce and Culture, Continuity and Change*, 2nd edn (Hong Kong: API Press, 1991).

Dicks, Anthony J., 'Macau: Legal Fiction and Gunboat Diplomacy', in Goran Aijmer (ed.), *Leadership on the China Coast* (London and Malmo: Curzon Press, 1984).

Duffy, James, *Portuguese Africa* (Cambridge, Mass.: Harvard University Press, 1959).

Eckstein, 'A Culturalist Theory of Political Changes', *American Political Science Review*, vol. 82, no. 3 (September 1988), pp. 789–804.

Edmonds, Richard Louis, *Macau* (Oxford: Uio Press, 1989).

——, 'Macau and Greater China', *The China Quarterly*, no. 136 (December 1993), pp. 878–906.

——and William John Kyle, 'Land Use in Macau: Changes between 1972 and 1884', *Land Use Policy*, vol. 15, no. 4 (1998), pp. 280–8.

——and Herbert S. Yee, 'Macau: From Portuguese Autonomous Territory to Chinese Special Administrative Region', *The China Quarterly*, no. 160 (December 1999), pp. 801–17.

Fei Chengkang, *Aomen 400 nian* (Four Hundred Years of Macau) (Shanghai: Remin chubanshe, 1988).

Feng Bangyan, *Aomen gailun* (A General Introduction to Macau) (Hong Kong: Joint Publishing, 1999).

Feng Ruoyi, *Aomen huixuan xianxiang fenxi* (An Analysis of Macau's Electoral Bribery Activities) (Guangzhou: Department of Politics and Public Administration, Zhongshan University, December 1997), unpublished MA thesis.

Fernandes, Moisés Silva, 'Portuguese Behaviour towards the Political Transition and the Regional Integration of Macau in the Pearl River Region', in Rufino Ramos, José Rocha Dinis, Rex Wilson and D.Y. Yuan (eds), *Macau and Its Neighbours in Transition* (Macau: Macau Foundation, 1997).

Gunn, Geoffrey C., *Encountering Macau: a Portuguese City-State on the Periphery of China, 1557–1999* (Boulder, Colorado: Westview, 1996).

——, 'A Few International Ambitions', in *China Perspectives*, no. 26 (November–December 1999), pp. 43–9.

Hargreaves, John D., *Decolonization in Africa* (London and New York: Longman, 1988).

Henry, Gerard, 'Frank Lei: the Sleeping City', *China Perspectives*, no. 26 (November–December, 1999), pp. 66–7.

Ho Yongan, 'Aomen gongwuyuan naru Puguo renyuan bianzhi de chengxu' (The Process of Integrating Macau's Civil Servants into Portugal's Civil Service), in Wu Zhiliang, Yang Yunzhong and Feng Shaorong (eds), *Aomen 1998* (Macau 1998) (Macau: The Macau Foundation, 1999).

Huang Hanjiang and Hu Zhiliang (eds), *Aomen zonglun* (A General Survey of Macau) (Macau: Macau Foundation, 1996).

Inglegart, Ronald, 'The Renaissance of Political Culture', *American Political Science Review*, vol. 82, no. 4 (December 1988), pp. 1203–30.

Kahler, Miles, *Decolonization in Britain and France: the Domestic Consequences of International Relations* (Princeton, New Jersey: Princeton University Press, 1984).

Lam, Jermain T.M. and Jane C.Y. Lee, *Research Report on the Political Culture of the Voters in Hong Kong: Part II – A Study of the Geographical Constituencies of the Legislative Council* (Hong Kong: Department of Public and Social Administration, City Polytechnic of Hong Kong, April 1992).

Lamas, Rosmarie Wank-Nolasco, *History of Macau – a Student's Manual* (Macau: Institute of Tourism Education, 1998).

Lau Siu-kai, 'Political opposition in the doldrums', *South China Morning Post*, 24 October 1999, p. 11.

Leng Xia, 'Eryuan zhengzhi de keguan cunzai yu chongxin zhenghe' (The Objective Existence of a Binary Politics and its Restructuring [in Macau]), *Aomen zhengce yanjiu* (A Study of Macau Policies) (Macau) (February 1999), pp. 21–9.

Li Bingshi, *Aomen zongdu yu lifahui* (The Governor and the Legislative Assembly in Macau) (Macau: The Macau Foundation, 1994).

Lin Chang, *Zhongpu guanxi yu Aomen qiantu* (Sino-Portuguese Relations and Macau's Future) (Macau: Macau Foundation, 1994).

Lo Shiu Hing, 'An Analysis of Sino-British Negotiations Over Hong Kong's Political Reform', *Contemporary Southeast Asia*, vol. 16, no. 2 (September 1994), pp. 178–209.

——, 'The Politics of Localization of the Civil Service in Hong Kong and Macau', *The Journal of Commonwealth & Comparative Politics*, vol. 33, no. 1 (March 1995), pp. 103–36.

——, *Political Development in Macau* (Hong Kong: Chinese University Press, 1995).

——, 'Democracy Movement in Hong Kong and Its Implications for South China', *Journal of Contemporary Asia*, vol. 27, no. 2 (1997), pp. 198– 215.

——, *Politics of Democratization in Hong Kong* (London and New York: Macmillan and St. Martin's Press (now jointly Palgrave), 1997).

——, 'Gambling and Organized Crime: Towards the end of the Stanley Ho Connection?' *China Perspectives*, no. 26 (November–December 1999), pp. 56–65.

——, 'Macao's Political System', in J.A. Berlie (ed.) *Macao 2000* (Hong Kong: Oxford University Press, 1999).

——, 'The Democratic Party in the Hong Kong Special Administrative Region', *The Round Table*, no. 352 (1999), pp. 635–58.

Loureiro, Rui Manual, 'Introduction: Reports on China in Iberian Literature (Sixteenth and Seventeenth Centuries)', *Review of Culture* (Macau), no. 32 (1997), English Edition, pp. 13–18.

Marreiros, Carlos, 'The Future of Intermarriages in Macau', *Journal of Culture* (Macau), no. 21 (Spring 1995), pp. 49–56.

McGivering, Jill, *Macao Remembers* (Hong Kong: Oxford University Press, 1999).

Min Qi, *Zhongguo zhengzhi wenhua: Minzhu zhengzhi nanchan de shehui xinli yinsu* (The Chinese Political Culture: Socio-Psychological Elements in the Difficult Birth of Democratic Politics) (Kunming: Yunnan renmin chubanshe, 1989).

Morbey, Jorge, *Macau 1999: O Desafio da Transicao* (Lisbao: Impressao e Acabento, 1990).

——, 'Macanese: Aspects of an Ethnic Group', *Review of Culture* (Macau), no. 20 (Autumn 1994), pp. 165–73.

Ng Kuok Cheong, *Minzhupai* (The Democratic Factions) (Hong Kong: Qingwen shuwu, 1990).

——, 'Lifahui zai Aomen zhuanbianzhong de fazhi yu zhengzhi yunzuo jiqi yu xingzhengquan de guanxi' (The Legislative Assembly's Changing Legal and Political Functions and its Relations with the Executive Power), in Herbert S. Yee (ed.), *Aomen huigui qianhou de wenti yu duice* (Macau at the Handover: Problems and Policies) (Hong Kong and Macau: Mingliu, 1999).

Ng Shiu Ka (Wu Shaojia), 'The Macanese Social Status and Their Attitudes Towards 1999', in Herbert S. Yee (ed.), *Aomen zhengzhi yu gonggong zhengce chutan* (An Exploratory of Politics and Public Policy in Macau) (Macau: The Macau Foundation, 1994).

Nunez, Cesar Guillen and Leong Ka Tai, *Macao Streets* (Hong Kong: Oxford University Press, 1999).

Oliveira, Jorge, 'A Lei Básica e o princípio da continuidade do ordenamento jurídico vigente em Macau', in *O Ordenamento Jurídico de Macau no Contexto da Lei Básica* (Macao: Associacão dos Advogados de Macau, 1991).

——, Rebelo Jessica, Paul Cardinal and Paulo Pereira Vidal, 'An Outline of the Macau Legal System', *Hong Kong Law Journal*, vol. 23, no. 3 (1993), pp. 358–94.

Pereira, Francisco Goncalves, *Portugal a China e a 'Questão de Macau'* (Macau: Livros do Orient, 1995).

Porter, Jonathan, 'The Transformation of Macau', *Pacific Affairs*, vol. 66, no. 1 (Spring 1993), pp. 7–20.

——, Macau: *The Imaginery City* (Boulder, Colorado: Westview, 1996).

——, 'A Question of Sovereignty', *China Perspectives*, no. 26 (November–December 1999), pp. 8–17.

Ramos, João de Deus, 'A Declaracao Conjunta sobre Macau no ambito das relacoes luso-chineas', *Politica Internacional*, no. 14 (1997), pp. 19–30.

Ramos, Rufino, D.Y. Yuan, John E.M. Barnes and Wong Hon Keong (eds), *Population and Development in Macau* (Macau: University of Macau, 1994).

——, José Rocha Dinis, Rex Wilson and D.Y. Yuan (eds), *Macau and Its Neighbour Toward the 21st Century* (Macau: University of Macau, 1998).

Scott, Ian, *Political Change and the Crisis of Legitimacy in Hong Kong* (Hong Kong: Oxford University Press, 1989).

Shipp, Steve, *Macau, China: a Political History of the Portuguese Colony's Transition to Chinese Rule* (Jefferson N.C.: McFarland and Company, 1997).

Silva Rego, Antonio da, *Macau: Perspectiva Historica* (Lisboa: Junta de Investigacoes do Ultramar, 1966).

Tan Zhijiang, *Aomen zhuquan wenti chimo* (1553–1993) (The Beginning and Ending of the Macau Sovereignty Question) (Taipei: Yongye chubanshe, 1994).

Wildavsky, Aaron, 'Choosing Preferences by Constructing Institutions: a Cultural Theory of Preference Formation', *American Political Science Review*, vol. 81, no. 1 (March 1987), pp. 3–21.

Wu Fo, *Zhengzhi wenhua yu zhengzhi shenghuo* (Political Culture and Political Life) (Taipei: Sanmin shuju, 1998).

Wu Zhiliang, *Aomen zhengzhi* (The Political System of Macau) (Macau: Macau Foundation, 1995).

——, *Shengcun zhido: lun Aomen zhengzhi zhidu yu zhengzhi fazhan* (The Path of Surviving: an Analysis of Macau's Political System and Political Development) (Macau: The Macau Adult Education Society, 1998).

——and Ieong Wan Chong (eds), *Aomen baike quanshu* (Encyclopedia of Macau) (Macau: Macau Foundation, 1999).

——, 'Aomen zhengzhi fazhanshi dui weilai de qishi' (The Evolution of Macau's Political System and its Implication for Future [Political Development]) in Herbert S. Yee (ed.), *Aomen huigui qianhou de wenti yu duice* (Macau at the Handover: Problems and Policies) (Hong Kong and Macau: Mingliu, 1999).

——, Ieong Wan Chong and Feng Xiaorong (eds), *Aomen 1999* (Macau 1999) (Macau: Macau Foundation, 1999).

Xu Chang, *Aomen guoduqi zhongyao falu wenti yanjiu* (A Study of Important Legal Issues During Macau's Transitional Period) (Beijing: Beijing University Press, 1999).

Ye Zhijiang, 'Aomen xingzhengquan yu lifaquan jijian de zhengheng' (The Balance of Power between the Executive and Relative Power Branches in Macau), in Herbert S. Yee (ed.), *Aomen zhengzhi yu gonggong zhengce chutan* (An Exploration of Politics and Public Policies in Macau) (Macau: Macau Foundation, 1994).

Yee, Herbert S. and Sonny S.H. Lo, 'Macau in Transition: the Politics of Decolonization', *Asian Survey*, vol. 31, no 10 (October 1991), pp. 905–19.

——, Liu Bo-long and Ngo Tak-wing, Macau's 'Mass Political Culture', *Asian Journal of Public Administration*, vol. 15, no. 2 (December 1993), pp. 177–200.

——, Liu Bo-long and Ngo Tak-wing, *Aomen Huaren zhengzhi wenhua* (The Political Culture of the Macau Chinese) (Macau: The Macau Foundation, 1993).

——(ed.), *Aomen chaoyue jiujiu* (Macau Beyond 1999) (Hong Kong: Wide Angle, 1993).

——, 'The Eurasians (Macanese) in Macau: the Neglected Minority', *Issues & Studies*, vol. 33, no. 6 (June 1997), pp. 113–32.

——, 'Money Politics and Political Mobilization in Macau: the 1996 Legislative Assembly Elections', *Asian Survey*, vol. 37, no. 10 (October 1997), pp. 944–60.

——(ed.), *Shuangchengji: Gang Ao de zhengzhi, jingji ji shehui fazhan* (A Tale of Two Cities: Political, Economic and Social Developments in Hong Kong and Macau) (Macau: The Macau Association of Social Sciences, 1998).

——, 'The Mass Political Culture of Macau and Hong Kong', in Danny S.L. Paau (ed.), *Reunification with China: Hong Kong Academics Speak* (Hong Kong: Asian Research Service, 1998).

——, 'Mass Political Culture in Macau: Continuity and Change', *Issues & Studies*, vol. 35, no. 2 (March–April 1999), pp. 174–97.

——(ed.), *Aomen huigui qianhou de wenti yu duice* (Macau at the Handover: Problems and Policies) (Macau, Hong Kong: Mingliu, June 1999).

——, 'Prospects of Democratization: an Open-Ended Game?' *China Perspectives*, no. 26 (November–December 1999), pp. 28–38.

——, *The Political Culture of China's University Students: a Comparative Study of University Students in Mainland China, Hong Kong, Macau, and Taiwan* (Commack, New York: Nova Science, 1999).

Zhang Hu, *Aomen jiujiu: wenti yu yanjiu* (Macau 1999: Issues and Studies) (Taipei: Guiguan tushu, 1999).

Index